*New Security Challenges in Asia*

# New Security Challenges in Asia

Edited by

## Michael Wills and Robert M. Hathaway

In association with
The National Bureau of Asian Research

Woodrow Wilson Center Press
Washington, D.C.

The Johns Hopkins University Press
Baltimore

EDITORIAL OFFICES

Woodrow Wilson Center Press
One Woodrow Wilson Plaza
1300 Pennsylvania Avenue, N.W.
Washington, D.C. 20004-3027
Telephone: 202-691-4029
www.wilsoncenter.org

ORDER FROM

The Johns Hopkins University Press
Hampden Station
P.O. Box 50370
Baltimore, Maryland 21211
Telephone: 1-800-537-5487
www.press.jhu.edu/books/

*Library of Congress Cataloging-in-Publication Data*

New security challenges in Asia / edited by Robert M. Hathaway
and Michael Wills.
    pages cm
  Includes bibliographical references and index.
  1. Security, International—Asia. 2. National security—Asia.
3. United States—Foreign relations—Asia. 4. Asia—Foreign
relations—United States. I. Hathaway, Robert M., 1947– editor of
compilation. II. Wills, Michael, 1970– editor of compilation. III.
Pomeranz, Kenneth. Drought, climate change, and the political economy of
Himalayan dam building.
  JZ6009.A75N48  2013
  355'.03305—dc23

2013006162

ISBN 978-1-4214-1010-4

# Contents

# Tables and Figures

# Acknowledgments

This volume is the product of the National Asia Research Program (NARP), a joint initiative of the National Bureau of Asian Research (NBR) and the Woodrow Wilson International Center for Scholars designed to reinvigorate and advance the policy-relevant study of contemporary Asia in the United States. The members of the NARP's inaugural class of twenty-seven research associates and twelve research fellows were chosen in March 2010 through a competitive, nationwide selection process based on their research on issues of strategic importance to U.S. interests in Asia. The chapters in this book, with the exception of the introductory chapter, were written by scholars from this class of NARP associates or fellows and were first presented at the Asia Policy Assembly held in Washington in June 2010.

As coeditors of this volume, we gratefully acknowledge the many individuals and institutions without whose encouragement and support this book, and the broader NARP initiative, would not have been possible. First, we would like to thank Richard Ellings, president of NBR, and Lee Hamilton, then the president of the Woodrow Wilson Center, for their vision and energy in designing and establishing the NARP. We have a huge debt of gratitude to the members of Congress whose support enabled the NARP to become a reality in 2010–11, and to those grant-making foundations—the Lynde and Harry Bradley Foundation, the Henry Luce Foundation, the Asia Foundation, and the Japan Foundation/Center for Global Partnership—for their backing of the initiative. In addition, we owe thanks to those scholars and scholar-practitioners who contributed their time and expertise through their service on the NARP's advisory board and selection committee. We would also like to thank Jane Harman, president of the Wilson Center, and Joe Brinley, director of the Woodrow Wilson Center Press, for their support of this book, one of the many outcomes of the NARP.

More colleagues at NBR helped to make the NARP a success than there is space to acknowledge individually, but particular thanks are due to Stephanie Renzi for her leadership of the program during its first year and her superb coordination of the Asia Policy Assembly; to Melissa Colonno and Sonia Luthra, for their management of the program during its second year; and to Jonathan Walton, for his careful and attentive editorial assistance in the preparation of this volume. At the Woodrow Wilson Center, we gratefully acknowledge the valuable contributions of Sue Levenstein and Jon Abramovic, and the support of the editorial-production team led by Alfred Imhoff.

Asia's resurgence marks a turning point in world history. In the decades ahead, many of the United States' greatest interests overseas—opportunities as well as challenges—will lie in Asia. Accordingly, we must be better prepared to understand the implications of developments in Asia for U.S. economic vitality, diplomacy, and security. Our hope is that this volume contributes to this goal.

Michael Wills
The National Bureau of Asian Research

Robert M. Hathaway
Woodrow Wilson International Center for Scholars

*New Security Challenges in Asia*

# Chapter 1

# Introduction:
# New Security Challenges
# for a New Century

*Robert M. Hathaway and Michael Wills*

Throughout history, diplomats and national security managers have thought of security primarily in geopolitical, state-centered terms. Threats have customarily been seen as emanating from other states. Implicit or explicit coercion, generally of a military or economic nature, has usually been involved. Military power has been regarded as the essential guarantor of a state's security. International relations theories focusing on the balance of power, deterrence, alliance management, preemptive force, and similar concepts have dominated discussions about security in both official and scholarly circles.

No more. The nature of security challenges worrying statesmen, military planners, and foreign policy analysts today has dramatically changed and expanded in recent years. This is not to suggest that traditional geopolitical threats have disappeared; the prospect of interstate conflict and its consequences remain very real concerns. But a new and markedly different set of challenges has risen alongside the traditional security challenges. As then–U.S. secretary of state Hillary Clinton marveled, "our parents never

1

dreamt of melting glaciers or dirty bombs" as threats to the security of the United States—or any other country.[1] U.S. president Barack Obama has warned that all of us face "a world that has changed—a world in which the international architecture of the 20th century is buckling under the weight of new threats."[2]

This volume features nine chapters looking at a selection of these new threats, particularly as they affect Asia. The security challenges considered here—which focus on water security, food security, pandemic disease, and crime/terrorism—are "new" in the sense that, unlike in previous eras, national rivalries and traditional geopolitical competition are not necessarily the primary source of the security challenge. They are "new" in the sense that they do not necessarily arise from the actions of other governments, although governmental action (e.g., Chinese dam building in the Himalayas) or inaction (Beijing's delay in acknowledging the extent of the outbreak of severe acute respiratory syndrome, or SARS) can certainly aggravate the challenge. Coercion or threats from other nation-states are not the defining element of these new security challenges. These challenges are by definition transnational, recognizing neither international borders nor traditional notions of sovereignty.

New security challenges can be defined not only by the source of the threat, but also by the preferred response. In most cases, unilateral action by individual states is insufficient to deal with these new threats; international cooperation is almost always a prerequisite for a successful response. In East Asia, this cooperation has frequently featured institution building, and several of the principal East Asian multilateral organizations, including the Association of Southeast Asian Nations (ASEAN) and the ASEAN Regional Forum, have been active in addressing these new transnational challenges. South Asia, conversely, has lagged behind in creating regional institutions to manage these new threats.

Admittedly, these threats are not entirely "new." The Spanish influenza epidemic at the end of World War I, which killed 50 million to 100 million people worldwide, certainly constituted a major threat to significant U.S. interests. Nor is piracy, for instance, a recent concern; the fledging United States, after all, went to war in the Mediterranean more than two centuries ago primarily because of piracy. What is unprecedented about today's new security challenges is the potentially catastrophic impact on vital national interests that these threats pose—imagine a nuclear weapon in the hands of a group like al-Qaeda—the seriousness with which national security managers view these threats, and the national resources mobilized to counter them.

No clear line divides traditional, geopolitical threats from these new security challenges, nor is there a widely held consensus on which threats should be considered new security challenges. During the past decade, the scholarly literature has begun to frame the parameters of what are often called nontraditional security threats, but so far with no clear definition. One Chinese scholar, for example, has noted a tendency "to lump almost everything into the basket" of new security threats, including traffic congestion, "identity ambiguity," and poverty relief.[3] Another analyst insists that domestic economic and social disparities comprise a nontraditional security threat to China.[4] Surely this is too elastic a definition of new security challenges; for one thing, these inequalities lack a transnational component. Similarly, some scholars would include demographic pressures—a fertility rate that is too low to produce the next generation of workers (as in Japan), or so high that a young population threatens to overwhelm the resources of a fragile state (as in Pakistan). In each of these instances as well, the transnational element is missing, which would seem to disqualify demographic pressures as a new security challenge, even though these pressures assuredly pose a strategic challenge to core Japanese and Pakistani interests.

No two states are likely to include precisely the same threats on their list of new security challenges, nor prioritize such threats in the same manner. During the past decade, international terrorism and the proliferation of weapons of mass destruction have resided at the very top of the U.S. government's list. North Korea and Thailand, conversely, have ranked these concerns far lower. In like manner, Singapore worries more about the consequences of maritime terrorism or a huge oil spill in the Strait of Malacca than does land-locked Nepal.

Defining these new security challenges is in part a matter of gradation. What constitutes an acceptable risk to one state may well be an intolerable threat to another. A six-inch rise in the sea level poses a rather different threat to Bhutan than to Bangladesh or the Maldives, for example. SARS with one hundred fatalities is a catastrophe for those families but represents no challenge to the state. SARS with a million fatalities is an altogether different matter.

These new security challenges have gained salience in part from global trends in international security: the end of the Cold War and the overall decline in traditional security threats occasioned by great power rivalry; globalization, with its dramatic rise in travel, trade, and the dissemination of ideas; and population growth, which has led to new pressures on natural resources and greater attention to energy, food, and water security for sustained economic growth. New security challenges are particularly important in Asia due to the concentration of global economic, political, and military power in the region and the potential of such challenges to exacerbate enduring suspicion and long histories of unresolved animosities among Asian states.

Over the past two decades, these challenges have also become an important element in the U.S. government's thinking about security planning in Asia, supplementing traditional security concerns that stem from Washington's post–World War II role as the region's security guarantor. Deployments of U.S. military forces in response to these new challenges, as during the 2004–5 Indian Ocean tsunami relief operation and following the 2011 Tohoku earthquake and tsunami, are now as much a part of U.S. contingency planning as preparations to deter aggression in Northeast Asia or protect freedom of the seas in the Indian and Pacific oceans.

This volume highlights four pressing new security challenges facing Asia today: water security, food security, pandemic disease, and crime/terrorism. It has been written with two distinct audiences in mind: Asians, who are called upon to wrestle with these challenges on a daily basis, and U.S. officials and scholars considering how best to safeguard U.S. interests in Asia. This introduction begins with a summary of the post–Cold War evolution of policy thinking on new security challenges in the United States and in Asia, and then reviews key characteristics of the four new security challenges addressed in this volume.

## Post–Cold War Policy Thinking on New Security Challenges

### Evolving U.S. Conceptions of New Security Challenges

It is not coincidental that the United States began to pay more systematic attention to new security challenges two decades ago, following the collapse of the Soviet Union and the conclusion of the Cold War. Indeed, the prominence given new security challenges in Washington was the direct result of the end of the Cold War and the dramatic diminution of any serious challenge from a traditional great power. The U.S. triumph in the great power arena opened the door, as it were, to an enhanced awareness of new threats. As the Pentagon's 1993 Bottom-Up Review flatly stated: "Most striking in the transition from the Cold War is the shift in the nature of the dangers to our interests."[5]

The emergence of new security challenges as a major preoccupation for U.S. policymakers also reflected broader international developments, most notably changes associated with globalization and the greater ease and frequency of global travel and trade. Though primarily beneficial, globalization also had a dark side. The connectivity of the modern world brings Americans not only Bollywood movies and mangoes but also germs and terrorism. The commonplace nature of international travel and commerce, for instance, made it far more difficult to localize potentially deadly viruses, as the 2002–3 SARS epidemic so vividly demonstrated. To take a different example, a fragile government in Somalia or Afghanistan that enables criminal or terrorist groups to operate from within its borders today affects important U.S. interests in a manner unimaginable to statesmen not many decades ago.

Although U.S. administrations during the Cold War had not totally ignored nontraditional threats, it was only during the administration of George H. W. Bush that these new security challenges began to figure regularly in the discourse of U.S. diplomacy and statecraft. Addressing the UN General Assembly in 1990, President Bush noted that even with the end of the Cold War, the world remained "a dangerous place. . . . We need serious international cooperative efforts," he warned, to counter "the threats to the environment, on terrorism, on managing the debt burden, on fighting the scourge of international drug trafficking, and on refugees, and peacekeeping efforts around the world."[6] Writing in the journal *Foreign Affairs* a few months later, Secretary of State James Baker underscored many of these same nontraditional dangers, highlighting drugs, the environment, and migration as "important components of a comprehensive approach to security."[7] The administration's National Security Strategy of the same year called for extending the United States–Japan partnership "beyond its traditional confines and into fields like refugee relief, nonproliferation and the environment."[8]

The administration of Bill Clinton elevated this concern with new security challenges still further. During his 1996 State of the Union Address, President Clinton warned: "The threats we face today as Americans respect no nation's borders. Think of them: terrorism, the spread of weapons of mass destruction, organized crime, drug trafficking, ethnic and religious hatred, aggression by rogue states, environmental degradation."[9] Here was a blend of traditional and nontraditional dangers that extended far beyond superpower rivalries. And as the years passed, administration officials kept expanding this list. The 1997 National Security Strategy added "intrusions in our critical information infrastructures" and listed corruption, money laundering, and international criminal cartels as additional threats.[10] Two years later, President Clinton upped the ante still further, informing the Congress that "our most fateful new challenge is the threat of global warming."[11]

Not that Washington lost sight of more traditional, state-based threats in the decade after the collapse of the Soviet Union, as the successive Balkan wars brought on by the breakup of Yugoslavia attest. In Asia, North Korea's efforts to acquire a nuclear arsenal brought the world dangerously close to war in 1994, and dominated Washington's regional diplomacy throughout the Clinton era. Continuing tensions on the Korean Peninsula "remain the principal threat to the peace and stability of the Asian region," the White House warned in 1997.[12] Missile tests, inflammatory rhetoric, and naval deployments in waters adjacent to the Taiwan Strait in 1995 and 1996 also reflected the continued relevance of more traditional, state-centered threats.[13] Although victorious in its superpower rivalry with Moscow, Washington was not afforded the luxury of leaving traditional geopolitical security concerns altogether behind.

Indeed, in important ways, the heightened emphasis on new security challenges gave relations among the major powers even greater salience. By definition these transnational nonstate challenges placed a new premium on international cooperation. "There are some issues that we really can't address without China's help," Secretary of State Warren Christopher told an interviewer in 1996, specifically listing drug trafficking, terrorism, and environmental degradation.[14] He could easily have substituted Russia, India, France, Saudi Arabia, Brazil, or any of dozens of other examples for China.

The September 11, 2001, terrorist attacks on the United States provided a horrific illustration of just how intertwined the mix of traditional and nontraditional security challenges had become. The September 11 attacks demonstrated the relative ease with which nonstate actors could use nontraditional weapons—hijacked commercial airliners—to strike at core U.S. interests. The response chosen by the George W. Bush administration—the employment of overwhelming military force against al-Qaeda and Taliban forces in Afghanistan—was very much a traditional one. Yet, the nature of U.S. opponents in Afghanistan (and subsequently in Iraq)—loosely organized private militias and terrorist groups outside the control of national governments—was a far cry from the foes envisaged in Cold War security plans that arrayed massive armies against one another. In this respect, these recent conflicts differ from the "wars of national liberation" that bedeviled U.S. Cold War strategists in Southeast Asia, Africa, and elsewhere, and that were viewed in Washington as part of the international communist challenge orchestrated by Moscow, Beijing, or Havana—a linkage to foreign rivals largely absent from the wars in Afghanistan and (albeit less so) Iraq.

Officials in the second Bush administration continued to work from the list of new security challenges that had been developed by their predecessors. "The phenomenon of weak and failing states is not new," Secretary of State Condoleezza Rice wrote in a 2005 *Washington Post* article, "but the danger they now pose is *unparalleled*" (emphasis added).[15] Although much of the administration's security strategy depended on deterrence, alliances, and even the preemptive use of force, Rice and her colleagues rightly understood that the twenty-first century proffered a very different—in her words, unparalleled—set of security challenges. In Afghanistan before the September 11 attacks, and in Pakistan's tribal areas since then, the threat arose not from national governments and organized armies, but from ungoverned areas largely beyond the control of national capitals.

The forces of globalization had exposed the world to new types of threats and changed the way old threats affected U.S. interests. As Rice observed: "When people, goods and information traverse the globe as fast as they do today, transnational threats such as disease or terrorism can inflict damage comparable to the standing armies of nation-states."[16] President Bush's 2006 National Security Strategy took up this same theme, specifically singling out public health challenges like HIV/AIDS and avian influenza that "recognize no borders" and pose risks to social order that "are so great that traditional public health approaches may be inadequate, necessitating new strategies and responses." The same document also warned about illicit trafficking "in drugs, human beings, or sex, that exploits the modern era's greater ease of transport and exchange" and "corrodes social order; bolsters crime and corruption; undermines effective governance; facilitates the illicit transfer of [weapons of mass destruction] and advanced conventional weapons technology; and compromises traditional security and law enforcement."[17]

The early years of the new century saw greater attention to an old threat, piracy, and a rapidly evolving new one: cyberattacks and other forms of information warfare. Asian waters, with their heavy maritime traffic channeled through narrow sea lanes, proved especially attractive to modern-day pirates; as a result, antipiracy measures have come to figure heavily in regional diplomatic discussions. Some of the threats in cyberspace have emanated from governments; China is frequently fingered as a culprit. But others appear to have been the work of individual hackers operating without their government's knowledge or consent. The notion that a single bored or antisocial teenager could cripple an entire U.S. industry or intelligence network carried the idea of nontraditional security threat to a whole new level of complexity.[18]

When it took office in 2009, the Barack Obama administration reprised the call of its predecessors for international cooperation to confront these new security challenges. "America cannot solve the problems of the world alone, and the world cannot solve them without America," Secretary of State Hillary Clinton declared in February 2009, in the administration's first extended statement on Asia. To illustrate her point, she listed three challenges—a mix of traditional and nontraditional security threats—that required international collaboration: the global financial crisis, North Korea's nuclear weapons program, and climate change. Old threats and new. She asked her audience to "consider the *gravest* global threats confronting us—financial instability and economic dislocation, terrorism and weapons of mass destruction, food security and health emergencies, climate change and energy vulnerability, stateless criminal cartels and human exploitation" (emphasis added). The items missing from this list—aggression across borders, bitter competition with ideological adversaries—demonstrated just how much the world had changed in the span of a generation.[19]

None of this is to suggest that old state-centered security concerns simply disappeared. President George W. Bush and then Obama found their national security calculations dominated by prolonged overseas wars. North Korea's nuclear weapons program and brinkmanship remained a pressing concern. And China's reemergence as a great power—with a roaring economy, a two decades–long military modernization program, and muscle-flexing in the South and East China seas—ensured that U.S. decisionmakers did not lose sight of the continued centrality of nation-states.

Indeed, at a time when oceans and national borders afforded less and less security, allies and old friends were just as important as before. President Obama's 2010 National Security Strategy declared that U.S. alliances with Japan, South Korea, Australia, the Philippines, and Thailand remained "the bedrock of security in Asia. . . . We are working together with our allies to develop a positive security agenda for the region, focused on regional security, combating the proliferation of weapons of mass destruction, terrorism, climate change, international piracy, epidemics, and cybersecurity, while achieving balanced growth and human rights."[20] Once more, one is struck by the prominence of new security challenges on this agenda. As President Obama told a Japanese audience during his first trip to Asia in November 2009, "we will stand with all of our Asian partners in combating the transnational threats of the 21st century," specifically mentioning extremism, piracy, infectious disease, poverty, and trafficking.[21] Two decades after the fall of the Berlin Wall, the basic American understanding of security, and U.S. security concerns in Asia, had undergone a profound alteration.

## *Asian Policy Understanding of New Security Challenges*

Broadly speaking, Asian nations have been slower than the United States to align budgetary resources and bureaucratic structures to reflect this new security paradigm. For the nations of Asia, the end of the Cold War competition between Washington and Moscow did not carry the same strategic significance it held for the United States, nor did it relieve them of traditional geopolitical security concerns. And in the two decades since then, national security planners in the region have not, as a group, focused as heavily on the new security challenges as their U.S. counterparts. More precisely, while Southeast Asian states have used ASEAN to highlight these challenges, they have not invested significant resources or otherwise demonstrated that they give precedence to this broader conception of security. To the contrary, traditional state-based threats continue to shape their strategic planning and spending priorities.

At first glance, this lag in responding to new security challenges may seem odd. In some respects Asia's geographic location and less advanced economic development make it more susceptible to such threats than Europe or the United States. Many of the most significant new security challenges over the past two decades have originated in Asia. Densely populated Asia has given rise to SARS, swine flu, and multiple contaminated food scares. The waters linking the Indian and Pacific oceans are a prime site for piracy. In 1997, the haze from burning forests in Indonesia shut down air traffic across Southeast Asia, created serious economic disruptions, and threatened the health of millions of people. Moreover, the modest economic resources available to many of the region's states make safeguarding against these transnational threats more difficult, a situation that, one might have assumed, would have encouraged more, not less, official scrutiny.

Nonetheless, traditional, state-centered definitions of security continue to occupy a large place in Asian discussions on security. The Taiwan Strait, the Korean Peninsula, and Indo-Pakistani tensions still demand the attention of regional security planners and analysts. Unresolved border disputes trouble relations between India and Pakistan, India and China, and

Cambodia and Thailand. Contested territorial claims in the South China Sea and East China Sea provide periodic reminders of the continued importance of more traditional, state-based security challenges.

China's astonishing economic growth and rapid military modernization have also served to remind Asian leaders that they cannot afford to ignore traditional, state-based threats. China is on the verge of acquiring capabilities that will enable it to project power beyond its territorial waters in a way that it has not for several centuries, a situation that makes a number of its neighbors uneasy. Partly as a consequence of China's strides in this area, other Asian nations have been on an arms-buying spree for much of the past decade, further evidence that they have not lost focus on traditional threats.

The global financial crisis that began in 2008 may also serve, in the coming years, to underscore traditional security anxieties in many Asian states. The heavy toll of the financial crisis on the U.S. economy, coupled with Washington's continued inability to align its expenditures with its revenues, the shaky domestic U.S. economy, and the strain of two wars, has placed new pressures on the U.S. defense budget. Notwithstanding the Obama administration's talk about "rebalancing" toward Asia, many Asian analysts worry that the U.S. military presence in their region might be scaled back in the years ahead just as China's military strength is increasing. Although in some Asian capitals this may encourage a reevaluation of the wisdom of a close partnership with the United States, it will also raise anxieties about traditional security threats emanating from China.

Finally, many Asian countries also see a danger in too extensive an incorporation of nontraditional concerns into a security agenda, for fear of giving stronger states an opening to intervene in sensitive matters that the target nation regards as "internal" or "domestic." At this moment in their respective histories, China, India, Malaysia, and Vietnam, among others, continue to place great premium on a concept of state sovereignty that limits the ability of stronger states to meddle in their internal affairs—even when such an adherence to sovereignty norms puts them at risk from threats arising within neighboring states. China, for instance, refuses to accept climate change as a legitimate security issue. "Climate change may affect security but it is fundamentally a sustainable development issue," a senior Chinese diplomat informed a United Nations audience in mid-2011.[22]

Although the September 11 terrorist attacks had a huge impact on U.S. thinking about the threat posed by nonstate actors, Washington's focus on terrorism and religious extremism in the decade since then has been met with varying degrees of enthusiasm, caution, or opposition by Asian governments, depending on their overall relationship with Washington, the size or importance of their own Muslim populations, and their own calculations about the threat posed by extremist groups or ideologies. Beijing, for instance, prioritizes terrorism and religion-based extremism as a threat because it worries about separatist activities in Xinjiang, but nonetheless shies away from becoming closely associated with the wars in Afghanistan and Iraq. Manila has worked actively with the United States in the fight against Islamist extremism because the Philippine government faces a similar threat in its Muslim-majority southern island of Mindanao. Indonesia, although it too has been victimized by Islamist terrorists, has been more ambivalent about the war on terrorism, perhaps a reflection of its large Muslim population skeptical of U.S. policies in the Middle East and the wars in Afghanistan and Iraq. Many Indian officials hoped that a common opposition to Islamist extremism might more closely align U.S. policies with India's, but have deeply resented Washington's insistence on regarding Pakistan as part of the solution in the war against terrorism rather than as a source of the problem. The September 11 attacks, in short, have had a mixed record in focusing Asian thinking on new security challenges posed by terrorist groups and other nonstate actors.

This is not to suggest that Asians have altogether overlooked these new types of challenges; Asia too has shifted from a geopolitical, state-centered definition of security to one encompassing a broader range of nonstate-based threats. In the mid-1990s, China introduced a "new security concept" that called for the replacement of traditional power politics by a new paradigm of mutual trust, mutual benefit, equality, and coordination. This did not mean that the communist government in Beijing had suddenly embraced a philosophy more associated with pacifists. Rather, China saw these principles as a way to insulate itself from pressures exerted by the far stronger United States. As part of this new international agenda promoting multilateralism and a rejection of coercion, the new security concept also gave increased emphasis to nontraditional security concerns. The Shanghai Cooperation Organization (SCO), established in 2001 and linking China, Russia, and four of the new Central Asian states, reflects the tenets and priorities of this new security concept. In addition to the SCO's initial focus on terrorism, separatism, and extremism, more recent SCO statements have highlighted transnational crime, drug trafficking, and cyberwarfare as security concerns.

The 2003 SARS crisis served as something of a milestone in Asian attitudes toward new security challenges. Until then, health security had not customarily been included among the region's principal security concerns. The SARS scare accelerated the reconceptualization of security across the region. The crisis generated unprecedented consultation and sometimes coordination among China, Japan, South Korea, and the ASEAN countries. Regional leaders, for example, worked to harmonize travel procedures to ensure adequate health screening at points of origin as a way of slowing the spread of the infection. As Yanzhong Huang writes of the 2009 H1N1 flu pandemic in chapter 6 of this volume, by the end of the twenty-first century's first decade, health had been transformed "from a humanitarian, technical, 'low politics' issue to one that featured prominently on the security agenda" of Asian nations.

The growing importance of these transnational threats and the increasingly interconnected character of modern society place a greater premium on international cooperation and the institutions that can promote such cooperation. But other compulsions also encouraged Asian leaders to pay greater heed to the new security challenges. For instance, consider the first ASEAN Defence Ministers' Meeting–Plus, which took place in Hanoi in October 2010 and brought together the defense ministers of the ten ASEAN states and those of Australia, China, India, Japan, New Zealand, Russia, South Korea, and the United States. The Vietnamese hosts deliberately steered discussions away from sensitive geopolitical issues, such as territorial disputes, in favor of a safer nontraditional security agenda featuring humanitarian aid, disaster relief, maritime security, counterterrorism, and peacekeeping operations. Similarly, other Asian-based security organizations, such as the ASEAN+3 and the ASEAN Regional Forum, have featured extensive discussion of these less sensitive nontraditional issues.

In recent years, Chinese officials have repeatedly spoken about the need for international cooperation as a way to address these new security challenges. However, this emphasis on international cooperation also offers Beijing a variety of other benefits. It is useful in assuring neighbors of Beijing's peaceful intent and in dampening anxieties about China's rapidly growing economic and military power. It can be used to counter U.S. military influence and security alliances in the region. And it can help neutralize demands from the United States and other Western countries for a greater voice on matters sensitive to China.

"Asia," of course, is not a singular geographical entity, and generalizations concerning "Asian thinking" about new or nontraditional security challenges inevitably fail to distinguish among the various regions of Asia, or among states within a particular region. South Korea, for instance, which shares a border with heavily militarized North Korea, is considerably more focused on the possibility of a cross-border invasion and full-fledged armed conflict than is China or Japan. As a general rule, the countries of Southeast Asia assign a higher priority to illegal migration and drug trafficking than do their Northeast Asian counterparts. Even within a country, definitions of what constitutes a new security challenge may vary considerably. Officials concerned primarily with economic development are likely to place less priority on air quality or other forms of environmental degradation than those working on health issues.

## A Review of New Security Challenges in Asia

Much of the recent scholarship on new security challenges in Asia has focused on a handful of issues: nuclear proliferation, transnational terrorism, climate change and environmental degradation, and energy security. Several other challenges, however, are emerging as critical concerns in Asia, and thus to U.S. interests in the region—water security, food security, pandemic disease, and transnational crime/terrorism (including drug trafficking, piracy, and cybercrime).

All four of these new security challenges are widespread, affecting all parts of Asia. Water security—the availability of sufficient volumes of clean water for human, agricultural, and industrial needs—is a concern for policymakers and communities across China, South Asia, and Southeast Asia. As Kenneth Pomeranz points out in chapter 2, the rivers arising on the Tibetan Plateau in the Himalayas serve almost half the world's population as they flow across China (especially the Yellow and Yangzi rivers), Southeast Asia (the Mekong and Irrawaddy), and South Asia (the Brahmaputra, Ganges, and Indus). Similarly, food security—the ability of states to provide sufficient nutrition to growing and, in many parts of Asia, increasingly affluent populations—is a mounting concern. In chapter 5, Robert Pomeroy explores one manifestation of this new preoccupation with food security in his examination of overfishing in Southeast Asia. And in chapter 8, Elizabeth Wishnick demonstrates how the related issue of food safety is having a worldwide impact with the growth of global food supply chains. Pandemic disease throughout history has transcended localities and become a global threat, but as Jonathan and Rachel Schwartz remind us in chapter 7, "Certain attributes of expanding globalization—such as the movement of goods, services, and people across the planet in ever-increasing numbers—have exacerbated human vulnerability to pandemics." In chapter 9, Justin Hastings examines the links between transnational crime and terrorism in maritime Southeast Asia, but these phenomena are just as much a problem in the borderlands of mainland Southeast Asia and South Asia. Cybersecurity threats, as Adam Segal ably describes them in chapter 10, arise in a realm that is universal and expanding in size. Although some states with a higher degree of dependence on the Internet are at greater risk now, these challenges will increasingly affect all states in the near future.

All four of these challenges can also have a huge impact in the event of a crisis—affecting tens or even hundreds of millions of people. Reduced water flow, silting, and pollution are critical problems for the populations concentrated along Asia's rivers. As Eric Strahorn notes in chapter 4, the 2010 flooding of the Indus River in Pakistan displaced 20 million people—more than 10 percent of the country's population. Pomeroy observes that about half of Southeast Asia's population of 540 million gets more than 20 percent of their animal protein from rapidly declining fish stocks. The three most recent instances of pandemics in Asia—SARS, H1N1 (avian influenza), and H5N1 (swine influenza)—fortunately did not reach the mortality/morbidity levels of the most severe pandemics recorded, such as the Spanish influenza catastrophe of 1918–19 that killed 50 million to 100 million worldwide. But most scientists fear that more lethal mutations of pandemic disease are almost inevitable, and that Asia stands a good chance of being the epicenter. Thus, policymakers and security planners see a potential future landscape of flood, drought, famine, disease, and major migration on scales almost unimaginable.

Even before reaching such a scale, however, these new security challenges are impeding political and economic stability within states. Recent years have witnessed an increase in unrest and disputes between people and their governments, between competing users of a resource, between upstream and downstream communities, and between business and government. Given the potential severity of the consequences, and the huge variations in political stability among Asian states, it is difficult to generalize about the potential effects of these new challenges. For instance, the December 2004 Indian Ocean tsunami killed 230,000 people, primarily in Indonesia, Thailand, and Sri Lanka, and in Indonesia led to a dramatic and unexpected resolution of the decades-long separatist struggle in Aceh. The March 2011 earthquake and tsunami of similar magnitude in Japan killed less than one-tenth this number—about 16,000 people—and even the subsequent Fukushima nuclear crisis did not put at risk Japan's stability, despite the enormous cost of the damage. These two illustrations suggest the range of consequences can prove manageable or catastrophic depending on the level of national preparedness, the strength and skill of crisis response teams, and the political, economic, and social resilience of the state.

These new security threats are significant also in that each carries the potential to affect relations among states. Yanzhong Huang notes that China's heavy-handed response to the H1N1 pandemic, which included large-scale suspension of flights and collective quarantines, damaged that country's relations with important trade partners. China's response to H1N1 was markedly different from its earlier handling of SARS, when Beijing refused to acknowledge the extent of the outbreak until multiple serious cases were diagnosed in Hong Kong. Wishnick demonstrates that suppression of information in China is still a problem, as during the 2008 melamine-tainted milk crisis, which required pressure from New Zealand before China was willing to act. Pomeranz likewise describes how China's management of rivers on the Tibetan Plateau colors its relations with countries across South and Southeast Asia, with suspicions heightened when information (in this case on water flow and dam-building plans) is not shared with downstream neighbors. Pomeranz also provides the example of Pakistani allegations of Indian manipulation of water resources as a cause of the devastating 2010 floods—in this case an illustration of how new security challenges intertwine with traditional political/security disputes. Such tensions are obvious, of course, in relation to water, which as Strahorn notes, does not neatly divide along national borders. Segal, meanwhile, demonstrates that cybersecurity challenges have the potential to lead to conflict as states work toward determinations that some cyberthreats will be viewed and responded to as acts of war.

Given the severity of these new security challenges, it is hardly surprising that these threats are no longer incidental policy concerns, but rather are being elevated, as evidenced in government responses and new strategy documents, to the level of high politics and international relations. The worst-case scenarios are staggering—the potential for tens of millions of casualties or refugees fleeing floods, drought, famine, disease, or interstate conflict triggered by these new transnational threats. A review of the four challenges in this volume suggests that U.S. and Asian policymakers and security planners are right to be focusing on them.

## Managing New Security Challenges

The importance and policy salience of these new security challenges are clear. Less obvious is how best to prepare for, manage, and mitigate their impact. Again, a review of the four challenges described in this volume allows us to identify four important reasons why fashioning an appropriate policy response has so far proved difficult.

The first reason arises from the sheer complexity of the new security challenges. As David Pietz clearly describes the situation in chapter 3, pressure on water resources in northern China stems from increasing population, rapid industrial development, growing agricultural demand, worsening pollution, climate change, and historical legacies in water management systems. Given the complex web of causal factors and relationships here, managing water security challenges requires more than simple solutions. To cite another example, Pietz notes that the transition to biofuels to alleviate energy security concerns can increase pressure on arable land and drive up food prices, thus contributing to food insecurity.

Second, these new challenges arise and threaten security much more rapidly than those faced by previous generations of policymakers and security planners. This is evident when looking at how quickly pandemic disease spreads because of international air travel, rendering even measures like quarantines only marginally effective, or at how cyberthreats can be unleashed within milliseconds at the click of a computer mouse. Segal argues, moreover, that this trend is on an ever-quickening trajectory, as the World Wide Web becomes a more central component of international trade and economic relations.

Third, and perhaps most troublesome, is the attribution problem. This is of course a particular challenge with cybersecurity threats, which Segal defines as "the use of computer power for intelligence gathering or to attack the computer, communications, transportation, and energy networks of states or nongovernmental groups," and which can be exceedingly difficult to trace to the source of the threat. For instance, states are joined in cyberspace by (sometimes independent) nonstate actors, which, even if just individuals, wield enormous power. The attribution problem reduces the salience of traditional deterrence policies in cyberspace. Attribution is similarly a challenge in water security. Pietz, for instance, describes how Pakistani allegations of Indian diversion of water resources (frequently characterized as water theft or water terrorism), even if unfounded, are widely cited by government and the media. Pomeroy illustrates how overfishing leads to the classic case of the tragedy of the commons, with increasing competition and pressure on resources, combined with an absence of frameworks to mitigate these new pressures, leading to a vicious cycle of overfishing.

Fourth, and perhaps most important, managing new security challenges is so difficult because success depends on integrating new frameworks of cooperation within governments, between governments, and between governments and the private sector. From the arguments presented in this volume, part of the solution to managing new security challenges is to adopt a "whole-of-government" response. Within states, different government agencies need to develop means to work with one another, and with private-sector actors, as Huang demonstrates in the realm of public health. In terms of water security, Pietz describes tensions within the Chinese government between national ministries and provincial authorities, further complicated by different interests among the provinces. Pomeranz similarly highlights this divergence of interest between central and local authorities, and notes that China's central government frequently cannot monitor implementation of its directives, while local authorities often have little reason to comply. Hastings describes the same phenomenon in Southeast Asia, when central authorities and local officials have different objectives and incentives in managing the challenge of smuggling. Schwartz and Schwartz provide a detailed assessment of the pros and cons of centralized (as in China) versus decentralized (as in the United States) public health systems in response to pandemic threats. Wishnick judges that decentralization of the food industry in China and inadequate regulation have worsened risk.

Shortcomings in government response may arise from either lack of policies and capabilities, or absence of oversight even when the policy frameworks and capabilities exist. On the policy side, many Asian states simply lack the capacity to respond effectively to new security challenges. Huang notes that inadequate planning and communication can lead governments to address threats like pandemics with heavy-handed responses like quarantine, and Pietz underscores the absence of institutional capacity in China to effectively manage water security. Alternatively, many of the threats arise from or are exacerbated by lack of state oversight. Hastings, for instance, describes the limitations of Indonesian and Philippine state control of customs and immigration networks, and argues that smuggling becomes easy in such environments, where more nefarious actors like the Jemaah Islamiyah terrorist group are quick to take advantage of these networks. The two shortcomings combine in gray areas beyond the effective control of the state, where new security challenges can emerge, grow, and metastasize before governments even become aware of them. Segal adds that cyberspace serves as the ultimate gray area, where lines of authority are unclear and blurred distinctions and still-emerging norms of behavior provide space for crime and security threats to flourish.

International cooperation poses even more challenges. Huang, citing Beijing's handling of the H1N1 pandemic, illustrates how political considerations can triumph over scientific realities, and lead governments to adopt broad trade and travel restrictions that turn out to be more expensive than are warranted and damage relations among states. Schwartz and Schwartz develop this idea further, arguing that new pandemics demand international coordination, preparedness, and response, because vaccines and quarantine-based, state-specific solutions will never meet demand or be able to address the challenges of a severe global pandemic. Both Pomeranz and Pietz note similar trends in water security, explaining that unchecked "water nationalism" is a potential source of interstate conflict, while Pomeroy provides parallel examples in food security, and the increase in international disputes over fishing rights following the establishment of exclusive economic zones in the 1970s.

There are some countervailing positive examples. Schwartz and Schwartz, for example, describe United States–China cooperation on pandemics in the years after the SARS and H5N1 pandemics; during the H1N1 outbreak the two countries enjoyed much closer interaction and placed health officials in each other's public health systems. Yet in general, the international trends are less collaborative. Pietz shows how Chinese investment in agricultural resources overseas through direct land ownership or long-term leases has the potential to cause international problems, which some authors have described as a new form of colonialism.[23] Segal details international cooperation in the face of cyberthreats along a spectrum from traditional Cold War–style deterrence to a more public health–style model dominated by prevention and resilience, and argues forcefully for the need to establish norms of behavior, as the United States and the Soviet Union did for nuclear postures and doctrines during the Cold War. Wishnick, meanwhile, echoes this recommendation with calls for an alignment of varying international standards of food safety—something ever more important as globalization deepens.

A final complicating issue is the need for various government agencies to work more effectively with private-sector actors, both within their own country and internationally. Such a requirement is clear in the case of pandemics, where, as Huang notes, governments must collaborate with private-sector vaccine manufacturers to secure supplies of vaccines, and with private shipping and transportation companies to move vaccines where needed. Public-private cooperation is also key for managing cyberthreats; Segal describes how Japan and South Korea have created a government–military–private sector triad system to bolster defense of networks (although this is still beset by conflicts among different agencies and between government and the private sector).

One common thread that emerges from all these chapters is a need for responsive, flexible systems to identify, respond to, and manage threats, rather than top-down centralized responses, which are better suited to establishing policy and regulatory frameworks. Pietz demonstrates how subsidies on agricultural water and grain distort market signals and affect production, which does little to help resolve water security tensions. Similar issues arise with energy subsidies—a common phenomenon across the region. Pomeranz points to the damaging impact of price subsidies as barriers to effective solutions. Segal highlights the dangers of moving away from the current form of the Internet—an open, relatively secure, globally connected network—to a patchwork of national or regional blocs.

At a fundamental level, managing new security challenges therefore becomes an issue of transparency and trust. Both Huang and Schwartz and Schwartz describe this phenomenon in relation to pandemic threats, where governments and the media have to strike a balance between conveying adequate amounts of accurate information without provoking panic. Schwartz and Schwartz take this one step further by assessing how propaganda affects information flows, and argue that the open U.S. system is more effective than China's system of censorship and suppression of news for political reasons. Wishnick, looking at food safety, notes that in crisis situations the Chinese media has a dual function: to assist in crisis control (as does the Western media), but also to help the state in image control, to preserve the reputation and authority of the government. Huang elucidates how increased transparency, cooperation among the government and the media, and improved surveillance networks can help accomplish other public health goals in addition to safeguarding against pandemic disease. Pietz cites China's reluctance to share water flow and rainfall data with downstream countries in Southeast Asia and South Asia as an impediment to effective cooperation on water security issues, while Pomeranz describes China's failure to respond to Indian requests for more information about dam-building plans in Tibet as a significant problem. Pomeranz argues persuasively that international exchange of information is often more important than building bilateral frameworks.

## The Tasks Ahead

Notwithstanding the increased emphasis U.S. security planners and policy-makers give these new security challenges, the job of redirecting mindsets and marshaling resources has barely begun. Leslie Gelb, one of the "wise men" of the U.S. foreign policy establishment, has complained that "Washington still principally thinks of its security in traditional military terms and responds to threats with military means." The United States, Gelb has written, must "redefine 'security' to harmonize with twenty-first-century realities."[24] Gelb had economics in mind as he penned these words. His advice, however, appears equally valid for new security challenges of the sort discussed in this volume.

Similarly, Asian governments have only just started to acknowledge the extent to which their security agendas have broadened in recent decades. It is one thing for Chinese president Hu Jintao to declare that "health security is part of national security," as Yanzhong Huang relates in chapter 6. It is an altogether different matter, even for an autocratic regime, to coax vast government bureaucracies out of established routines. Less centralized governments in the region, especially those anxious about the rising power of one or another of their neighbors, confront an even more daunting task in encouraging national security managers to abandon old ideas.

If outdated modes of thought pose one obstacle for redefining security, budgetary constraints are another. The United States in particular has entered an era of relative austerity; even its defense budget can no longer expect to emerge unscathed from the scalpels of those who would scale back spending. The specific circumstances in each Asian country differ, but defense planners in even the richest countries in the region also compete for budgetary resources with a host of other claimants, many enjoying substantial domestic political influence. Those arguing for greater allocation of resources for nontraditional or less familiar threats face an especially difficult task. No doubt they will not obtain all the resources they think these risks demand. Nonetheless, it is likely that defense spending in the coming years will reflect a concern about these new security challenges in a manner unimaginable just a decade ago.

The heightened importance of these new security challenges is, to some extent, a reflection of past successes. The United States would not be nearly so likely to think about drug trafficking and environmental degradation in security terms if it still faced tens of thousands of Soviet nuclear warheads poised atop intercontinental ballistic missiles on hair-trigger alert. Similarly, for the first time in history, Chinese leaders now worry as much about food safety as about food security—but only because China has finally defeated the age-old scourge of famine and widespread hunger. Unprecedented success in providing China's people with enough to eat now necessitates new attention to the safety of what they eat.

The contributors to this book recognize that the twenty-first century offers a considerably broader menu of challenges and threats than any earlier era. They argue that new challenges demand new responses—something traditional bureaucracies struggle to produce. They maintain that old notions of national autonomy and state sovereignty must give way to fresh ways of conceptualizing problems and devising solutions. They underscore the incomplete nature of the regional response to these new challenges, including the failure to build robust frameworks and organizations.

In like fashion, Hillary Clinton has spoken of the need to craft new regional organizations and global institutions that are "durable and dynamic enough to help us meet today's challenges and adapt to threats that we cannot even conceive of." Referring to the network of alliances, partnerships, and institutions created in the years after World War II, she has observed that this architecture "served a different time and a different world."[25] The "complex transnational challenges" offered by the new century, she adds, "requires a set of institutions capable of mustering collective action."[26]

The now-former U.S. secretary of state is correct. If the United States and its Asian partners are to surmount the challenges of a new century, they must break out of the thought patterns of the previous one. How well they succeed in this task will go far to determining whether the twenty-first century escapes many of the calamities of the twentieth.

## Notes

1. Hillary Rodham Clinton, "Remarks on United States Foreign Policy," September 8, 2010, transcript, U.S. Department of State, http://www.state.gov/secretary/rm/2010/09/146917.htm.

2. Barack H. Obama, *National Security Strategy of the United States* (Washington, D.C.: White House, 2010), http://www.whitehouse.gov/sites/default/files/rss_viewer/national_security_strategy.pdf.

3. Yizhou Wang, "Defining Non-Traditional Security and Its Implications for China," http://www.irchina.org/en/pdf/wyz07a.pdf.

4. Susan L. Craig, "Chinese Perceptions of Traditional and Nontraditional Security Threats," March 2007, http://www.strategicstudiesinstitute.army.mil/pdffiles/pub 765.pdf.

5. Les Aspin, *Report on the Bottom-Up Review* (Washington, D.C.: Federation of American Scientists, 1993), http://www.fas.org/man/docs/bur/part01.htm. This early document was strikingly limited and traditional in its definition of these new dangers, compared with the wide sweep of transnational threats that were soon regularly evoked by American policymakers.

6. George H. W. Bush, "Address to the United Nations," October 1, 1990, transcript and Adobe Flash audio, 23:25, Miller Center of Public Affairs, University of Virginia, http://millercenter.org/scripps/archive/speeches/detail/3426.

7. James A. Baker III, "America in Asia: Emerging Architecture for a Pacific Community," *Foreign Affairs* 70 (1991): 2, http://www.gwu.edu/~power/literature/dbase/baker1.pdf.

8. George H. W. Bush, *National Security Strategy of the United States* (Washington, D.C.: White House, 1991), http://www.fas.org/man/docs/918015-nss.htm.

9. William J. Clinton, "State of the Union Address," January 23, 1996, transcript and Windows Media video, 62:09, Miller Center of Public Affairs, University of Virginia, http://millercenter.org/scripps/archive/speeches/detail/5494.

10. William J. Clinton, *A National Security Strategy for a New Century* (Washington, D.C.: White House, 1997), http://clinton2.nara.gov/WH/EOP/NSC/Strategy/.

11. William J. Clinton, "State of the Union Address," January 19, 1999, transcript, Office of the Press Secretary, White House, http://clinton2.nara.gov/WH/SOTU99/.

12. Clinton, *National Security Strategy*.

13. Joseph S. Nye Jr., "Strategy for East Asia and the U.S.-Japan Security Alliance," presentation, Pacific Forum Center for Strategic and International Studies/Japanese Institute of International Affairs, Washington, D.C., March 29, 1995, http://www.defense.gov/Speeches/Speech.aspx?SpeechID=878.

14. Warren Christopher, interview by Jim Lehrer, *PBS NewsHour*, PBS, November 26, 1996, http://www.pbs.org/newshour/bb/asia/july-dec96/christopher_11-26.html.

15. Condoleezza Rice, "The Promise of Democratic Peace," *Washington Post*, December 11, 2005, http://www.washingtonpost.com/wp-dyn/content/article/2005/12/09/AR2005120901711.html.

16. Ibid.

17. George W. Bush, *National Security Strategy of the United States* (Washington, D.C.: White House, 2006), http://georgewbush-whitehouse.archives.gov/nsc/nss/2006/sectionX.html.

18. For one expression of official thinking about this new threat, see William J. Lynn III, "Defending a New Domain: The Pentagon's Cyberstrategy," *Foreign Affairs* 89, no. 5 (September–October 2010), http://www.usna.edu/AcResearch/William_Lynn_III_Defending_a_New_Domain.pdf.

19. Hillary Rodham Clinton, "U.S.-Asia Relations: Indispensable to Our Future," February 13, 2009, transcript, U.S. Department of State, http://www.state.gov/secretary/rm/2009a/02/117333.htm.

20. Obama, *National Security Strategy*.

21. Barack H. Obama, "Remarks by President Barack Obama at Suntory Hall," November 14, 2009, transcript, Office of the Press Secretary, White House, http://www.whitehouse.gov/the-press-office/remarks-president-barack-obama-suntory-hall.

22. Neil MacFarquhar, "UN Deadlock on Addressing Climate Shift," *New York Times*, July 21, 2011, http://www.nytimes.com/2011/07/21/world/21nations.html.

23. See chapter 3 in this volume by David Pietz, in which he cites Ely Ratner, "The Emergent Security Threats Reshaping China's Rise," *Washington Quarterly* 34, no. 1 (Winter 2011): 29–44, http://www.twq.com/11winter/docs/11winter_Ratner.pdf.

24. Leslie H. Gelb, "GDP Now Matters More Than Force," *Foreign Affairs* 89, no. 6 (November–December 2010): 35.

25. Clinton, "Remarks."

26. Hillary Clinton, "America's Pacific Century," *Foreign Policy*, November 2011, http://www.foreignpolicy.com/articles/2011/10/11/americas_pacific_century.

# Chapter 2

# Drought, Climate Change, and the Political Economy of Himalayan Dam Building

*Kenneth Pomeranz*

The Himalaya–Tibet region is Asia's water tower. Rivers beginning here serve 47 percent of the world's people and huge amounts of irrigated agriculture.[1] The heights from which the waters descend create unmatched hydropower potential, most of it still untapped. By one simple measure—power potential divided by number of people to be displaced—Himalayan dam sites are among the most desirable in the world; they also avoid some serious environmental complications of lowland dams in warm areas. But they also involve high risks, difficult trade-offs, and great potential for conflict.

Increased manipulation of these waters is central to development planning in China, India, Pakistan, Bangladesh, Vietnam, Thailand, and elsewhere. But many of these plans are mutually incompatible; even current levels and modes of water use may be unsustainable. While no violent international conflicts seem imminent, unchecked "water nationalism" could easily lead to future clashes.[2] Meanwhile, Pakistan's horrific 2010 floods showed that the existing infrastructure cannot handle increasingly volatile weather, that those same fluctuations make the costs and benefits of new projects increasingly uncertain, and that failure can threaten both popular welfare and state security.

Unsurprisingly, China and India loom largest in this story, and most of this chapter focuses on them. Their economic and social gains both before and since economic liberalization have depended on unsustainable rates of groundwater extraction, especially for irrigation. Both governments also see hydropower as essential to continuing rapid growth while curbing carbon emissions and limiting dependence on imported energy. Some of the enormous Himalayan projects under consideration will probably do less to relieve water stress than would spending comparable sums on less heroic measures, such as fixing leaky pipes or tightening enforcement of wastewater treatment standards, but they seem likely to go ahead nonetheless.

China's choices will be the most important of all. Nine of Asia's ten largest rivers (all but the Ganges) have at least one source on China's side of the border—in Tibet, where water politics interacts with other sensitive political and security issues. Along with having the leverage that comes from being upstream, China has the technical capacity and financial resources to build any project it chooses, without needing international lenders or engineers. This gives it greater freedom of action than any other state involved, and makes it logical for us to view these issues from a Chinese perspective first. But China's freedom of action is not absolute, and is shaped by regional relationships and its own long history of water management.

## Chinese Water Policy in Historical Perspective

For more than a thousand years, Chinese governments have transferred resources from well-watered southern regions to dryer northern ones where agricultural yields were insufficient to support the armies and capitals that states placed there. For centuries, this mostly involved transferring vast amounts of grain along the 1,000-mile Grand Canal; the Qing Dynasty (1644–1912) added further mechanisms through which southern taxes paid for ecological stabilization projects in the north and northwest. These subsidized projects included flood control on various northern rivers, subsidies for well-digging in semiarid northern and northwestern areas, and so on. Although the flood control measures were more famous and more expensive (the Yellow River alone consumed 10 to 20 percent of Qing spending, ca. 1780–1840), combating water shortages was equally significant. Government-sponsored and -subsidized campaigns added at least 600,000 wells in five northern provinces during the Qianlong reign (1736–96) alone; deep and thus expensive wells became ever more important as the population grew and the water table fell.[3] Today North and Northwest China have about 30 percent of China's population and half of its farmland, but only 6 to 7 percent of its water supply.

For a long time, these efforts helped stabilize poorer regions, though some measures failed, and costs rose as population growth increased ecological fragility.[4] But in the nineteenth century, the entire system crashed. Costs soared and administration weakened, while internal rebellion and foreign incursions raised military spending sharply, so that China could no longer spend relatively generously on infrastructure while taxing lightly.[5] The resulting problems were most severe and most enduring in the North and Northwest. Floods increased sharply with declining river control spending; but the big killer was drought, exacerbated by population growth, by the loss of some state subsidies for deep wells, and by a decline in public order. Xia Mingfang has estimated that famine caused 38 million deaths from 1865 to 1949, more than 80 percent in the North and Northwest.[6]

Water attracted considerable government attention again after 1949, with efforts again concentrated in the North and Northwest. Irrigated area tripled between 1949 and 1980 (growing only slightly since then); about two-thirds of the gains came in northern and northwestern areas.[7] Many technologies were employed, but deep wells with power-driven pumps were especially important. Large-scale groundwater withdrawals began circa 1960, peaking in the 1970s at ten times the 1949–61 annual rate; today's rate is about quadruple that of 1949–61.[8] This extraction vastly exceeds the natural recharge rate of the aquifers; meanwhile, almost all the North's surface water is in use, and demand keeps growing. Consequently, water shortages and falling water tables are common throughout northern China.

Waste-reducing technologies exist (e.g., drip irrigation systems), but most are expensive, and some—when implemented elsewhere—actually made irrigation so much more efficient (and therefore profitable) that demand rose.[9] More mundane measures—fixing leaky faucets, lining irrigation ditches, and improving wastewater treatment to allow more reuse—could make a big difference, but the central government cannot monitor implementation closely, and local actors often have little reason to comply. More commercially realistic pricing of irrigation water would help, but such measures could make many marginal farms uneconomical, accelerating China's already rapid urbanization.

This last point is worth emphasizing. It would not be a huge *economic* problem if higher water prices reduced China's farm output. China can certainly afford to import more food, and diverting more water to cities might increase its overall output. Studies suggest that a gallon of water generates up to sixty times more output in Tianjin industry as in North China agriculture.[10] But the government does not want to become dependent on foreign grain, and has consequently kept net imports at around 5 percent of total supply. Other food purchasers might not welcome vastly higher Chinese imports, either. Moreover, reduced farm output raises social concerns, which probably worry Chinese leaders more. The People's Republic of China has consistently sought to avoid developing large peri-urban shantytowns—characteristic of many third world countries—and has largely succeeded, using both spending and repression. But with annual net migration to cities now over 15 million and rising, maintaining that record will be difficult.[11] Raising water prices sharply would accelerate exit from the countryside, making it even harder to avoid the growth of slums. Consequently, while agricultural water use has become more efficient, rapid further improvements are unlikely, and industrial and domestic use is almost certain to continue rising with increasing population and incomes.[12]

## Chinese Water Diversion Plans and Their International Implications

Unable to reduce demand sufficiently, the state is again focusing on increasing supply, in part through centrally directed megaprojects. The most significant of these, a three-pronged effort to move water from South to North China, the so-called South-North Water Transfer Project, represents the largest construction project in history (figure 2.1).[13] The eastern route began operating in 2008, although it is having water quality problems. The central route is under way but behind schedule, facing both unanticipated environmental challenges and difficulties relocating displaced people.[14]

In the long run, the most internationally significant problems will probably come from the western routes, designed to tap the currently plentiful water of China's far southwest, where Tibet alone has 30 percent of China's freshwater (figure 2.2). The engineering challenges in that region are enormous, but so are the potential rewards, both in water supply and

*Figure 2.1. Proposed Routes for South-North Water Diversion in China*

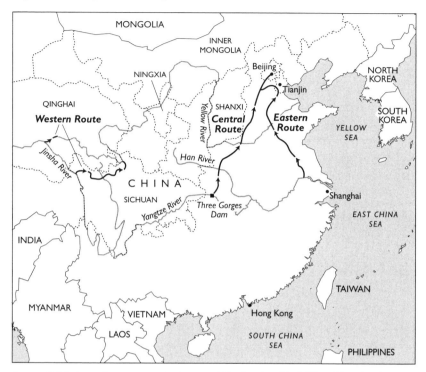

*Source:* Original map from water-technology.net, "The South-to-North Water Diversion Project, China," http://www.water-technology.net/projects/south_north/south_north1.html, modified by Kenneth Pomeranz and Christopher Heselton. Cartography by Bill Nelson.

in hydropower, because the Yangzi completes 90 percent of its drop to the sea before it enters China proper. The social, political, and environmental uncertainties involved touch places from Karachi to Saigon to Tianjin.[15]

China is considering a dam of 38,000 to 40,000 megawatts—almost twice the capacity of Three Gorges—on the Yarlong Zangbo River in Tibet (figure 2.3). The Yarlong Zangbo runs west to east up to its Great Bend, and then flows *south* into Assam to help form the Brahmaputra and Ganges, serving more than 300 million people. It is currently far less polluted than the Ganges, Yellow, Yangzi, or other major Asian rivers, making its waters especially valuable.[16] China recently disclosed that it has been building a smaller dam upstream from the Great Bend, at Zangmu—a development which it had previously refused to confirm even though construction was

*Figure 2.2. Chinese Water Supply by Region*

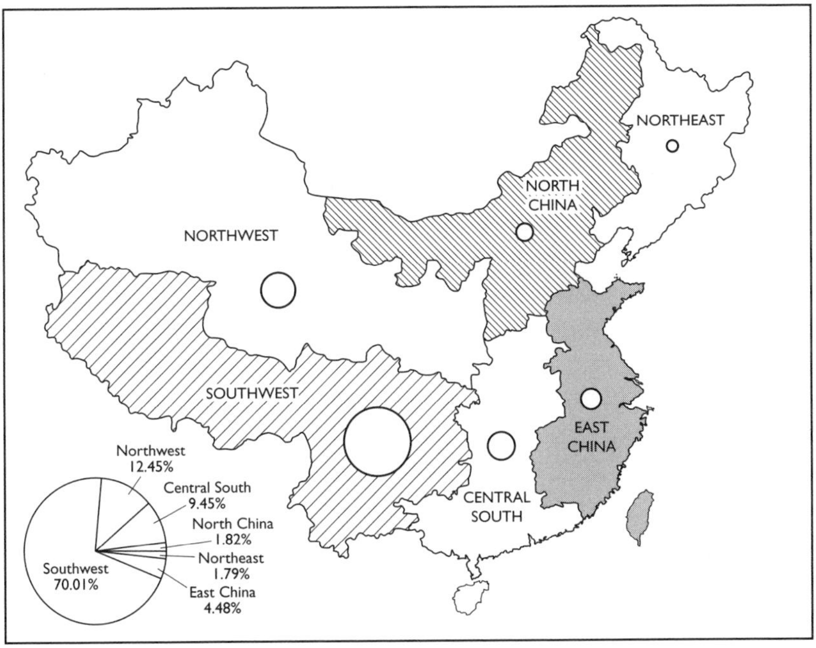

*Source:* Pan Jiazheng (Chinese National Committee on Large Dams), ed., *Large Dams in China: History, Achievement, Prospect* (Beijing: China Water Resources and Electric Power Press, 1987).

visible in satellite photos—and this smaller dam could provide power for a future Great Bend construction effort.[17]

Even if the Great Bend Dam is only a hydropower project, involving no diversion of water, it could affect Indians and Bangladeshis downstream. It would trap silt that currently enriches soils farther south; moreover, any significant water storage capacity would give China significant influence over fluctuations in water supply below the dam.[18] For instance, if China retained water to keep generators running in the early spring (before the monsoon rains arrived), water could become scarce during the planting season downstream; releasing water during the monsoon could exacerbate downstream floods. More Yarlong Zangbo dams are planned, apparently including one that would occupy some territory still disputed from the 1962 India-China war.[19]

If, however, as some sources claim, water will be diverted northward after it passes turbines at the Great Bend—or at any other point—then the

*Figure 2.3. The Yarlong Zangbo River and Other Rivers in Eastern Tibet*

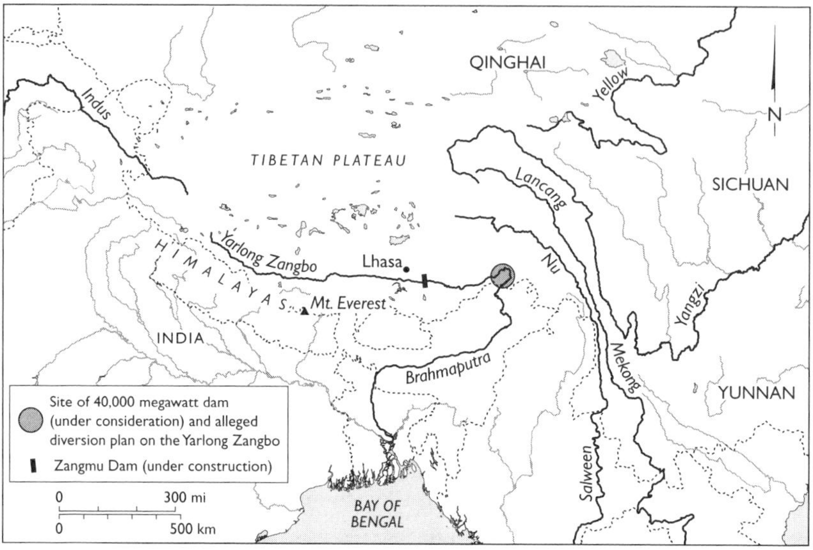

*Source:* Original map from Pete Winn, "Geology and Geography of Tibet and Western China," http://www.shangri-la-river-expeditions.com/wchinageo/wchinageo.html, modified by Kenneth Pomeranz and Christopher Heselton. Cartography by Bill Nelson.

implications for South Asians would become vastly more serious. In the worst case scenario, large parts of Northeast India and Bangladesh would be devastated. Though South Asians have long worried about such diversions, the Chinese government repeatedly denied such intentions until 2008. Since then, the picture has become murkier; China has not publicly replied to recent Indian requests for more information about its plans, though it has repeated its assurances that they will not affect the Brahmaputra in India.[20] No treaty for sharing this river exists, though Indian officials say they have sought one. Nor does it help the situation that while Chinese officials have said that the Zangmu project is a run-of-the-river dam, with no effect on water volumes downstream, Xinhua news agency's story revealing the dam (in Chinese) said that it would also benefit flood control and irrigation—goals that would require some water diversion.[21] And with growing uncertainty about whether the Yangzi can meet even the current demands on it, some fear that the overall south-north river diversion plan—which is definitely moving ahead—may ultimately require a large-scale diversion from some other river beginning in the Himalayas.[22] That climate change also threatens the sources of the Yangzi and Yellow rivers increases the temptation for China to divert the Yarlong Zangbo.

### Chinese Institutions and Incentives

While international water diversions are the projects that would most certainly lead to conflicts with its neighbors, many Chinese hydropower projects also raise border-crossing issues. It is thus important to note that Chinese water and energy policy has institutional biases that favor large hydro projects, including some that would otherwise probably not make economic or environmental sense. The semiprivate system governing watershed use since 2002 makes it easy for state agencies to quietly subsidize private dam builders through collusive transactions—and all the dam-building firms have high-level political connections.[23] Spectacular projects are also more useful for career building and stoking nationalism than improved maintenance and unglamorous conservation measures.

Moreover, Beijing sees hydropower from China's far southwest as a linchpin of its strategy, not only for economic growth but for maintaining leverage on China's fast-growing and increasingly outward-oriented coastal regions. Planning for Guangdong Province (including the industrial hub of the Pearl River Delta) to consume hydropower from Yunnan began in the 1980s; deliveries began in the 1990s. Starting in 2001, the central government began vetoing additional coal-fired power plants in Guangdong, thus ensuring that this booming province's energy infrastructure keeps it dependent on the rest of China rather than on imports.[24] The planned dams on the Yarlong Zangbo would apparently also send much of their power to the Pearl River Delta and Hong Kong.[25] Two maps of hydroelectric power projects—those built before 1987 and those begun or announced right after that—tell much of the story (figures 2.4 and 2.5). The pre-1987 projects (most of them pre-1976) reflect both limited technical capacity and cautions about introducing rapid change to ethnic minorities in the far west. More recently, increasing economic urgency and technical competence have placed engineering criteria in command, and Beijing's strategy for minority regions has increasingly emphasized raising incomes as the key to political loyalty rather than—as was still true until about twenty years ago—seeing cultural paternalism and a slower pace of change as politically stabilizing. The recent unbridled development of water projects represents only one aspect of that shift, but an important and potentially explosive one—especially when we also consider the implications for China's neighbors.

*Figure 2.4. Major Hydropower Projects in China Constructed before 1987*

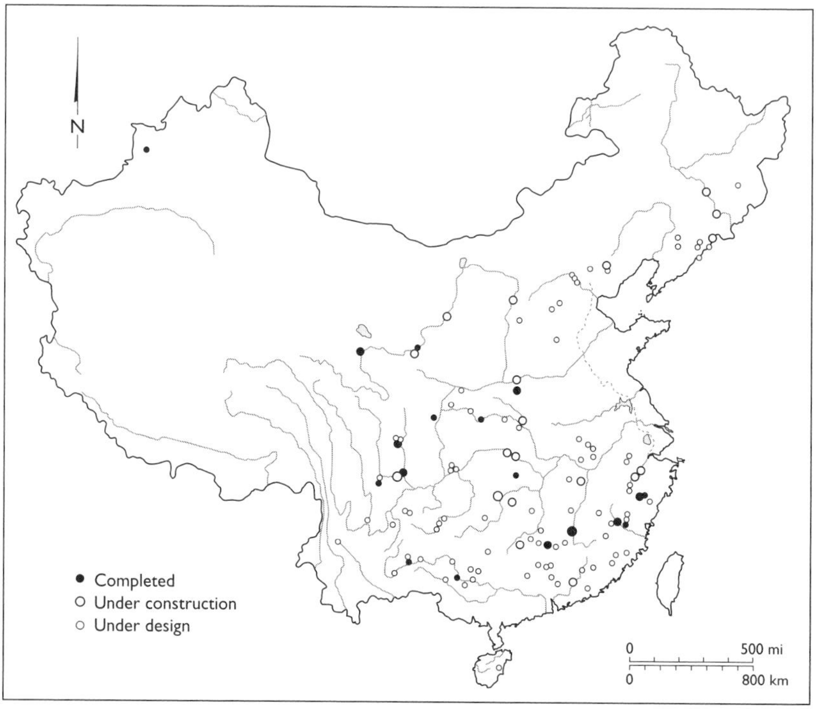

• Completed
○ Under construction
○ Under design

0 —————— 500 mi
0 —————— 800 km

*Source:* Pan Jiazheng (Chinese National Committee on Large Dams), ed., *Large Dams in China: History, Achievement, Prospect* (Beijing: China Water Resources and Electric Power Press, 1987). Cartography by Bill Nelson.

## South Asian Concerns

Having briefly outlined China's Himalayan water interests and outlook, let us now look at how South Asian water needs and projects intersect with them. South Asia's Green Revolution, like China's roughly contemporary agricultural gains, was essential to reducing hunger while its population continued to grow. Because parts of northern India and Pakistan (plus parts of South India) are significantly drier than North China—roughly half of Pakistan gets less rain than Phoenix, and about 80 percent gets less than Tel Aviv—South Asian agricultural growth depends on massive amounts of irrigation.[26]

Year-round irrigation systems, reducing reliance on seasonal floods, generally began in the late nineteenth century, especially in Punjab, a

*Figure 2.5.  Hydropower Projects in China Planned for Construction after 1987, as of 1988*

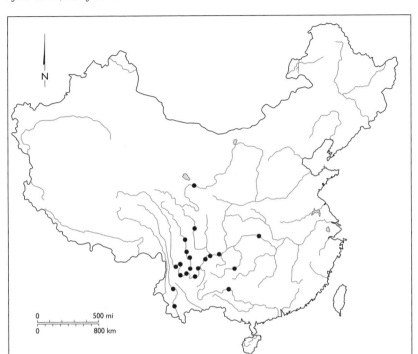

*Source:* Pan Jiazheng (Chinese National Committee on Large Dams), ed., *Large Dams in China: History, Achievement, Prospect* (Beijing: China Water Resources and Electric Power Press, 1987). Cartography by Bill Nelson.

major breadbasket for both India and Pakistan since then. Today, many of the surface-water-based systems are old, undermaintained, polluted, and inadequate for current needs.[27] As any country's installed base of water infrastructure grows, resources are expected to be reallocated from new construction to maintenance. But neither India nor Pakistan has done this to the predicted extent. The World Bank argues that water management in both countries is overstaffed and inefficient, and describes them as following a "'build/neglect/rebuild' philosophy of public works."[28] The Indus barely reaches the ocean much of the year, and can no longer flush its pollutants effectively.[29] These problems, coupled with population growth and reliance on high-yielding but thirsty crops, have created very serious water shortages, as well as flood control dangers.

Consequently, just as in northern China, northern India and Pakistan have increasingly relied on deep wells since 1960, leading to similar but even more severe problems. The charges paid for water in rural India are essentially the costs of powering the pumps, and rural electricity is heavily subsidized.[30] Groundwater supplies more than 70 percent of irrigation and 80 percent of water for domestic use in northern India,[31] and accounts for 50 percent of irrigation in Pakistan.[32] Most wells in both countries are private, and owners have every incentive to take whatever water they can reach from their land before somebody else drains the aquifer, a classic tragedy of the commons.[33] At the same time, many people have no electricity and/or no land on which to drill, so even very cheap power does not allow them to access groundwater; they buy water at hefty markups. Raising prices significantly for publicly controlled water is even harder than in China, because rural South Asians vote in national elections (more consequently, thus far, in India than in Pakistan). And while Chinese agriculture is reducing its water use, albeit not enough, all categories of Indian and Pakistani water use continue to increase.[34]

South Asia also faces particularly acute flood dangers. Monsoons create exceptionally large seasonal differences in water supply and, thus, water storage needs. Yet both India and Pakistan have unusually limited water storage capacity. The United States and Australia—wealthy countries with significant arid areas—can store more than 5,000 cubic meters of water per capita, and China about 2,200; the official figure for India is 200 and for Pakistan 150. The Indian figure probably underestimates capacity by missing many small facilities, but the general picture is nonetheless severe.[35] Being relatively young and increasingly deforested, the Himalayas erode relatively rapidly; consequently reservoirs silt up quickly, even with optimal care. Moreover, the Himalayan glaciers are shrinking—although how fast is unclear—raising the specter of increased flooding problems in the near and medium terms, followed by devastating droughts once the glaciers are gravely diminished.

Unsurprisingly, then, India has also considered massive water diversions, hoping they would address regional water shortages, generate hydropower, and perhaps reduce flood dangers. The largest plan, the "Inter-Linking of Rivers" project, was strongly supported by the government led by the Bharatiya Janata Party from 1998 to 2004. It would have taken water from Himalayan parts of the Brahmaputra and its tributaries, irrigating 35 million hectares (almost the area of Japan), mostly in the Northwest, at an officially estimated cost of $120 billion.[36] The current Congress Party–led government has shelved this idea, for a variety of reasons, but less grandiose diversion plans appear to be going forward.[37] Significantly, India would need some external financing to revive the large-scale Inter-Linking project, while China can finance its megaprojects internally. Thus China— being upriver and having the money and expertise to build on its own—is very much in the driver's seat, both with respect to India and with respect to countries along the Mekong, Salween, and so on.[38]

*Southeast Asian Concerns*

Mainland Southeast Asia has different, albeit related, water issues. On the whole, none of these countries is short of water in a "normal" year. Regional and seasonal droughts are a problem, however, and may prove more frequent; both 2009 and 2010 were particularly bad, although whether this indicates a trend is unclear.[39] Unlike in China and India, Southeast Asia has very few large dams, in part due to periods of warfare, civil unrest, limited state control, and isolation. However, Thailand and Vietnam are now considering major hydropower projects to reduce electricity shortages. Meanwhile, almost all of Southeast Asia's major rivers start in China, making these countries vulnerable in ways similar to Pakistan, Bangladesh, and (to a lesser extent) India. The timing of Chinese impoundment and release of upper Mekong waters, with multiple implications for Southeast Asia, has become increasingly contentious.

It is worth noting that even what might seem obviously desirable— evening out seasonal fluctuations in Southeast Asia's water supply—poses many potential problems. This is partly because freshwater fisheries in the Tonle Sap and Mekong Delta—the largest in the world—are hugely important for Southeast Asia diets and export earnings;[40] they account for roughly 80 percent of Cambodia's protein consumption, by one estimate.[41] The Tonle Sap has been shrinking, and the Mekong Delta suffers increased saltwater invasions as the river's flow decreases. Additionally, many fish lay and fertilize their eggs in response to seasonal changes in water levels, and can be seriously affected even if total annual flow is unchanged. Finally, dams—especially dams in Southeast Asia—would seriously hamper fish migration and reproduction. Technologies that have had some success in reducing these effects elsewhere, such as the fish ladders and elevators on the Columbia River, are unlikely to work here.

*Climate Change, Water Shortages, and Himalayan "Green" Power*

Meanwhile, climate change and other developments threaten the Himalayan water sources themselves, crucial for nine of Asia's ten largest rivers.[42] The likelihood of fewer days of rain per year in South Asia, but more
extreme precipitation events, makes increased water storage capacity even
more important. That does not mean that such capacity has to be built in
the mountains.[43] However, if it has to be built anyway, having a water-
storage project also generate sorely needed power is attractive. One can
certainly argue that global warming makes it all the more important that
major hydropower opportunities be exploited as a partial alternative to fossil fuels. Zhang Boting, deputy secretary general of the Chinese Society
for Hydropower Engineering, has said that the Great Bend Dam on the
Yarlong Zangbo would save roughly 200 million tons of carbon emissions
per year, equivalent to more than one-third of the United Kingdom's total
emissions.[44] Dams at high altitudes also drown relatively little vegetation in
their reservoirs; in subtropical or tropical lowlands, submerged, rotting vegetation can emit so much methane that carbon emissions from such dams
exceed those of fossil fuels burned for a comparable amount of electricity.[45]

Because diversions, unlike power generation, are a zero-sum game, officials are much less likely to tell international media that the likelihood of
greater future scarcities makes them more inclined toward "water nationalism." It is hard to believe, however, that this does not increase the appeal of
presenting others with a fait accompli, at least for some actors. But changes
already underway on the Himalayan Plateau may also frustrate these projects or make them even more risky. All that seems reasonably certain is that
climate change will put increasing pressure on water supplies.

Himalayan glaciers are shrinking. Recent samples from Tibetan glaciers
suggest that they have lost all the ice built up since the mid-1940s.[46] The
Intergovernmental Panel on Climate Change estimates that the Himalayan
highlands are warming at about twice the average global rate (and soot
deposits are making the glaciers themselves absorb more sunlight), so this
retreat will probably accelerate. One estimate has one-third of the Himalayan glaciers disappearing by 2050, and two-thirds by 2100.[47] Meanwhile,
large numbers of Tibetan lakes have disappeared—although the spottiness
of earlier mapping makes counting difficult—including some that fed the
Yellow River and Yangzi River.[48] There has also been considerable damage to parts of Tibet's permafrost layer, perhaps exacerbated by recent

road and railway building; this increases evaporation rates for water in the adjacent soil.[49]

Thus, even if all the engineering goes right, these projects might not deliver enough water and/or hydropower for long enough to be worthwhile. A number of the projects—particularly the Chinese ones—are also planned for seismically active areas, raising the possibility of catastrophic dam failures affecting millions. Increased glacial melting and the likelihood (in some climate models) of greater year-to-year variations in the size of monsoon rains also increase the risk of dam failures due to glacial outburst floods.[50] In short, climate change increases both the pressure to do something and the risks of making the wrong choice.

## Security Implications

The security implications of these problems are divided here into three categories: (1) the effects of water problems on food supplies and international markets, (2) possibilities for unrest within single countries, and (3) possibilities for cross-border conflict. This ordering goes from most to least likely to occur in the immediate future, but none of these threats can be dismissed.

### Food Security Issues

Because none of these projects can be built overnight, they cannot soon ameliorate the water problems plaguing Indian, Pakistani, or Chinese farmers; for the same reason, no area is likely to be immediately prejudiced by a massive water diversion. Thus the short-term question is the extent to which either existing water problems or water-price increases—implemented to ration water—make one of these countries into a much bigger buyer on international markets. China would seem most likely to voluntarily implement a price increase sharp enough to reduce domestic grain production, and could certainly offset such a decline by purchasing grain; but even in China's case this seems unlikely in the near term. The more likely danger, for now, is some combination of extreme weather (like the Pakistani floods in the summer of 2010) and the failure of *existing* infrastructure. More such events could certainly occur, and could be exacerbated by upstream water retention/release in another country. Some Pakistanis and Southeast Asians believe this has already happened due to projects on tributaries of the Indus and Mekong, respectively. Publicly available evidence does not confirm these accusations, but incomplete information fuels continued suspicions.[51]

In the longer term, rivers beginning in the Himalayas will be placed under enormous strain, and this pressure is likely to be exacerbated by climate change and glacial melting. The Strategic Forecasting Group (Mumbai) concludes that "the cumulative effect of water scarcity, glacial melting, disruptive precipitation patterns, flooding, desertification, pollution and soil erosion will be a massive reduction in the production of rice, wheat, maize and fish. . . . [By 2050], China and India alone will need to import more than 200–300 million [metric] tons of wheat and rice."[52] This projected shortfall, based on very modest assumptions about demand increases, is about five times the amount of wheat exported by the United States, Canada, and Australia combined last year, and thus would be hard to compensate for. If India and/or China eventually needs imports on anything close to this scale, and somehow managed to obtain them, many millions of people elsewhere would suffer unless global output unexpectedly soared. Such scenarios make some argue that river diversions are worth the substantial risks involved.

But many other possible palliatives exist. Some, like the megaprojects themselves, involve counting on advanced technology and taking on environmental risks of unknown magnitude. For example, crops genetically engineered for drought resistance could conceivably make a major contribution, but the probabilities and scale of both the relief and the complications are currently unknown. Meanwhile, low-risk palliatives, using well-known technologies—such as reducing water waste by lining more irrigation ditches, fixing and maintaining leaky pipes, and improving basic wastewater treatment—could theoretically solve much of the problem. However, they would require institutional reforms aimed at broad-based implementation of these measures and at removing existing disincentives to water savings.[53] They would also require sharp increases in water prices, which could create serious unrest among farmers, accelerate rural-urban migration, and, in the short run, increase agricultural shortfalls by causing the abandonment of marginal lands and/or crops (e.g., winter wheat in much of northern China). It is not clear that even the Chinese central government can force these sorts of changes on local governments and millions of people; the likelihood of success is considerably lower in South and Southeast Asia. Large river diversions may thus become the sole remaining option.

*Possibilities for Domestic Unrest*

Water insecurity is thus likely to exacerbate unrest in several countries in the region. The risks are probably smallest in China, although even there serious risks exist. First, to the extent that China either fails to solve North China's water shortages or relies on large rural price increases to do so, this will interfere with the government's efforts to moderate rural-urban inequality. Local water price increases have been quite unpopular, without being nearly enough to solve the problem.[54] Rural violence could target cadres (especially if allocations are perceived as unfair), water-using and water-polluting industries, or upstream/downstream communities. And if further development of the South-North Water Transfer Project coincides with more frequent water shortages in the south, as could well happen, unrest could appear there, too. Incidents would probably be local in nature, rather than targeted at Beijing; but enough of them, combined with other sources of discontent, could be hard to handle.

Further accelerating China's already very rapid urbanization could also strain the social fabric in some cities. China has thus far been relatively successful at preventing the growth of large slums lacking basic services, but the speed at which urbanization is now occurring makes this increasingly challenging. If water problems greatly increased the rate of exit from agriculture, keeping up would be still more difficult.

Worsening environmental problems in Tibet may exacerbate unrest there as well. The drying out of wetlands and disappearance of lakes directly affect Tibet's many herders and upsets many Tibetan Buddhists, for whom rivers and lakes are sacred. Big, visible water control projects could be lightning rods, especially insofar as good jobs on the projects are given to Han Chinese from other regions and the water and power are sent out of Tibet.

The threat to domestic order is still greater in downstream countries. Pakistan offers the most plausible nightmare scenarios. It is very dependent on a single river, which has been steadily drying up over the last few decades but can also have huge seasonal floods. The government had limited success in delivering relief in 2010, intensifying popular anger; and parts of the country already host an active insurgency. Some Islamist and military hardliners have blamed both the current floods and earlier droughts on Indian manipulations (with some, including a former head of the powerful Directorate for Inter-Services Intelligence, adding the United States and Israel to an alleged anti-Pakistan conspiracy), making these problems even more fraught for the current government.[55] Floods and droughts could also create large movements of internal or cross-border refugees, while upstream diversions could make such dislocations permanent. There is also potential for serious food crises if chronic droughts should continue to worsen in Pakistan or in northwestern India. Punjab, where agriculture is almost completely dependent on intensive irrigation, produces India's largest agricultural surpluses, including roughly half the wheat and rice procured by the central government for its food-price stabilization program.[56]

If either China or India deals with its problems through large-scale diversions, the big losers would be in Assam and especially Bangladesh. India is obligated not to reduce the flow of the Brahmaputra/Ganges into Bangladesh, but—in the event of a Chinese diversion—this would involve sacrificing many of its own citizens. One Indian commentator writes of "one hundred million" people in Assam and Bangladesh becoming refugees in the event that China diverts the Yarlong Zangbo / Brahmaputra, but this appears to be an off-the-cuff guess rather than a careful projection.[57] Of course, a project could adversely affect far fewer people than that and still be catastrophic.

*International Confrontations*

This brings us to the possibility that one or more Himalayan water projects could lead to major international confrontations. Among other things, this would probably be the scenario most threatening to U.S. interests. But even far short of outright "water wars," tensions exacerbated by water projects pose problems for the United States. If, for instance, fear of India is a major reason why Pakistan will neither stop supporting insurgents in Kashmir nor abandon the Taliban in Afghanistan, it seems logical that escalating anxieties about Indian dams worsen both situations.

India and Pakistan have the most difficult relationship of any pair of countries in the region, and water has become an increasingly important part of the problem. Although the 1960 Indus Waters Treaty has been largely respected by both sides, it dates from a time when the Indus had far more water than the signatories needed, and nonetheless took a decade to negotiate.[58] The Indus is now seriously depleted, while demands on its waters continue to grow. After a long period in which little new infrastructure was built on the Indus and its tributaries, both countries—but especially India—now have multiple large projects. Pakistan is mostly downstream from India, but some corners of India are downstream from Pakistani projects. Pakistan's accusation that Indian construction violated the Indus treaty was rejected by an international arbitrator in 2007, to the dismay of many Pakistanis. A subsequent set of complaints are under negotiation. While experts have been unconvinced by Pakistani charges that India is retaining water that belongs to them under the treaty, current projects would give the Indians enough storage capacity to hold about one month's flow of the Indus;[59] were they to do so during the spring planting season, they could devastate Pakistani agriculture. (India has held back water on some past occasions, but not on anything like the scale that these projects would allow it to do.[60]) Many Pakistani commentators and politicians (including the retired but still-powerful Hamid Gul, the hawkish former Inter-Services Intelligence chief) have said that this is an unacceptable situation, and should be dealt with militarily if necessary.[61] That some of the projects in question are in hotly disputed Kashmir makes the situation even more tense. Hard-line Pakistani groups—including some linked to terrorism—have increasingly emphasized water issues in their calls to arms, using slogans such as "Water flows or blood." Their insistence that India wants the water, not just for its own use, but to turn Pakistan into "a Sudan or a Somalia" are reminiscent of claims in the 1950s that India aimed at a "slow strangulation" by which Pakistan would be turned into a "desert."[62] While attempts to settle these disputes peacefully continue,[63] the long hostility between the two countries, the worsening shortages, the recent acceleration of construction, the insistence by some politicians in both countries that their own government is not doing enough to protect the nation, and the wild cards of global warming and extreme weather events make this an extremely dangerous situation.

Chinese/Indian water tensions also involve vital interests and disputed territory. Some Indian suspicions about Chinese intentions are reminiscent of hard-line Pakistani comments about India's, and people in both countries have suggested building big projects now to preempt the other.[64] Even if China has no intentions of actually redirecting the Yarlong Zangbo, the hydropower dams that it is building (after initial denials) might need to hold back water in the months before the monsoon to keep their generators going; because this would coincide with spring planting in eastern India and Bangladesh, it creates the same vulnerability that worries many Pakistanis vis-à-vis India's Kashmir dams.[65] But the Chinese projects that most alarm South Asians are either in early stages or not yet begun; some people doubt that a major water diversion from Tibet to North China is even technically feasible.[66] Thus far the most provocative comments about the Yarlong Zangbo / Brahmaputra, both in India and China, have come from people outside government; official comment has been more restrained.[67] In short, there is still time to avoid major international confrontations.

## U.S. Interests and Policy Options

Even if one assumes that overt conflict will be avoided, tensions related to Himalayan water complicate other security issues for China and the United States. Chinese uncertainty about whether it can tap Himalayan water and hydropower—and do so without greatly increasing tensions with its neighbors—presumably adds impetus to the People's Republic of China's "resource diplomacy" elsewhere, complicating issues ranging from the Diaoyu/Senkaku Islands to international attempts to pressure Iran and Sudan. It seems less likely that Himalayan-related tensions will lead downstream countries (with the exception of Pakistan, discussed above) to act in ways that bring them into conflict with the United States. For one thing, none of them has international influence and resource-driven diplomatic strategies comparable to China's. However, some Southeast Asian countries have stakes in border and island disputes with China, which could be exacerbated by tensions over Himalayan water.

The U.S. stake in Himalayan water goes beyond avoiding uses of it that might trigger political conflict, environmental catastrophe, or both; it includes seeing these resources utilized to alleviate existing economic and environmental problems, to the extent that they can be used sustainably and without creating international conflict. This is just as well, because it is unlikely that the United States could prevent expanded use of Himalayan water. Can the United States, then, do anything to make this use environmentally and politically safer?

For the most part, decisions about what environmental risks countries accept will be made internally, especially in China. Some international measures could matter at the margin; for instance, making sure that the UN Kyoto Protocol's Clean Development Mechanism credits go only to projects that have been carefully assessed across all possible effects, which is clearly desirable regardless of specifically Himalayan issues. And China does continue to use World Bank and Asian Development Bank funds and expertise on many water projects—especially projects undertaken by less prosperous provincial governments. But because the central government does not absolutely need to have external partners on a project to which it assigns high priority, outsiders are probably not able to block any particular Chinese project.

Where external funding is required, outside leverage is somewhat greater, although this still varies by country. India, according to recent figures, had financing in place for only a fraction of its planned dam construction projects through 2017. Chinese and Middle Eastern money, which has been crucial for Pakistan's expensive Diamer Bhasha Dam on the Indus, is unlikely to be available for Indian projects.[68] Smaller countries—both Himalayan states like Nepal and Bhutan and downstream countries—need outside financing and technical help. This gives the United States some opportunities for influence, at least in concert with other developed countries. How could that influence best be used?

A central aim should be to avoid having projects built hastily in order to preempt other projects[69]—a pattern that would increase both environmental and political risk—and, more generally, to minimize the number of risky projects undertaken despite the existence of technically superior options. As far as the latter, broader, aim goes, the United States is obviously not going to guarantee governments' security against farmers angered by water price increases. However, foundations and multilateral agencies can be encouraged to help with projects that reduce water waste at local levels and generate replacement income for poor farmers dependent on intensive irrigation. Because there are politically significant groups within all the relevant countries that are well aware of the risks of megaprojects, anything that promotes other palliatives also buys time for a more careful exploration and evaluation of the environmental and political risks. To some extent, the evaluation process itself may be another place where foreign groups can have an impact, although this will vary from country to country. China, for instance, has been more willing to consider environmental assessments from multilateral agencies or from experts it hires than from independent nongovernmental organizations. In all cases, though, there is some room for participation, especially at subnational levels.

With respect to international politics, encouraging more exchange of information is a crucial first step toward avoiding hasty claim-staking projects. But beyond that, some framework needs to be established to replace the current reliance on bilateral treaties (which have been rare in this region) and reliance on general principles that favor the claims of first movers. One challenging but potentially promising approach is to try to encourage joint projects, rather than focusing exclusively on agreements that specify what parts of a river each nation is allowed to use unilaterally. This is a point suggested for the Indus specifically by Eric Strahorn in chapter 4 of this volume, but it is of more general applicability. Ben Crow and Nirvikar Singh have, in fact, proposed such a transnational commission to manage Himalayan waters.[70]

There are at least three reasons why a move from water sharing to joint development seems desirable. First, transborder cooperation offers some possibilities for solutions that combine efficiency and equity better than a simple division of waters. For instance, dams on the Chinese part of the Mekong offer more hydropower potential with less danger to fisheries than dams farther downstream, but because downstream countries would have no claim on the power from a purely Chinese dam, they might well decide to build at technically inferior sites within their borders. An agreement to share an upstream dam would make more sense for downstream countries, and might also appeal to China if it eased tensions with its neighbors. (A more complex scenario could ensue if China agreed to share a dam with one neighbor in order to isolate another affected country.) A multilateral framework might also make it easier to include nonstate actors in the discussions (something Crow and Singh emphasize) and thus create more space for small-scale projects and local interests to be more thoroughly considered. Second, shared projects require at least the sharing of information, and create structures for technical collaboration that can be an important supplement to formal state-to-state channels for cooperation and trust building. Third, it is worth reiterating that even some very basic features of the physical environment are now of dubious certainty: How fast will glaciers recede, or how will quantities and seasonality of rainfall patterns change? In some cases, there are gaps in knowledge of even present conditions. Continued growth in water demand is the only (near) certainty, and its scale cannot be precisely known, either. Thus, agreements that create fixed rules for dividing resources are quite likely to be superseded before long or become much less fair than at the time of signing. Agreements for joint management build in considerably more flexibility to deal with this high likelihood of environmental surprises.

That does not, of course, make the creation of such institutions easy; the same problems of conflicting interests, very limited trust, and the potential of discussions to touch on other sensitive matters (e.g., Tibet and Kashmir) all pose significant obstacles. Moreover, both India and China have preferred bilateral dealings with their neighbors—in which, being much larger, they generally have a bargaining advantage—to multilateral arrangements.

Indian rejection of any third-party mediation on Kashmir on the eve of President Obama's 2010 visit is just one example. It is possible that the need to deal with China, which has the many bargaining advantages discussed above, will make India more receptive to a multilateral framework, but it is less obvious why China would change its historic approach to such matters. The United States could conceivably play a role in getting such discussions going, or in encouraging some existing multilateral entity, such as the World Bank, to do so. U.S.-based private parties (nongovernmental organizations, academic experts, etc.) could also play a role once discussions got going. It is also possible that China could be nudged toward cooperation on these matters if it perceived that this would influence the U.S. stance on related issues that it cares about. Tibet is the obvious example here, although a host of other matters must be considered in contemplating any change in the U.S. position on that topic. Overall, parties outside the region probably have very limited leverage on these issues, but limited leverage is better than none at all.

One possible place for useful outside involvement is in making information available to all parties. As several of the more restrained comments in India and China have suggested, greater sharing of information could be an important first step to preventing these tensions from escalating. For instance, China currently shares data on water levels and flows in Yarlong Zangbo with India and Bangladesh only during the monsoon months, and even that started fairly recently.[71] If one of the major fears of downstream countries about hydropower dams is that China would retain water to keep the turbines running during the spring planting season—when the rains have just begun and water levels are still low—then moving to year-round data sharing could be a very useful trust-building measure.

At this point there is still time for a better relationship to be built gradually—especially if China also takes more aggressive steps to solve its water shortages by managing demand and reducing waste, and thus makes it less likely that a Yarlong Zangbo diversion would be needed to supplement the Yangzi diversions already underway. But such an easing of tension will become more difficult if it does not start soon, while the objective problems that need to be managed, and thus the temptation to grab opportunities unilaterally, continue to mount. And if it becomes clear at some point that China plans not only hydropower dams but a large-scale water diversion, it is hard to imagine any negotiated solution. In sum, then, all the countries that use Himalayan waters will no doubt continue to build new water projects, some of them huge, to increase their supplies of both water and energy—but too exclusive a reliance on expanding supply is both environmentally and politically dangerous. Unless all affected countries take steps toward serious demand management and improve their communication and cooperation in using these vital resources, major conflicts will become inevitable.

## Notes

1. Sudha Ramachandran, "Greater China: India Quakes Over China's Water Plan," *Asia Times Online*, December 9, 2008, http://www.atimes.com/atimes/China/JL09Ad01.html.

2. This term appears to have been coined in Jeremy Allouche, "Water Nationalism: An Explanation of the Past and Present Conflicts in Central Asia, the Middle East, and the Indian Subcontinent" (Ph.D. diss., Université de Genève, 2005), but subsequent use differs from his, which pointed to how nations "imagined" water as integral to their "bodies." Common usage now seems to refer simply to states pursuing their perceived self-interest in water issues, sometimes at the expense of other countries.

3. For a brief summary of the historical arguments covering the early modern and modern periods, see Kenneth Pomeranz, "Chinese Development in Long-Run Perspective," *Proceedings of the American Philosophical Society* 152, no. 1 (2008): 83–100. For earlier periods, and the history of the Grand Canal in particular, see Hoshi Ayao, *Dai Unga* (The Grand Canal) (Tokyo: Kundo shuppansha, 1971). On wells, see Chen Shuping, "Ming Qing shiqi de jingguan" (Wells in the Ming-Qing Period), *Zhongguo shehui jingji yanjiu* 4, no. 1 (1983): 29–43.

4. See, e.g., Lillian Li, *Fighting Famine in North China: State, Market, and Environmental Decline, 1690s–1990s* (Cambridge, Mass.: Harvard University Press, 2007).

5. For a similar argument about imperial China's military security, fiscal practices, and spending on infrastructure and social services in comparative perspective, see Jean-Laurent Rosenthal and R. Bin Wong, *Before and Beyond Divergence* (Cambridge, Mass.: Harvard University Press, 2011).

6. Xia Mingfang, *Minguo shiqi ziran hai yu xiangcun shehui* (Natural disasters and village society in the Republican era) (Beijing: Zhonghua shuju, 2000), 78–79, 400–402.

7. On changes in irrigation rates, see James Nickum, "Is China Living on the Water Margin?" *China Quarterly* 156 (1998), 884; and Vaclav Smil, "Will There Be Enough Chinese Food?" *New York Review of Books*, February 1, 1995, 32–34. Regional boundaries and water endowments can be defined various ways, but the resulting proportions do not vary much. For a good overview, see Mark Elvin, "Water in China's Past and Present: Cooperation and Competition," *Nouveaux Mondes* 12 (2003): 117–20.

8. Eloise Kendy et al., "Combining Urban and Rural Water Use for a Sustainable North China Plain," International Water Management Institute, Colombo, Sri Lanka, 2003, 4, http://www.iwmi.cgiar.org/Assessment/files_new/publications/Workshop percent20Papers/IYRF_2003_Kendy.pdf.

9. Frank Ward and Manuel Pulido-Velazquez, "Water Conservation in Irrigation Can Increase Water Use," *Proceedings of the National Academy of Sciences* 105, no. 47 (2008): 18215–20, http://www.pnas.org/content/early/2008/11/17/0805554105.full.pdf+html?sid=cdce4d4d-d3fb-4759-a8a6-19dd6369759d.

10. The sixty-times figure comes from Sandra Postel, "China's Unquenchable Thirst," *Alternet*, January 24, 2008, http://www.alternet.org/story/74608. I have seen lower figures, but none below twenty.

11. Wang Feng and Anthony Mason, "Population Aging in China: Challenges, Opportunities, and Institutions," in *China's Economic Transitions: Origins, Mechanisms, and Consequences*, edited by Loren Brandt and Thomas Rawski (Cambridge: Cambridge University Press, 2008), 136–66.

12. Li Zijun, "China Issues New Regulation on Water Management, Sets Fees for Usage," WorldWatch Institute, March 14, 2006, http://www.worldwatch.org/node/3892; Elvin, "Water in China," 113. Combining these sources, agricultural water use seems to have fallen almost 20 percent since the late 1980s, without a decline in yields.

13. A good description of the project in English is given by Liu Changming, "Environmental Issues and the South–North Water Transfer Scheme," *China Quarterly*, no. 156 (1998): 900–904. See also Gavan McCormack, "Water Margins: Competing Paradigms in China," *Critical Asian Studies* 33, no. 1 (2001): 19–20; James Nickum, "The Status of the South to North Water Transfer Plans in China," http://hdr.undp.org/en/reports/global/hdr2006/papers/james_nickum_china_water_transfer.pdf.

14. See Water Technology Net, "China's Giant Water Scheme Creates Torrent of Discontent," March 9, 2009, http://www.water-technology.net/features/feature506 49/; BBC, "Delays Block China's Giant Water Scheme," February 8, 2009, http://news.bbc.co.uk/2/hi/asia-pacific/7864390.stm; Jane Macartney, "Progress Anything But Smooth on China's Ambitious, and Costly, Water Plan," *The Australian*, September 20, 2010, http://www.theaustralian.com.au/news/world/progress-anything-but-smooth-on-chinas-ambitious-and-costly-water-plan/story-e6frg6so-1225926385461.

15. Water transfers from basins along the Russian and Kazakh borders to North China have also been discussed, leading Kazakhstan to protest. But these ideas are smaller scale and less advanced. See, e.g., Frédéric Asserre, "The Amur River Border: Once a Symbol of Conflict, Could It Turn into a Water Resource Stake?" *Cybergeo: European Journal of Geography, Environnement, Nature, Paysage*, 9, article 242, July 30, 2003, http://cybergeo.revues.org/index 4141.html.

16. Strategic Forecast Group, *The Himalayan Challenge: Water Security in Emerging Asia* (Mumbai: Strategic Forecasting Group, 2010), "Executive Summary," 3.

17. Ramachandran, "Greater China"; Jonathan Watts, "Chinese Engineers Propose World's Biggest Hydro-Electric Project in Tibet," *The Guardian*, May 24, 2010, http://www.guardian.co.uk/environment/2010/may/24/chinese-hydroengineers-propose-tibet-dam.

18. Preethy Vignesh, "Brahmaputra River: Dispute between India and China," Jeywin (Indian Civil Service Exam Preparatory Materials), http://www.jeywin.com/blog/brahmaputra-river- percentE2 percent80 percent93-dispute-between-india-and-china/; Joydeep Gupta, "Nervous Neighbours," *China Dialogue*, November 24, 2010, http://www.chinadialogue.net/article/show/single/en/3959.

19. Estimates of how many dams vary; see, e.g., Y. C. Dhardhowa, "China's Controversial Plan for Dam on Yarlung Tsangpo in Tibet," *Tibet Post*, May 24, 2010, http://www.thetibetpost.com/en/features/environment-and-health/898-chinas-controversial-plans-for-dam-on-yarlung-tsangpo-in-tibet; and International Rivers, "Brahmaputra (Yarlung Tsangpo) River," http://www.internationalrivers.org/china/china-other-projects. *Asia News*, April 24, 2010, refers to a small disputed area (90,000 square meters) that would be occupied.

20. Vignesh, "Brahmaputra River"; *Tribune* (Chandigarh) October 16, 2009. The dam may have been discussed at a private meeting with the Indian foreign minister; see *Asia News*, April 24, 2010. For the 2006 assurances, see the excerpt from *Hindustan Times*, November 22, 2006, http://www.ipcs.org/pdf_file/news_archive/nov_06_india external.pdf. For former minister of water resources Wang Shucheng's denial that China intends to do this, see Xinhua, "Nation Won't Divert Yarlung Tsangpo River to Thirsty North," China.org.cn, May 26, 2009, http://www.china.org.cn/environment/news/2009-05/26/content_17838473.htm. For the earlier rumors that China would move forward on this project beginning in 2009, see McCormack, "Water Margins," 18.

21. This is pointed out by Gupta, "Nervous Neighbours," November 24, 2010. When I checked the Web a few days later, I found various Chinese reprints of the Xinhua story that did indeed mention irrigation and flood control, in the story's fourth paragraph. (All the stories were identical.) See, for instance, Huanqiu ribao, "Xizang kai jian diyizuo daxing shuidianzhan Yalu Zangbu jiang bei jieiliu" (Tibet begins building first hydrostation; flow of Yalong Zangbo River blocked), November 14, 2010, http://news.163.com/10/1114/22/6LG1VUFO00014AEE.html; and "Xizang kai jian diyizuo shuidianzhan Yalu Zangbu jiang bei jieiliu" (Tibet begins building first hydrostation; flow of Yalong Zangbo River blocked), *China News,* November 14, 2010, http://military.china.com/zh_cn/important/64/20101115/16241636.html. The Xinhua Web site itself, however, had only the first three paragraphs of the story. See "'Shuidian xiangjun'" weizhen gaoyuan Yalu Zangbu jiang shouci jieiliu" ("Hydroelectric Hunan Army" brings awesome power to plateau; Yalong Zangbo River is blocked for first time"), November 14, 2010, http://www.hn.xinhuanet.com/newscenter/2010-11/14/content_21386993.htm; and Yang Xuyi, "Changjiang zai zheli shicong le," *Nanfang zhoumo*, February 18, 2009, http://www.infzm.com/content/24061.

22. For one among many recent discussions, see Yang Xuyi, "Changjiang zai zheli shicong le," *Nanfang zhoumo,* February 18, 2009, http://www.infzm.com/content/24061Yang 2009.

23. Darrin Magee, "Powershed Politics: Yunnan Hydropower under Great Western Development," *China Quarterly* 185, March 2006, 35; Xinhua, " Li Xiaopeng Appointed Vice Governor of Shanxi Province," Xinhua Economic News Service, June 12, 2008; ShanghaiDaily.com, June 12, 2008; Isabel Hilton, "Still Waters Run Deep," *China Dialogue*, June 29, 2009, http://www.chinadialogue.net/article/show/single/en/3125--Still-waters-run-deep. Grainne Ryder, "Skyscraper Dams in Yunnan: China's New Electricity Regulator Should Step In," *Probe International Special Report*, May 12, 2006, 9, http://www.greengrants.org.cn/read.php?id=66, raises doubts about the economic rationality of both Three Gorges and various Yunnan hydroprojects on this basis. See also Grainne Ryder, "China's New Dam Builders and the Emerging Regulatory Framework for Competitive Power Markets," draft paper for Mekong Region Waters Dialogue meeting, Vientiane, July 2006, 2–3, 8–9, http://www.probeinternational.org/files/pdfs/muw/GRMekongpaper2006.pdf. The Yarlong Zangbo project now under way belongs to Huaneng Power, perhaps the best-connected firm of all. Until 2008, Huaneng was headed by the son of former premier (and chief advocate of Three Gorges) Li Peng; the son then moved on to a provincial vice-governorship. His sister heads Huaneng's Hong Kong subsidiary, which is the company's principal arm for raising money abroad; she is also a member of the Chinese People's Political Consultative Conference and a member of the Copenhagen Climate Council. See Xinhua, "Li Xiaopeng"; ShanghaiDaily.com; and Hilton, "Still Waters."

24. Magee, "Powershed Politics," 25–26; Ryder, "Skyscraper Dams," 3.

25. *Asia News*, April 24, 2010.

26. See, e.g., Punjab, Government Department, Food, Civil Supplies, and Consumer Affairs Department, http://punjabgovt.nic.in/GOVERNMENT/food_civil_supplies_consumer_affairs.htm, accessed April 23, 2009; and http://pakistamweb.com/html/agriculture.htm.

27. P. K. Jensen et al., "Domestic Use of Irrigation Water in Punjab," 297–98, paper from twenty-fourth WEDC conference on "Sanitation and Water for All," Islamabad, 1998, http://www.wedc-knowledge.org/wedcopac/opacreq.dll/fullnf?Search_link=AAAA:7417:35998192.

28. On Pakistan, see World Bank, "Better Management of Indus Basin Waters: Strategic Issues and Challenges," 2006, 2; on India, see John Briscoe et al., "India's Water Economy: Bracing for a Turbulent Future," draft report, World Bank, 2005, 43, http://www.worldbank.org.in/WBSITE/EXTERNAL/COUNTRIES/SOUTHASIAEXT/INDIAEXTN/0,,contentMDK:20674796~pagePK:141137~piPK:141127~theSitePK:295584,00.html).

29. "Pakistan's Water Crisis," *PRI's The World*, April 13, 2009, http://www.pri.org/theworld/node/25692.

30. Briscoe et al., "India's Water Economy," 3–24, gives figures relative to the fiscal deficits of various Indian state governments. "India's Water Shortage," *Fortune*, January 24, 2008, 2, http://money.cnn.com/2008/01/24/news/international/India_water_shortage.fortune/index.htm, puts the cost of subsidizing farmers' electricity at $9 billion per year.

31. Briscoe et al., "India's Water Economy," 23.

32. John Briscoe and Usman Qamar, *Pakistan's Water Economy: Running Dry* (Washington, D.C.: World Bank, 2006), 1.

33. See, e.g., Daniel Zwerdling, "'Green Revolution' Trapping India's Farmers in Debt," and "India's Farming 'Revolution' Heading for Collapse," May 11, 2009, http://www.npr.org/templates/story/story.php?storyId=102893816 and http://www.npr.org/templates/story/story.php?storyId=102944731.

34. N. K. Garg and Q. Hassan, "Alarming Scarcity of Water in India," *Current Science* 93, no. 7 (2007): 935; Briscoe et al., "India's Water Economy," 30.

35. Briscoe and Qamar, *Pakistan's Water Economy*, 5–6; Briscoe et al., "India's Water Economy," 34. On undercounting, see Himanshu Thakkar, "The World Bank's Misguided Advocacy of Large Water Storage Facilities," Infochange, 1–2, http://infochangeindia.org/20051029383/Water-Resources/Analysis/The-World-Bank-s-misguided-advocacy-of-large-water-storage-facilities.html.

36. N. Prasad, "A Bird's Eye View on Interlinking of Rivers in India," in *Interlinking of Rivers in India*, edited by A. K. Thakur and P. Kumari (New Delhi: Deep and Deep, 2007).

37. On the cancellation, see Sudha Ramachandran, "India Sweats Over China's Water Plans," India Defence Forum, February 5, 2010, http://www.defenceforumin./forum/showthread.php?t=6082&page=9; for a memorandum of understanding to go forward on a smaller version, see Aarti Kapur, "River Inter-Linking to Help Ease Water Crisis: Bansal," *The Tribune* (Chandigarh), September 18, 2010, http://www.tribuneindia.com/2010/20100919/main4.htm.

38. For an overview, see Kenneth Pomeranz, "The Great Himalayan Watershed: Agrarian Crisis, Mega-Dams and the Environment," *Asia-Pacific Journal: Japan Focus*, July 27, 2009, http://japanfocus.org/-Kenneth-Pomeranz/3195.

39. P. Nuorteva, M. Keskinen, and O. Varis, "Water, Livelihoods and Climate Change Adaptation in the Tonle Sap Lake Area, Cambodia: Learning from the Past to Understand the Future," *Journal of Water and Climate Change* 1, no. 1 (2010): 93; Khouth Sophakchakrya, "Japan Offers Support for Farmers in Three Tonle Sap Provinces," *Phnom Penh Post*, August 19, 2010, http://www.phnompenhpost.com/index.php/2010081941349/National-news/japan-offers-support-for-farmers-in-three-tonle-sap-provinces.html; Radio Free Asia, "Dams or Drought: An Interview." August 24, 2010, http://www.rfamobile.org/english/news/china/osborne-08232010150911.html.

40. Seasonal floods are also important for rice growing, although agriculture can more easily adjust to changes in those floods than fish can.

41. Radio Free Asia, "Dams or Drought: An Interview"; "Dam the Consequences," *Guardian Weekly*, April 6, 2007, http://www.guardian.co.uk/world/2007/apr/06/outlook.development.

42. Ramachandran, "Greater China."

43. Briscoe et al., "India's Water Economy," 33–34.

44. Watts, "Chinese Engineers." This estimate implies a surprisingly high rate of carbon emissions per watt of coal-derived electricity, and so probably exaggerates the amount of emissions the dam would save; but the basic point stands nonetheless.

45. For Indian examples, see South Asia Network on Dams, Rivers, and People, "India Dams Methane Emissions," May 18, 2007, http://www.sandrp.in/dams/India_Dams_Methane_Emissions_PR180507, citing a study by Ivan Lima et al., "Methane Emissions from Large Dams as Renewable Energy Resources: A Developing Nation Perspective," *Mitigation and Adaptation Strategies for Global Change* 13, no. 2 (February, 2008): 193–206.

46. N. Kehrwald et al., "Mass Loss on Himalayan Glacier Endangers Water Resources," *Geophysical Review Letters* 35, L22503, doi:10.1029/2008GL035556, 2008.

47. T. Gardner, "Tibetan Glacial Shrink to Cut Water Supply by 2050," Reuters, January 6, 2009, http://www.reuters.com/article/environmentNews/idUSTRE50F76420090116.

48. Yang Xuyi, "Changjiang zai zheli shicong le," *Nanfang zhoumo*, February 18, 2009, http://www.infzm.com/content/24061; see also Chen Xiqing et al., "Secular Changes in Yearly Minimum Flows from the Upper Yangtze River, China, since 1882," Chinese-German Joint Symposium on Hydraulic and Ocean Engineering, August 24–30, 2008, Darmstadt, http://www.comc.ncku.edu.tw/joint/joint2008/papers/34.pdf.

49. See http://www.asiasociety.org/chinagreen/origins-of-rivers-omens-of-a-crisis/. See also "Permafrost Soil in Yangtze River Area Disappearing," English Xinhuanet, www.chinaview.cn, February 13, 2009; and Jane Qiu, China: The Third Pole," *Nature* 454 (2008): 393–96, http://www.nature.com/news/2008/080723/full/454393a.html.

50. Shripad Dharmadikary, *Mountains of Concrete: Dam Building in the Himalayas* (Berkeley, Calif.: International Rivers, 2008), 33; Ann-Kathrin Schneider, "Dam Boom in Himalayas Will Create Mountains of Risk," *World Rivers Review*, March 2009, 10.

51. On the Mekong accusations, see Radio Free Asia, "Dams or Droughts." On the Indus, see, e.g., chapter 4 in the present volume by Eric Strahorn; Gargi Parasai, "India, Pakistan, Look to Settle Water Dispute," *The Hindu*, July 23, 2010, and Lydia Polgreen and Sabrina Tavernise, "Water Dispute Increases India–Pakistan Tension," *New York Times*, July 23, 2010, http://www.nytimes.com/2010/07/21/world/asia/21kashmir.html.

52. Strategic Forecasting Group, *Himalayan Challenge*, iv.

53. E.g., water-sharing arrangements for rivers that cross more than one Indian state base future allocations on recent usage, so that a state that conserves water reduces its future entitlements vis-à-vis other states; these rules also do not include ecological services, such as maintaining existing wetlands, as a recognized "use" for which a state receives credit.

54. See, e.g., Tian Lei, "Water Crisis in North China," *Nanfeng chuan*, June 21, 2008, translated and republished by Three Gorges Probe, www.probeinternational.org/beijing-water/water-crisis-north-china.

55. Tufail Ahmad, "Water Disputes between India and Pakistan: A Potential Casus Belli," executive summary of Report of the Henry Jackson Society, July 31, 2009, 5–6, http://www.henryjacksonsociety.org/stories.asp?id=1230); Strahorn, this volume.

56. See Punjab, Government Department, Food, Civil Supplies, and Consumer Affairs Department, http://punjabgovt.nic.in/GOVERNMENT/food_civil_supplies_consumer_affairs.htm.

57. Hari Sud, "China's Future Water War with India," UPI Asia, May 13, 2008, http://www.upiasia.com/Security/2008/05/13/chinas_future_water_war_ with_india/3300/.

58. Allouche, "Water Nationalism," 196–238.

59. Polgreen and Tavennise, "Water Dispute Increases India-Pakistan Tension."

60. Allouche, "Water Nationalism," 209–12. They also released some water during the 2010 floods to relieve pressure on their own dams. Karin Brulliard, "Rhetoric Grows Heated in Water Dispute between India, Pakistan," *Washington Post*, May 28, 2010; Ahmad, "Water Disputes," 4–7.

61. Brulliard, "Rhetoric Grows Heated." Ahmad, "Water Disputes," 4–7.

62. Ahmad, "Water Disputes," 4–7; Allouche, "Water Nationalism," 228–29.

63. Parsai, "India, Pakistan, Look to Settle Water Dispute."

64. Hari Sud, "China's Future Water War with India," UPI Asia, May 13, 2008, http://www.upiasia.com/Security/2008/050/13/chinas_future_water_war_with_india/3300/; Watts, "Chinese Engineers" (quoting India's environment minister and a leading member of the China Society for Hydropower Engineering); Edward Wong, "China and India Dispute Enclave on Edge of Tibet," *New York Times*, September 4, 2009, http://www.nytimes.com/2009/09/04/world/asia/o4chinaindia.html.

65. "Mother of Hydro Electric Power Plants: China Plans the Biggest Hydro Power of 38,000 MW in Tibet," May 27, 2010, Hydropowerstation.com/?p=487; *Hindustan Times*, May 26, 2010, http://www.hindustantims.com/StoryPage/Print/548572.aspx.

66. See, e.g., *Hindustan Times*, May 26, 2010, quoting the Tibetan-Canadian scholar Tashi Tsering and Saira Kurup, "Water Wars: India, China, and the Great Thirst," *Times of India,* July 25, 2010, http://timesofindia.com/articleshow/6212014.cms?prtpage+1&fbc_channel=1; Zhang Boting quoted by Watts, "Chinese Engineers."

67. E.g., "Red Flag Up for Bangladesh, India," *Sulekha*, September 9, 2010, http://chandrashekhar.sulekha.com/blog/post/2010/09/red-flag-up-for-bangladesh-india.htm; Amit Ranjun, "Beijing's Threat to India's Water Security," *Asia Sentinel*, November 10, 2010, http://www.asiasentinel.com/index.php?option=com_content&task=view&id=2812&Itemid=174 vs. the people, quoted by Kurup, "Water Wars."

68. Dharmadikary, *Mountains of Concrete*, 11–15. See also Ann-Kathrin Schneider, "South Asia's Most Costly Dam Gets an Infusion," *International Rivers World River Review*, December 15, 2008, http://internationalrivers.org/en/node/3663, citing a consortium involving Chinese companies and "some Arab countries."

69. For a few recent discussions of the possibility of building to preempt another country's project, see S. Padmanabhan, "China, The Brahmaputra, and India," *Hindu Business Line*, April 14, 2009, http://wwww.thehindubusinessline.com/2009/04/14/stories/2009041450250900.htm; "Dam on Brahmaputra: Consequence and Reality Check," June 28, 2009, http://horizonspeaks.wordpress.com/2009/06/28/dam-on-brahmaputra-consequence-and-reality-check/; and B. K. Rana, "China and India Race for Dams on Brahmaputra River," *Himalayan Voice*, July 20, 2010, http://thehimalayanvoice.blogspot.com/2010_07_20_archive.html.

70. Ben Crow and Nirvikar Singh, "The Management of International Rivers as Demand Grows and Supplies Tighten: India, China, Nepal, Pakistan, Bangladesh," *India Review* 8, no. 3 (2009): 306–39.

71. Strategic Foresight Group, *Himalayan Challenge*, iv.

# Chapter 3

# Domestic, Regional, and Global Implications of Water Scarcity in China

*David Pietz*

Environmental degradation in China has received wide attention in recent years. A plethora of images and stories have fueled a pervasive image of China as an environmental wasteland, as extensive scholarship and media coverage have inventoried China's air, water, and land problems. Although reasonable observers can disagree on the prescriptive responses necessary to address such challenges, it seems there is little disagreement that there is indeed a fundamental tension between China's breakneck economic development and its environmental context. These economic and ecological dynamics implicated in the reemergence of China will critically shape the evolution of United States–China relations and the position of the United States in the world system. One question that must be addressed is whether this growth will be conditioned by resource constraints. A second issue, which lay at the heart of this research, are the policy implications for the United States as China explores the range of options available to address resource scarcity.

Although there has been substantial analysis of China's role in recent international climate change compacts, this discussion lacks a thorough-going exploration of how China's environmental challenges may have an impact on the country's internal economic, political, and social trajectories, along with its external relationships. Ultimately, the domestic and international repercussions of China's resource challenges will implicate the United States. In its assessment of global challenges in the period up to 2025, the U.S. National Intelligence Council lists resource nationalism as a "key uncertainty" that contains "the risk of great power confrontations."[1] Indeed, some estimates suggest that by 2030 nearly half the world's population will be living in areas of acute water shortage.[2] A particular challenge for policy analysts is the interconnectedness of water with a variety of contemporary challenges such as food security, energy security, and environmental security.[3] Indeed, this nexus of issues is at play in China and will continue to shape China's internal economic and political dynamics—as well as its role in international networks—for the foreseeable future.

Accordingly, this chapter explores the trajectories of China's global interactions as it grapples with water resource constraints. The goal of the chapter is not to provide an exhaustive catalog of policy considerations arising from China's water predicament, but instead to highlight several key examples to suggest the range of water-related issues affecting China, and to suggest the critical importance that nontraditional foreign policy concerns may have in shaping China's internal and external dynamics. This analysis also suggests a range of opportunities and challenges for U.S. policy actors in light of China's water scarcity.

Before exploring these critical policy-related questions, the chapter begins by examining the biophysical setting of water on the North China Plain—one of the most water-challenged regions of China and the world.

## The Biophysical Context

Water scarcity is one of the central environmental challenges that will shape the future trajectory of China's development. Although China ranks fourth in global freshwater reserves, it possesses the second lowest per capita water supply of any country in the world.[4] One of the most critical areas of the development-resource nexus in China is the North China Plain, a region covering approximately 409,500 square kilometers (158,000 square miles). Though the Yellow River flows through the heart of the North China Plain, compared to the more humid south, North China's limited water resources have been a persistent challenge to human communities inhabiting the plain. The Yellow River Valley and the North China Plain constitute one of the economic and social cores of China—generating more than 20 percent of the nation's grain supply and being among the most densely populated regions in the world. However, water in the region has become an endangered commodity. The North China Plain accounts for less than 10 percent of China's total water resources, despite sustaining more than 30 percent of its population. Per capita water availability on the North China Plain is 225 cubic meters per year, while China's average per capita water supply is 2,300 cubic meters. In 1995, per capita water resources in North China averaged one-tenth the world average. Rapid economic development since 1978 has had profound consequences for the limited water resources of the North China Plain region. Water tables have declined by an average of 1.5 meters per year since 1990. Industrial, agricultural, and urban pollutants have rendered water in downstream segments of the river unsafe for any use. In 1997, the river ran dry 780 kilometers upstream from its mouth.[5] Temporal availability of water is also a problem. The vast majority of annual rainfall occurs in the summer months—often in heavy downpours. Thus, drought and flooding have traditionally been the dual scourges of the North China Plain. In short, North China is facing an acute water dilemma that will shape politics, society, and culture.

What forces have generated these increasingly severe water problems on the North China Plain? Degradation of water in the Yellow River Valley is a consequence of water management practices since 1949. Human communities along the river have struggled with drought, floods, and famine for centuries. The government of the People's Republic of China sought to address these problems with the application of technology, political social organization, and cultural expressions that were consistent with building "communist modernity." These approaches had long-term environmental consequences that affected water supply and use.

Many observers of contemporary China have identified the quickened industrial development and urbanization of the post–Mao Zedong period (1978 to the present) as the agents responsible for water problems on the North China Plain. However, in order to understand water scarcity in North China, we must also examine water management during the Mao period (1949–78). The entire matrix of values and power in which hydraulic engineering and technology were socially embedded during the Mao era generated water problems before and during the present reform period.[6] In other words, the manipulation of water in the Maoist period casts a long shadow over water resources in the post-Mao era.

One headline-grabbing event occurred in 1995, as domestic and international attention to water issues in China was awakened by Lester Brown's book, *Who Will Feed China?*[7] Brown predicted that, due to water scarcity and the shortage of arable land, China would have to import between 200 million and 369 million tons of grain by 2030. Brown further argued that the poor countries of Sub-Saharan Africa and South Asia would be priced out of the international grain market by China's growing appetite for imported grain.[8] Although subsequent scholarship revised the data on which Brown premised the immediacy of the challenge, his emphasis on the impact of water scarcity on China's food security was prescient.[9] In China, significant funding was extended to research institutes to explore water, land, and food security issues.

## Domestic and International Implications of Water Scarcity in China

The 1978 reconceptualization of social and economic priorities ("market socialism") imparted differing conceptions of water on the North China Plain. The introduction of market forces had a potent transformative effect on the social and economic landscape of China. The consequences of urbanization and rapid urban and rural industrialization generated environmental dynamics that were transposed onto a landscape/waterscape fundamentally transformed by the hydraulic practices of the Mao period (1949–78). Water shortages resulting from expanded agricultural, urban, and industrial demand combined with conflicting spatial disagreements (provincial disputes) over water rights. All these problems began to challenge further economic restructuring, while water pollution severely compounded existing water scarcity problems and became an impediment to the aggressive economic development plans of the state.

China has pursued a dual policy of demand management and continued faith in engineering solutions to manage water scarcity. In the past several years, China has aggressively engaged in land conservation policies such as reforestation, as well as limited pricing reforms. Such policies, however, are tempered by the added demands upon the rural sector and the potential for social instability as the increased cost of water eats into rural incomes. At the same time, an abiding faith in large engineering solutions to supply management is evident by the construction of mammoth projects such as the Three Gorges Dam and the South-to-North Water Diversion Scheme. In addition to issues of energy security, China has historically been critically sensitive to issues of food security. Although the two concerns can generate conflict about the best way to manage water resources, because hydroelectricity and irrigation entail different management regimes, together they exert a powerful influence on resource development. The sense of vulnerability generated by these twin concerns will likely continue to fuel aggressive water resource engineering, including the South-North Water Transfer Project and the development of transboundary rivers in Southwest China.

On the demand side, policy innovations such as integrated river basin management and allocation policies have been introduced, but bureaucratic fragmentation mitigates the full implementation of integrated management, while concerns for the economic welfare of agricultural interests have limited price reform in the water sector. China's leadership and water sector experts are well aware of the potential impact of water shortages on economic and social stability. But structural approaches to demand management (e.g., water pricing) bring potential social problems such as rural dissatisfaction. Engineering solutions to supply management are also accompanied by social consequences (e.g., population resettlement) and failure to address resource shortage. The challenge for China is to negotiate both demand and supply options. However, solutions to more effective water management face fundamental institutional and social obstacles, suggesting that water problems will continue to plague the country for some time. What follows, then, is an exploration of how water scarcity in China shapes national, regional, and international security challenges for China and the United States.

*Water Issues and the Conditioning of Political Discourse*

Water scarcity—and environmental degradation more generally—will be a key component of China's internal political discourse. Data on rural disturbances released at the end of 2006 suggest that the number of resource-related protests is substantial. For both rural and urban protests, water degradation concerns were among the leading causes of localized discontent. Water constraints and their deleterious impact on economic opportunity may be an important fault line in political stability.

During the past two decades, economic liberalization and environmental transformations have introduced new values and actors to resource development in China. The human, material, and cultural costs of the Three Gorges Dam project is widely seen as galvanizing a growing sensitivity toward the environmental consequences of breakneck economic development. From the pathbreaking activism of individuals such as the journalist Dai Qing to the formation of nongovernmental organizations such as "Friends of Nature," the state and Communist Party were faced with prominent individuals (some with an impeccable party pedigree, e.g., Dai) and well-organized grassroots environmental organizations that political elites were ambivalent about. On one hand, opposition to "key" engineering projects would not be tolerated. Dai was imprisoned in 1989, in part for her opposition to the Three Gorges Project, which she called the "the most environmentally and socially destructive project in the world."[10] On the other hand, the state was occasionally more ambivalent, because local environmental activism can help identify and pressure local polluters where local environmental regulators are powerless. The individuals and nongovernmental organizations engaged in environmental activism reflect a pervasive growth in frustration at lack of clean water, frustration evident in virtually every corner of China. Although projects such as the Three Gorges Dam and the South-North River Transfer Project continue to suggest continuities in state assumptions about the mutually supportive role between the state and hydraulic engineering, the emergence of domestic and international conservationists and international technical partners— such as the World Bank and Asian Development Bank—has introduced values with the potential to further shape the relationship between water and politics in China.

Water quality and quantity problems have generated tensions within the bureaucratic and social fabric of China. The authority to allocate scarce water resources is administratively distributed across economic sectors and political units. Urbanization and industrial development have led to increased pressures on China's delicate water balance. The Ministry of Water Resources reports that 60 percent of China's cities face water shortages, while Beijing (on the North China Plain) has access to one-third the world average per capita water supply. In rural sectors, it is estimated that 500 million people are exposed to contaminated drinking water. The decisions that the state makes in allocating water resources between these two sectors are fraught with competing internal interests. The fact that much of this allocated resource is scarce and often degraded only compounds the importance of these decisions. Consistent with China's fragmented bureaucratic structure, responsibility for water administration is dispersed through various functional ministries—including, among others, the Ministry of Water Resources and the Ministry of Agriculture. Thus, bureaucratic constituencies fracture and coalesce around water policy. In the same spirit, province-level compacts regulating water withdrawals from interprovincial waterways are notoriously contentious and lack effective oversight mechanisms. A water accord reached in 1999 among riparian Yellow River provinces was already considered precarious shortly after the ink dried.[11] Thus, water constraints hold the potential to create disequilibria within a state administrative structure already stressed by bureaucratic fault lines. But generally it is at the local level where state and party concerns are focused on the potential for water stress to generate social and political instability.

As alluded to above, in a moment of genuine transparency the state issued data on annual public disturbances in China during 2006 and 2007. The number of mass incidents surprised many, but the number of public disputes associated with water was particularly striking. As Elizabeth Economy noted, "disputes over water reportedly rose from 16,747 cases in 1986 to 94,405 in 2004."[12] Clearly, access to ample quantities of clean water is a major component of China's growing urban/rural divide. As with virtually all polities, water allocation decisions bias urban and industrial interests over rural and agricultural consumers. Furthermore, water available to rural users is often polluted from agricultural runoff or from insufficiently regulated rural enterprises. Although the headline-grabbing spill of 100 tons of benzene into the Songhua River in 2006 suggested that urban residents are not immune to severe pollution issues, in most cases rural Chinese lack the institutional structures to cope with the economic and health consequences of water degradation. For example, public health systems in rural China are hard-pressed to manage waterborne diseases such as diarrhea, the leading cause of death among children under five years of age.[13] Thus, water constraints constitute one component of a "perfect storm"—combining with other environmental issues, corruption, income disparities, and fraying social safety nets—that could "present a unifying focal point for dissent that crosses geographic, cultural, socioeconomic, and political lines."[14]

In terms of economic stability, a critical water dilemma facing China is agricultural production (addressed more fully below). However, the investment needed to alleviate pollution and increase water supply to agricultural, urban, and industrial users will have a negative impact on China's overall growth rates. Although one might argue that China's growth rates are sufficient to absorb such state expenditure, the scale of engineering

solutions being implemented in China is extraordinarily large. Designed
to bring Yangzi River Valley water to the North China Plain, the South-
North Water Transfer Project is estimated to cost between $25 billion and
$30 billion. Government tax revenue will also continue to be negatively
affected as water scarcity makes an impact on economic productivity. In
addition, pollution abatement costs, the significant investment needed to
upgrade aging urban and rural water infrastructure, and the burden of massive health care costs and lost labor due to waterborne illnesses will collectively have an impact on China's economic performance.[15] Maintaining
high annual growth in gross domestic product (usually defined as 8 percent
or more) has been deemed by China's leadership as providing sufficient
employment necessary to compensate for the dislocation resulting from
economic restructuring. But if indeed China's growth rates decline due to
various internal and external factors, postponement of these investments in
water management will perpetuate adverse environmental conditions that
will continue to provide a flashpoint for social and political grievances.

## Water Constraints and the Development of "Resource Diplomacy"

Although there has been much attention paid to China's impact on global
energy markets during the past decade, there has been comparatively little analysis of how China's concerns over water and food security may
shape its relations with other states, particularly in Southeast Asia and Sub-
Saharan Africa.[16] Along with concerns about energy dependence, China is
acutely sensitive to issues of food security—sensitivities that are a legacy of
insecurities about its global standing and of more contemporary misgivings
over the reliability of international energy and commodity markets. With
just 7 percent of the world's arable land, China attempts to feed roughly
one-quarter of the world's population. Maintaining grain self-sufficiency
requires preserving sufficient land under cultivation while having access
to clean water resources for irrigation. Indeed, more than half of China's
farmland is irrigated. During the past several decades, estimates of China's
agricultural acreage have diverged rather dramatically, but a central concern of state leaders has been limiting the impact of rapid urbanization
and industrial development on land resources. With the incessant pressure
of these forces in the post-Mao era and the limited reach of the central
government in regulating unchecked urban and industrial expansion, any
central mandates intent on preserving agricultural land were bound for certain frustration.

In addition to urban sprawl and industrial development in rural areas, two more developments threaten China's capacity to feed itself. First, farmers are eagerly moving up the value-added production chain to make the switch from staple grains to fruits, vegetables, and nuts, largely as increasingly affluent urban consumers have quickly developed a taste for such products. Second, grain that continues to be grown on shrinking farmland is increasingly being fed to livestock as the palates of urban Chinese consumers increasingly favor animal protein. With available grain for human consumption stressed by land and water constraints, and production and consumption patterns influenced by the postreform domestic market, the challenge for China is to maximize grain production by preventing loss of agricultural farmland, having access to sufficient water for irrigation, and at the same time, increasing yields. Indeed, in 2007, Premier Wen Jiabao announced to the National People's Congress that China must maintain 120 million hectares of arable land. At the same time, Chinese agriculturalists have been engaging in practices to expand productivity by intensifying irrigation development and the application of inputs including chemical fertilizers. The sum of such efforts is that China maintains a precarious balance of grain self-sufficiency. As late as 2008, Chinese farmers produced roughly 95 percent of the country's staple agricultural products.

A critical variable in China's food security dilemma is water. The historical experience of developing regions suggests that agriculture usually loses to urban and industrial needs in decisions about allocating water. The reasons are well documented: the growing impulse to placate a potentially politically activist urban population and the desire to allocate material (and human) resources to value-added economic output. Roughly 75 percent of water usage in China occurs in the agricultural sector, but competing demands in the industrial and urban sector continue to whittle this percentage down—placing further stress on agricultural productivity. The critical problem, however, is that these sources will be difficult to increase. To be sure, there is significant capacity in the agricultural sector for increased water efficiency, but improvements have been hindered by the lack of unified bureaucratic planning and implementation. Furthermore, much of the surface water is polluted, while groundwater resources have been significantly compromised by overuse and pollution.[17] According to Ma Jun, a leading environmental observer in China, between the 1980s and 2005, the volume of wastewater flowing into the Yellow River increased from about 2 billion tons to 4.3 billion tons.[18] Intensification of fertilizer use has also generated significant pollution of farmland irrigation sources and waterways. As reported by Renmin University, China produced roughly 24 percent of world grain output, but "its use of fertilizer accounted for more than 35 percent of total global consumption," suggesting the significant increase in chemical inputs necessary to feed China's growing population. The report goes on to note that China's grain production had increased more than eightfold from the 1960s, while use of nitrogen fertilizers had surged by about 55 times.[19] The consequences of heavy chemical use in the farm sector have been devastating to water quality throughout China, but particularly in North China.

Finally, an additional stressor on water supply as it relates to China's drive for food independence arises from the energy-water nexus. As has been well documented, China has aggressively invested in alternative and renewable sources of energy. These measures are in response to a variety of projections that show China consuming upward of 14 million barrels per day of petroleum by 2030.[20] In addition to concerns about oil import dependence, environmental concerns are clearly impelling Chinese investments in clean energy sources. The International Energy Agency forecasts that China will emit nearly 30 percent of the world's "energy-related $CO_2$ [carbon dioxide]" emissions by 2030,[21] and that "use of vehicles is projected to expand from roughly 24 million vehicles [in 2006] to 90–140 million by 2020 due to a nationwide promotion of the automobile industry, increasing the demand for transportation energy from 33 percent of total Chinese petroleum use to about 57 percent."[22]

Ethanol production has been targeted as an area of accelerated investment to address the supply and environmental concerns resulting from this rapid expansion of the transportation sector. Although there are a variety of vegetable feedstocks under consideration, corn (grain and stover) has emerged as "a more attractive feedstock for making ethanol in the medium and long term due to their extensive availability in North China."[23] Although there are more recent reports that China may be moderating expectations, in late 2007 that state announced plans to meet roughly 10 percent of its national gasoline demand with biofuels by 2020. This would represent a 400-percent increase in biofuel production. The meeting of such a target would require a 26 percent increase in corn production. Such an increase in corn production would require massive additional inputs of water. As Elizabeth Economy notes, to produce "1 liter of maize-based ethanol in China requires 6 times more irrigation water than in the United States, and over 25 times more than in Brazil."[24] Clearly, the mutual influence of the water-energy nexus in China will force state leaders to reckon with critical dilemmas as it seeks to *simultaneously* avoid food and energy import dependence.

What are the implications of water and food (and energy) security concerns for China's foreign policy? One option available to China is to invest in agricultural resources abroad through direct landownership or long-term leases. Indeed, during the last decade China has engaged in such activities. But to better understand the present and future dynamics of these investments one needs to comprehend the global context of agriculture and agricultural policies. According to the World Bank, global population growth, rising levels of affluence, and the spread of Western dietary patterns will contribute to a 50 percent increase in global food demand by 2030. Agricultural productivity, however, may struggle to keep up with this demand as agricultural subsidies in many regions will suppress market signals. These subsidies are likely to continue as developing regions remain sensitive to politically volatile urban populations and the need to redirect wealth from agriculture to expanding industrial sectors. In its analysis of how the world "will have to juggle competing and conflicting energy security and food security concerns" between now and 2015, the National Intelligence Council argues that in grain surplus areas such as the United States, Canada, Argentina, and Australia, "demand for biofuels—enhanced by government subsidies—will claim larger areas of cropland and greater volumes of irrigation water, even as biofuel production and processing technologies are made more efficient. This 'fuel/farming' trade-off, coupled with periodic export controls among Asian producers and rising demand for protein among growing middle classes worldwide, will force grain prices in the global market to fluctuate at levels above today's highs."[25] A critical variable left mostly unaddressed in this calculus is the potential impact of degraded water quality and poorly managed water resources.

In China, these global dynamics are very much in play. Subsidies on agricultural water and grains distort market signals and ultimately have an impact on production, whereas the prospect of volatile international grain prices reinforces distrust of these markets. As a consequence, similar to its response in the realm of oil, China has sought to ameliorate domestic production bottlenecks, reduce reliance on international markets, and minimize future price volatility by investing in agricultural land and production abroad. These efforts have mixed consequences for U.S. interests. On one hand, farmers in the U.S. Midwest and West have witnessed strong commodity prices as a consequence of large Chinese purchases of U.S. corn and soybeans.[26] On the other hand, in agricultural regions of Africa and

Southeast Asia, China's "going abroad" strategy will likely pose challenges to U.S. policy planners.

Although the Chinese Ministry of Agriculture stated in 2009 that China preferred to be self-sufficient and would not aggressively pursue land deals, China had by that time leased more than 1.5 million hectares of farmland abroad, second only to South Korea.[27] China has invested in farmland in Kazakhstan, Laos, Australia, the Philippines, and Mexico, and in the African countries of Mozambique, Zimbabwe, and Tanzania. In addition, there are an estimated twenty-three Chinese-owned farms in Zambia.[28] The impulse for such investments has been to secure farmland for the production of biofuel crops like sugar, cassava, and sorghum, as well as for direct export to the Chinese domestic market. To be sure, there was a flurry of investment in global agricultural farmland during the first decade of this century, conducted by a variety of institutions (e.g., government funds, private investment funds) from a variety of countries. The International Food Policy Research Institute estimates "that 15 to 20 million hectares of farmland have been subject to negotiations or transactions over the last few years."[29] One analyst "estimated that by the end of 2008, China, South Korea, the United Arab Emirates, Japan, and Saudi Arabia controlled more than 7.6 million cultivable hectares overseas—more than five times the usable agricultural surface of Belgium."[30]

There has been considerable debate over the consequences of such investments. The estimated 15 to 20 million hectares of global farmland that have been subject to negotiations or transactions in the last several years have sparked charges from some quarters of a "new colonialism" by traditional powers and newly minted petrocolonists such as Saudi Arabia and the United Arab Emirates.[31] Much of this investment is sponsored by states that seek to bypass world markets to secure grain for consumption and biofuel feedstocks, lending greater force to charges that the purchasing or long-term leasing of land in developing countries leads to dependence and the withdrawal of land from local control, as well as demonstrating little concern for the long-term health of land and water resources. These critics' fundamental argument is that foreign land acquisition creates conditions for continued economic immiseration of countries in Southeast Asia and Africa. Conversely, many developing nations see foreign investment in land as providing much-needed technology and technological know-how, advanced agricultural practices for local emulation, and ultimately creating employment in the form of wage labor. These are the classic terms of debate over the colonial project of the nineteenth century and foreign investment regimes in the twentieth and twenty-first centuries.

The particular foreign policy challenge for the United States—in current and future investments by China in Africa and Southeast Asia—is, in many ways, similar to the challenges of China's global energy investments. As many have argued, global movement of agricultural commodities is really trade in water. Thus, it is no coincidence that many of the most aggressive government-sponsored investments in agricultural farmland emanate from regions that are water poor. And China's "resource diplomacy" is generally conducted in rational economic terms, little encumbered with issues such as human rights, terrorism, and so on. As is well known, this has generated much discussion and exhortations in U.S. policy circles for China to become a "responsible stakeholder" in global affairs. Significant farmland investment by China occurs in areas in Africa and Southeast Asia that are important to U.S. security and economic interests. One obvious example is the U.S. focus on these areas as part of its "war on global terrorism," but, perhaps more subtly, these are areas where U.S. interests are strong and where U.S. and China foreign policy reflect divergent national interests.

*Developing Himalayan Water Resources
and Its Effect on Regional Relationships*

Climate change is the single greatest threat to China's precarious water balance. Continued recession of Himalayan glaciers and snowpack on the Tibetan-Qinghai Plateau will have a profound effect on several key transboundary river systems that have their respective sources in China. Two of these major rivers, the Yellow and the Yangzi, flow through China proper and are critical sources of water in the agricultural, industrial, and demographic heartland of China. State leaders are well aware of the consequences of climate change on the Tibetan Plateau and are pursuing an aggressive agenda of developing the water resources of rivers that emanate in the Himalayas and the Tibetan Plateau. Many of these rivers are transnational and flow through Southeast Asian states after leaving China. Thus, how China manages these rivers will have critical consequences for China's relations with these states and Southeast Asian economic security. Compounding the potential effects of climate change are growing water shortages on the North China Plain and the desire to develop the Western regions. All these forces have impelled state leaders to cast their eyes upon the largely unregulated rivers descending from the Tibetan highlands.

One response to the challenges of water scarcity on the North China Plain is to divert water from the Tibet-Qinghai Plateau to the Yellow River Valley, ultimately conveying water to the North China Plain region. Indeed, this is the so-called western route of the South-North Water Transfer Project that aims to bring water from the Yarlong Zangbo, Dadu, Tongtian, and Jinsha rivers by canal over complex geography to the Yellow River Valley.[32] Although work was scheduled to begin in 2010, with completion slated for 2050, it remains unclear whether the government is willing to expend the enormous cost and effort to initiate the project. The entire water transfer project was initially conceived in the 1950s, but the successful exploitation of groundwater on the North China Plain, beginning in the 1960s, delayed serious consideration of the plan until the 1990s. With the near-completion of the eastern route and continued debate over both the central and eastern routes, it is clear that state leaders continue to be smitten by the promises of massive engineering solutions to China's water problems. This continued emphasis on managing supply is precisely what is making Southeast Asian leaders nervous, as they see China's predilection for aggressively developing water resources negatively affect downstream ecosystems in their region.

The second reason for China to look to its Himalayan water resources is the long-term plan to develop the western regions of the country. Premised on expanding internal markets and mitigating growing income gaps between the West and coastal regions, state planners see hydroelectric generation as a source of cheap energy to develop Tibet and the southwest provinces, as well as to send electricity to industrial centers in Guangdong Province. Both private capital markets and power generation corporations with significant state ties have capitalized on improved transportation infrastructure and technical capacities to target Himalayan rivers for the development of hydroelectric facilities.[33] Aside from their relative distance from population and industrial centers, one could not find better prospects for power generation than these rivers. Rising high out of the Tibetan Plateau, the steep gradient of these rivers provides hydroelectric potential unmatched in China. As of 2007, more than two hundred dams were under construction or in planning stages in Southwest China.[34]

It would be a mistake simply to suggest that dam building is not a contested undertaking in China. The fragmented nature of the state bureaucracy creates competing interests over water resources, and there is growing environmental concern over critical resources like air, land, and water. Indeed, these concerns have clearly entered China's administrative structure through agencies like the State Environmental Protection Agency and through international and domestic nongovernmental organizations. Projects in Southwest China, such as plans to dam the Nujiang River, have faced delays over ecological concerns. However, beyond a predilection for large engineering projects, an additional source of momentum for hydroelectric generation has emerged—hydroelectricity is seen as a clean alternative to coal-powered power generation. Thus there are new but conflicting sensibilities that have arisen over large hydroelectric projects in China that may result in sufficient momentum to continue aggressive water development projects in the southwest.

However, perhaps the greatest impulse propelling water development projects forward is growing concern about the impact of climate change on China's water supply. In the past decade, the state has channeled substantial money to research institutions like the Academy of Sciences to forecast the potential consequences of climate change. Of particular concern in this research agenda is the fate of precipitation, glaciers, and snowpack on the Tibet-Qinghai Plateau. As Ken Pomeranz points out, "glaciers and annual snowfalls in this area feed rivers serving 47 percent of the world's people."[35] There is little agreement on the precise outcomes of climate change, but a growing body of Chinese and international research suggests that the Himalayan region will be substantially affected by rising temperatures. Greater runoff will initially generate increased flows that will augment water supplies, but at the same time potentially increase flood risk. Over the long term, however, runoff will decrease and other potential consequences of climate change such as reduced precipitation in the Yellow River Valley and North China Plain will intensify water scarcity. According to a study in China published in 2007, at the current observed rates of melt, Himalayan glaciers could decline by one-third by 2050, and by one-half by 2090. The anticipated loss of water resources would have a negative impact on China's food production. According to Tang Huajun, deputy dean of the Chinese Academy of Agricultural Sciences, "a 5 to 10 percent crop loss is foreseeable by 2030 if climate change continues." The *China Daily* story continues, "The impact of climate change, coupled with arable land loss and water shortages, will cause a bigger grain production fluctuation and pose a threat to reaching output targets. . . . China, which recorded a grain output of 530.8 million tons in 2009, plans to increase output to 550 million tons by 2020 to ensure grain security for the world's most populous country. China is likely to face an inadequate food supply by 2030 and its overall food production could fall by 23 percent by 2050."[36] In addition to responses such as accelerating use of genetically modified, drought-resistant grains, China will more aggressively increase reservoir capacity on international waterways in Southwest China.

What will the consequences be for regional economic and political stability as increasing water security issues lead China to aggressively develop transboundary water resources? Asia's nine largest rivers originate on the Tibetan Plateau. Often referred to as the Asian "water tower," rivers from this region sustain the lives of 1.3 billion people in South and Southeast Asia.[37] For example, "60 percent of the Brahmaptura River flows through this region, although most of the users are downstream in India, Nepal, and Bangladesh. Due both to climate change and to brown soot raising the temperatures on their surfaces, at the current rate of melting, these glaciers [on the Tibetan Plateau] are predicted to retreat by 30–50 percent by 2050."[38] Although transboundary water conflicts have invariably been solved without resort to war, the National Intelligence Council concludes in its assessment of global trends to 2025 that "with water becoming more scarce in several regions, cooperation over changing water resources is likely to be increasingly difficult within and between states, straining regional relations."[39] Transboundary rivers such as the Mekong (Lancang), Brahmaputra (Zangbo), and Salween (Nujiang) are the lifelines of South and Southeast Asia. For example, the Mekong runs through China, Myanmar, Laos, Thailand, Cambodia, and Vietnam. In the lower basin, 60 million people rely on aquatic food sources for 80 percent of their protein needs.[40] In addition to aggressive plans for main-stem and tributary dams by Laos, Vietnam, and other downstream countries, the International Rivers Network reports that China is building a cascade of eight dams in the upper reaches of the Mekong River, four of them completed, including the massive Xiaowan Dam.[41]

The Mekong River Commission—made up of the member countries Cambodia, Laos, Thailand, and Vietnam—was established in 1957 "to promote and co-ordinate sustainable management and development of water and related resources for the countries' mutual benefit and the people's well-being by implementing strategic programmes and activities and providing scientific information and policy advice."[42] The Mekong River Commission's current structure and mission were institutionalized with the 1995 Mekong Agreement, which formally created an intergovernmental panel tasked with managing and developing the basin. China and Myanmar are officially "dialogue partners," with little immediate prospect of becoming full member countries. After a number of false starts, China began sharing significant flow and rainfall data beginning in 2007, but thus far, the calculus of China's water security interests precludes a full commitment to member status in the commission. Indeed, this security calculation has led to China's being "one of only three UN-member countries to reject the notion that states have the right not to be adversely affected by activities of upstream countries. Beijing asserts complete sovereignty over resources with its boundaries."[43]

The economic and political stability of South and Southeast Asia is clearly in the short- and long-term national interests of the United States. The stability of Pakistan is of obvious interest to present concerns related to the war on terror as manifested in Central Asia. The simmering Pakistan-India conflict also directly implicates U.S. security objectives in the region. Although the outcome of these instabilities does not solely depend upon water resources, water is a critical component of a suite of issues that collectively can influence the trajectory of these challenges. In addition, Southeast Asia's economic vitality and political stability are increasingly critical to U.S. global economic interests and geopolitical concerns related to terrorism and freedom of movement in important sea lanes, such as those connecting to some of our most important allies in the region (e.g., Japan). Water constraints, especially compounded by the potential effects of global climate change, will likely be a key input to economic and, ultimately, political stability in these regions. The fact that China holds the position of "water tower" to the political economy of these regions makes it a key player in the U.S. strategic calculus.

Recently, U.S. reengagement with India and Southeast Asia seems to be encouraging China to be a more "responsible stakeholder" in the region. In July 2009 during the inaugural U.S.–Lower Mekong Ministerial Meeting in Phuket, Secretary of State Hillary Clinton announced the framework for collaboration between the Mekong River Commission and the Mississippi River Commission. During this visit the United States also signed the Treaty of Amity and Cooperation. Renewed U.S. diplomatic activism in Southeast Asia seemed to pay immediate dividends. In April 2010, China participated in a Mekong summit in the Thai resort town of Hua Hin to mark the fifteenth anniversary of the Mekong Agreement. At the summit Chinese officials shared runoff and other data—information that they had not shared previously. In response to charges that China's upstream dams were responsible for serious dry-ups during recent dry seasons, Chinese officials also offered data on reservoir levels that disputed these charges.[44] Although China has not suggested that aggressive water development plans will abate, the relative eagerness of China to engage in dialogue appears to be a direct response to U.S. diplomatic efforts in the region. Indeed, engagement by the United States in the critical water issues in South and Southeast Asia can be one platform for augmenting current diplomatic efforts to strengthen U.S. relations with the countries of South Asia and Southeast Asia as a means of conditioning China's behavior in the region.

## The Impact of Water Constraints on Global Food and Health

Intensified use and reuse of degraded water resources are directly linked to food quality and health issues within and beyond China. The United States imports significant amounts of Chinese food products, and zoonotic diseases like severe acute respiratory syndrome (SARS) and avian flu are intimately associated with water quantity and quality conditions.

Much of the concern about the safety of food imports to the United States centers on fish. During the past decade China has become the world's leading exporter of fish. Acute water shortages have intensified fish production in concentrated production areas, and agricultural runoff, municipal waste, and industrial effluents have severely compromised fish-rearing waters. In mid-2010 the *China Daily* highlighted a particularly serious incident in Fujian Province where toxic waste from a local copper mine resulted in the loss of 1,890 tons of fish. The same article reported that "statistics from the Ministry of Environmental Protection show 9,123 enterprises were involved in heavy metal pollution during production in 2009. Almost 2,200 were found to be harmful to the environment, with 231 closed down and 641 ordered to halt all operations."[45] In many instances, on top of such degraded water, waste from fish-producing ponds is again cycled into local water systems. Further compounding the problem is the broadcasting of antibiotics and other drugs into fish feed to maintain the health of fish in these contaminated waters. These types of drugs tend to concentrate in muscle tissue, leaving potentially carcinogenic residue in fish that are marketed domestically and internationally.

The importance of farm-raised fish has become increasingly critical to global food production. Stocks of consumable ocean fish have declined substantially in the face of ravenous global demand for seafood. China has capitalized on the opportunities in aquaculture in a major way, producing 117 billion pounds of seafood in 2006, representing 70 percent of all farm-raised seafood in the world.[46] The state was eager to encourage the development of aquaculture operations, seeing them as an opportunity to provide rural employment to a chronically underemployed workforce and thus preempt further migration to urban areas. As of 2007, there were reportedly 4.5 million fish farmers in China.[47] But the quality of exports from these operations quickly caught the attention of importing countries. Japan, in particular, set stringent restrictions on residual traces of veterinary drugs, resulting in a 50-percent decline in eel imports in 2007.[48] One response to severe water problems in Chinese aquaculture is to move inland to areas where cleaner sources of water do not require heavy medication of fish stocks. The concern, however, is that inadequate enforcement of environmental regulations will ultimately reproduce practices near the coastal areas.

A second global health problem related to China's water scarcity is the development and spread of zoonotic diseases. The recent outbreaks of SARS and avian flu have focused global attention on virus transmission from animals to humans. The emergence of pandemic diseases is likely to occur in regions with high population densities and "close association between human and animals."[49] The SARS outbreak in China during 2003 reflected many of these conditions. In addition, "scientists have become increasingly aware of the linkage between emergence of outbreaks in zoonotic diseases and the destruction of natural habitat of animal hosts, climatic changes due to global warming, and other environmental changes caused by humans."[50] Water shortages are among the outcomes of environmental change that may be critical to the development of pandemic diseases. As has been definitively researched in areas of Africa, water shortages have intensified the human-animal interface, thereby providing appropriate environmental conditions for the spread of disease from animals to humans.[51] China clearly fits the profile of ecological transformations, high population densities, and close human-animal interface potentially fostering the emergence of pandemic diseases that do not respect national borders.

## Engaging China on Water Issues

Environmental security is becoming a global concern as local ecological transitions have effects reaching far beyond region and nation. Thus, water scarcity in China implicates a variety of U.S. interests including global economic health, as well as regional and international security. Ultimately, these are national security issues, as they directly affect the domestic vitality of the U.S. economy and its position in international trade and diplomatic networks. As such, U.S. policy actors have an opportunity to engage China in dialogue about water management and climate change. Chinese leaders are well aware of the challenges the country faces in more effectively managing its water. A comprehensive regulatory program has been established, and the government is fully aware of existing problems in regulatory enforcement, conservation, and pricing. The critical challenge in China is building the institutional capacity to effectively pursue reforms in the water sector. The U.S. water sector has considerable experience in these realms, but the two countries also face similar unresolved problems—such as in the water-energy nexus—which a mutually beneficial dialogue can be constructed around. A structured exchange of information on technological approaches and institutional arrangements can lead to a set of confidence-building exchanges that might ultimately advance agendas focused on military-to-military dialogue, intellectual property protection, and currency and trade issues.

## Conclusion

This chapter has attempted to explore several national, regional, and international security dimensions of China's water scarcity challenges. At each level, U.S. interests are implicated. Domestically, water shortages have had and will continue to have an impact on economic growth rates in China. The remarkable degree of integration between the respective economies means that the continued health of the U.S. economy depends on a stable and vibrant Chinese economy. The domestic economic consequences, combined with health safety concerns, of polluted and diminished water resources also have the potential to have an impact on political stability in China. It is certainly unclear whether frustration over environmental issues will threaten the Communist Party's monopoly on power, but such frustrations can be one component of a set of grievances that can collectively contribute to political instability. A politically unstable China unquestionably translates into an entire host of concerns for U.S. security.

At the regional and international levels, global climate change will likely condition China's relations with South and Southeast Asian countries as the challenges of managing these relationships are accentuated by diminishing water resources emanating from the Tibetan-Himalayan region.

Incorporating China into regional governance organizations such as the Mekong River Commission can help stabilize growing U.S. strategic and economic interests in the region. Globally, continued economic expansion coupled with demographic growth and climate change will intensify water resource constraints and impel a more aggressive Chinese posture in international grain markets and increased investment in agricultural resources like land. Finally, China's water quality and quantity issues are directly connected with global food safety and health issues. Given the spate of serious food and health incidents that have embarrassed the government at home and abroad during the past several years, China is keenly interested in creating better governance structures to monitor food safety. This is but one area that suggests that the United States and China have mutual interests in the management of water issues.

By virtue of their large economic and strategic footprints, China and the United States have the opportunity to forge a dialogue centered on water and water-related issues that can advance the bilateral, regional, and global interests of both states. First, bilaterally, the United States can and should identify the water sector as one area for policy and technical collaboration, just as it is doing in the clean energy sector. As Kenneth Lieberthal has noted in regard to the latter, such cooperation can further the building of mutual trust that can benefit the relationship in all its dimensions. The United States can offer technical and organizational support to assist China in increasing the efficiency of water-intensive industries like steel and cement. Second, the United States can provide support and expertise to regional basin organizations such as the Mekong River Commission, encouraging China to be a responsible stakeholder in international river basin governance structures. Last, the United States can encourage broad momentum for international agreement on climate change. U.S. diplomats and other officials can help prevent insularity in China by demonstrating a strong resolve to reach multilateral openings for agreement on climate change framework and principles.

Although China is indeed experiencing an acute set of water issues, there is no corresponding set of inevitable outcomes that will result from these challenges. The North China Plain has historically been a region plagued by water scarcity, and in the past China has managed this reality with remarkable success. To be sure, the rapid urbanization, industrialization, intensified agriculture, and demographic change in the post-Mao era have introduced pressures heretofore unseen on scarce water resources. Thus far, China has managed to delicately maintain impressive economic growth and political stability through a variety of mechanisms, including demand management and engineering solutions. The central question for U.S. policymakers is whether China can maintain this balance in the light of continued economic growth and climate change. The sheer pace of economic change coupled with demographic pressures over the next several decades suggests that maintaining this balance may indeed be a precarious proposition.

But what has clearly changed the calculus of the potential environmental impact on China's future economic growth is the degree to which China has become incorporated into international markets during the past two decades. Put simply, environmental constraints in China have international ramifications. For example, international wheat prices hovered near record highs in early 2011 as reports of serious drought conditions on the North China Plain ignited speculation that China would embark on aggressive buying on international commodity markets.[52] Food prices in China increased by double digits in January 2011, a potential source of domestic insecurity in that country. Moreover, the possible impact on world food prices may threaten stability in other critical areas around the globe. This appears to have already occurred in Egypt, where the price of wheat and other commodities was widely reported as one factor impelling protests in early 2011.[53] In short, in today's globalized world, U.S. policymakers must be increasingly cognizant that China's acute water difficulties are not simply a problem for China alone.

## Notes

1. National Intelligence Council, *Global Trends 2025: A Transformed World* (Washington, D.C.: National Intelligence Council, 2008), v.

2. UNESCO, *Water in a Changing World: The United Nations World Water Development Report* (Paris: UNESCO, 2007).

3. Dorothy C. Zibicz, *Asia's Future: Critical Thinking for a Changing Environment* (Washington, D.C.: Woodrow Wilson International Center for Scholars, 2009), 46.

4. Nathan Nankivell, *The National Security Implications of China's Emerging Water Crisis* (Washington, D.C.: Jamestown Foundation, 2005), http://www.asianresearch.org/articles/2694.html.

5. For these and other data, see "Yellow River Management: Continuity and Change," in *River Basins: Trajectories, Societies and Environments*, edited by François Molle and Philippus Wester (London: CABI, 2009).

6. For a compendium of environmental challenges in the post-Mao era, see Judith Shapiro, *Mao's War on Nature: Politics and the Environment in Revolutionary China* (New York: Cambridge University Press, 2001); and Elizabeth Economy, *The River*

*Runs Black: The Environmental Challenge to China's Future*, 2nd ed. (Ithaca, N.Y.: Cornell University Press, 2010).

7. Lester Brown, *Who Will Feed China? Wake-Up Call for a Small Planet* (New York: W. W. Norton, 1995).

8. For a critique, see also Jerry McBeath and Jennifer Huang McBeath, "Environmental Stressors and Food Security in China," *Journal of Chinese Political Science* 14 (2009), 49–80.

9. See Vaclev Smil, "Research Note: China's Arable Land," *China Quarterly* 158 (1999): 414–29.

10. See Dai Qing, *Yangtze! Yangtze!* (London: Earthscan, 1994); and Dai Qing, *The River Dragon Has Come!* (Armonk, N.Y.: M. E. Sharpe, 1998).

11. See Ma Jun, *China's Water Crisis* (New York: Eastbridge, 2004).

12. Elizabeth Economy, "Asia's Water Security Crisis: China, India, and the United States," in *Strategic Asia 2008–09: Challenges and Choices*, edited by Ashley Tellis et al. (Seattle: National Bureau of Asian Research, 2009), 373.

13. Ibid., 372.

14. Nankivell, *National Security Implications*.

15. Ibid.

16. For more on China's interaction with global energy markets, see David Pietz, "The Past, Present, and Future of China's Energy Sector," in *China's Energy Strategy: The Impact on Beijing's Maritime Policies*, edited by Andrew Erickson and Gabriel Collins et al. (Newport, R.I.: Naval Institute Press, 2008).

17. McBeath and McBeath, "Environmental Stressors," 65.

18. Quoted in "Yellow River Is 10 Percent Sewage: Official," *China Daily*, May 11, 2007, http://www.chinadaily.com.cn/china/2007-05/11/content_870093.htm.

19. Report cited in "China Needs to Cut Use of Chemical Fertilizer: Research," Reuters, n.d., http://www.reuters.com/article/idUSTRE60D20T20100114.

20. Bin Yang and Lu Yanpin, "The Promise of Cellulosic Ethanol Production in China," *Journal of Chemical Technology and Biotechnology* 82, no. 1 (2007): 6.

21. IEA chief economist Fatih Biros, as quoted in the *New York Times*, July 5, 2010, http://www.iea.org/journalists/headlines.asp?offset=20.

22. Jeffrey Logan of IEA, as quoted in ibid.

23. See E. Gnansounou, A. Dauriat, and C. E. Wyman, "Refining Sweet Sorghum to Ethanol and Sugar: Economic Trade-Offs in the Context of North China," *Bioresource Technology* 96 (2005): 985–1002.

24. Economy, "Asia's Water Security Crisis," 370.

25. National Intelligence Council, *Global Trends 2025*, 52.

26. On corn purchases, see "China Corn Buys May Exceed 1 Million Tons, U.S. Says," Bloomberg, June 17, 2010, http://www.businessweek.com/news/2010-06-17/china-corn-buys-may-exceed-1-million-tons-u-s-says-update1-.html). On soybean purchases, see "Grains: Soy Up Half Percent on Chinese Buying," Reuters, October 19, 2010, http://in.reuters.com/article/idINSGE69I03S20101019.

27. Javier Blas, "China Rules Out Pursuit of African Farmland," *Financial Times*, April 20, 2009, http://www.ft.com/cms/s/0/9d2cdee8-2dcf-11de-9eba-00144feabdc0.html.

28. Alexandra Spiedloch and Sophia Murphy, "Agricultural Land Acquisitions: Implications for Food Security and Poverty Alleviation," in *Land Grab? The Race for the World's Farmland*, edited by Michael Kugelman and Susan Levenstein (Washington, D.C.: Woodrow Wilson International Center for Scholars, 2009), 42.

29. Michael Kugelman, "Introduction," in *Land Grab?* ed. Kugelman and Levenstein, 1.

30. Ibid.

31. Ibid.

32. On the water diversion project, see Liu Changming, "Environmental Issues and the South–North Water Transfer Scheme," *China Quarterly* 156 (1998): 899–910.

33. Kenneth Pomeranz, "The Great Himalayan Watershed: Water Shortages, Mega-Projects and Environmental Politics in China, India, and Southeast Asia," *Japan Focus*, http://japanfocus.org/articles/3195.

34. Jennifer Turner and Linden Ellis, "China's Growing Ecological Footprint," *China Monitor*, March 2007, 9.

35. Pomeranz, "Great Himalayan Watershed," 1.

36. "Climate Change Takes Toll on Grain Harvest," *China Daily*, November 11, 2010, http://www.chinadaily.com.cn/china/2010-11/05/content_11505107.htm.

37. Xu Jianchu, "The Highlands: A Shared Water Tower in a Changing Climate and a Changing Asia," working paper, World Agroforestry Centre, 2007, 1.

38. Ibid, 18.

39. National Intelligence Council, *Global Trends 2025*, 66.

40. International Rivers; see http://www.internationalrivers.org/southeast-asia.

41. Ibid.

42. See http://www.mrcmekong.org/about_mrc.htm.

43. Economy, "Asia's Water Security Crisis," 379–80.

44. See "China Goes for Friendly Giant Role in Mekong," Inter Press Service, http://ipsnews.net/news.asp?idnews=51808; Mercle David Kellerhals, "U.S. to Spend $187 Million on Lower Mekong Initiative," Bureau of International Information Programs, U.S. Department of State, July 22, 2010, http://www.america.gov/st/develop-english/2010/July/20100722134433dmslahrellek0.2057459.html.

45. "Contaminated Waters That Kill," *China Daily*, July 16, 2010, http://www.chinadaily.com.cn/cndy/2010-07/16/content_10113959.htm.

46. "In China, Farming Fish in Toxic Waters," *New York Times*, December 15, 2007, http://www.nytimes.com/2007/12/15/world/asia/15fish.html.

47. Ibid.

48. Ibid.

49. National Intelligence Council, *Global Trends 2025*, 75.

50. See "The Impact of Environmental Changes on Zoonotic Diseases," http://serendipt.brynmawr.edu/exchange/node/5327. For a general discussion, see Sonia Shah, "The Spread of New Diseases: The Climate Connection," *Yale Environment 360*, October 15, 2009, http://e360.yale.edu/content/feature.msp?id=2199.

51. Joshua Brown, "When Rivers Run Dry," http://www.uvm.edu/~uvmpr/?Page=News&storyID=15205#.

52. See "China Drought Has Global Implications," *Globe and Mail*, February 16, 2011, http://www.theglobeandmail.com/report-on-business/economy/chinas-drought-has-global-implications/article1910465/.

53. See "UN Food Agency Issues Warning on China Drought," February 8, 2011, http://www.nytimes.com/2011/02/09/business/global/09food.html?_r=1&pagewanted=all.

# Chapter 4

# The Indus River Basin in the Twenty-First Century

*Eric A. Strahorn*

This chapter examines ecological and political relations in the Indus River Basin and their implications for the United States. The Indus Waters Treaty (IWT) has been reasonably successful at managing political conflict over water resources between India and Pakistan, but it is inadequate to manage the ecological challenges the region now faces. As a result, the IWT may grow less effective at managing political conflict as demands on water resources continue to increase.

The Indus River Basin is a critical watershed area with a population of over 100 million people (figure 4.1). It includes territory in Pakistan, India, Afghanistan, and China, crossing three disputed international borders—Afghanistan/Pakistan, India/Pakistan, and India/China.[1] In the past half century, the basin has been the site for wars between India and its largest neighbors (Pakistan and China), separatist movements in the Indian states of Kashmir and Punjab, and the current conflict with the Taliban in eastern Afghanistan and Pakistan. Since the partition of South Asia in 1947, the basin has been subject to numerous hydropower development projects,

*Figure 4.1. The Indus River Basin*

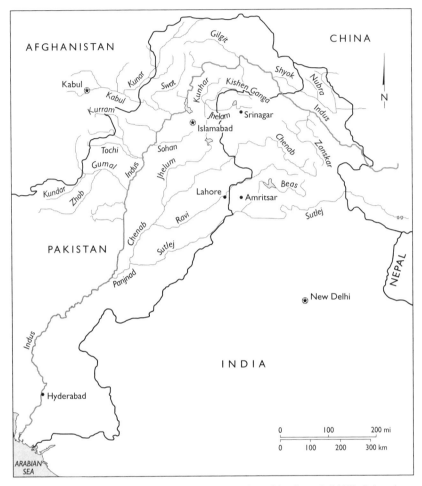

*Source:* Wikipedia user "Kmhkmh," May 29, 2009, http://en.wikipedia.org/wiki/File:Indus_river. svg. Cartography by Bill Nelson.

including dams, canals, and large-scale irrigation works, along with serious earthquakes, droughts, and floods.

The United States has been directly and continuously involved in water issues in the basin since the early 1950s, beginning with a request from the government of Pakistan to mediate the dispute with India over Indus Basin water.[2] Despite this involvement, the United States has rarely had a coherent policy toward the basin as an ecological and political whole, tending to deal with issues piecemeal. As recent events like the 2010 floods have shown, U.S. policy has tended to be reactive to events in the short run, sacrificing long-term goals for ad hoc crisis management. It is likely that the United States will remain involved in the region through at least 2015, due to the U.S. military presence in Afghanistan as well as U.S. commitments to Pakistan and India.[3] It is in the interest of the United States to encourage development of a successor treaty, providing a regulatory framework that would reduce the potential for conflict within and between the four countries, especially as increased exploitation of limited resources and the effects of climate change alter the ecological conditions of the basin over the next fifty years.[4]

U.S. interests in the Indus River Basin do not originate primarily from concerns over water issues. Rather, U.S. attention toward South Asia was initially motivated by Cold War concerns and is driven today by the war on terrorism. The United States first articulated a formal interest in South Asia in 1951 with the adoption of "The Position of the United States with Respect to South Asia," a policy drawn up by the National Security Council.[5] Among that policy's numerous objectives, which have remained relatively unchanged over six decades, are efforts to improve Indo-Pakistan and Afghan-Pakistan relations.[6] It was at this point in time that water issues, especially in the Indus Basin, were identified as critical to U.S. interests, because disputes over the region's various rivers and canals were seen as a source of instability and conflict.

Since the beginning of the war on terrorism in 2001, the understanding of U.S. interests in South Asia has been defined in similar ways. Essentially, the argument is that success in the war on terrorism is vital to U.S. security and that such success can be achieved only if Afghanistan, India, and Pakistan are stable and conflict among them is at a minimum. In a 2002 report to Congress on Kashmir, the Congressional Research Service argued that, "for the United States, the issue of Kashmir is how to prevent an all-out war between India and Pakistan while concurrently maintaining Indian and Pakistani cooperation in the antiterror campaign and *keeping bilateral relations with the two nations on an improving trend*" (emphasis added).[7] This was confirmed in a 2009 Congressional Research Service report, which noted that "a stable, democratic, prosperous Pakistan actively working to counter Islamist militancy is considered vital to U.S. interests."[8]

Managing water in the Indus Basin has been a major part of improving relations between countries in South Asia since the 1950s, and even more so in recent years due to "the inability of the states in the region to de-link the functional aspect of water sharing from other political issues affecting their relations."[9] As Michael Kugelman notes, "The U.S. government has recognized that Pakistan's economic and development challenges—including those of water—are linked to its combustible political and security situation, and that stabilizing the latter will require tackling the former."[10] Moreover, the security implications of terrorism and water issues became directly linked in 2009 when "Taliban forces launched an offensive that got within 35 miles of the giant Tarbela Dam [on the Indus River in Khyber Pakhtunkhwa Province], the linchpin of Pakistan's hydroelectric and irrigation system."[11]

This chapter begins with an analysis of the overall political ecology of the Indus River Basin, which is followed by an examination of the history and development of the IWT. It then addresses the ecological consequences of the IWT, with an emphasis on the connectedness of environmental problems throughout the basin rather than looking at each issue in isolation. This is followed by a discussion of whether a new treaty is necessary and what it may entail.

## The Political Ecology of the Indus River Basin

The political ecology of the Indus River Basin is divided such that there is little coordination between all of the riparian states, resulting in numerous disputes over existing water usage in addition to ongoing controversies over the causes and consequences of various natural disasters.[12] One thing the four states do agree on is that the volume of water in the basin's rivers is declining and is projected to decline still further over the next several decades.[13] As Uttam Kumar Sinha notes:

> In South Asia, rivers, with their distribution, agricultural utilization and potential for hydroelectric power projects, are increasingly defining interstate relations. Correspondingly, the existing structures of trans-boundary river treaties and agreements are being tested and influenced by growing water scarcity and competition on the one side and efforts to increase availability through water transfer on the other.[14]

The availability of water flow data throughout the basin is inadequate, given the overwhelming importance of the basin's rivers as sources of water. According to one recent study, while there are river gauges throughout the lower basin, very few of them are actually located in irrigation channels and canals where most of the increase in water consumption is taking place.[15] Meanwhile, there are few if any river gauges in much of the Upper Indus River Basin (upriver from Tarbela Dam) because of the difficulty of access due to the steep terrain as well as contentious political borders.[16] However, available data are more than sufficient to indicate the general scope of the problem. For example, the average annual water discharge has declined from 126 billion cubic meters in 1955 to just 10 billion cubic meters in 2003.[17] As a result, the Indus delta is undergoing desertification, with seawater intrusion into underground aquifers up to 100 kilometers inland leaving the groundwater too salty to drink or use for agriculture.[18] This is a separate process from the salinization of the soil elsewhere in the Indus Basin, which is caused by the application of too much irrigation water or waterlogging that dissolves the salts naturally occurring in the earth.

The decline in water flow is especially a cause for concern when combined with population growth in Pakistan. In 1950, the average volume of water available per capita was 5,000 cubic meters, but by 2009 it had dropped to approximately 1,200 cubic meters, resulting in the Indus River Basin within Pakistan fitting the United Nations' definition of being "water stressed." The volume of water is expected to decline further, making the situation in the basin one of "water scarcity." Estimates of when the water availability in Pakistan will reach this point vary from 2015 to 2035.[19] One study estimates that by 2050, the number of people who can be fed by the agricultural production of the Indus Basin will have decreased by 23 to 29 million. This represents a threat to the food security of 4.5 percent of the total population of the region, just due to declining water availability.[20]

Even before the major drought of 2009 and devastating floods of 2010, interstate tension over water was increasing. In addition to long-standing disputes between India and Pakistan, both Afghanistan and China have launched various development projects in their respective parts of the basin. The Kabul River is a major tributary of the Indus, and until recently very little of the water was utilized in Afghanistan but flowed instead into Pakistan. In recent years, this has begun to change as the Afghani government has turned to the Kabul River in its efforts to deal with water shortages. The city of Kabul and the surrounding area have relied too heavily on underground aquifers, resulting in a substantial decline in the water table (6 to 7 meters) since 1965.[21] The government of Afghanistan "has formulated plans for significant water infrastructure development . . . to mitigate floods and droughts and to fully exploit its irrigation and energy potential."[22] The government has recognized that its development plans could reduce the volume of water in the Kabul River available for use by Pakistan, but so far has been reluctant to engage the Pakistanis in dialogue to establish greater cooperation in managing the water flow. Pakistan has tended to downplay the merits of the proposed development works in Afghanistan and instead views them as part of an Indian plot to use water as a weapon against Pakistan.[23] Regardless—as noted by a former World Bank official, John Briscoe—this represents a serious threat to Pakistan's water security, because up to 20 percent of the flow of the Indus comes from the Kabul River.[24]

China has also begun to expand its use of the Indus and Sutlej rivers in western Tibet with the construction of hydroelectric dams on the Sutlej in 2004 and the Indus in 2005. These dams do not alter the volume of water in either river, but it is increasingly likely that China will begin to draw water from both in order to combat spreading desertification in the Tibetan Plateau. One of the most significant antidesertification projects in centered on the town of Shiquanhe, which is located just downriver of the dam built on the Indus in 2005. Published studies on the project do not mention large-scale water withdrawals, but it is unlikely that the water required by the project could come from anywhere else.[25] Up until now, there has been little communication between China and India regarding water use in the Indus Basin. In 2005, the two argued over the relationship, if any, between China's construction of hydroelectric dams on the Sutlej River and flood conditions in the Indian state of Himachel Pradesh during 2000 and 2004.[26] India's complaint was partially about the lack of water flow data made available by China, eventually leading to an agreement between the two to regularly exchange water flow information.[27] In 2009, China and India signed the "Agreement on Cooperation on Addressing Climate Change between the Government of the Republic of India and the Government of the People's Republic of China," which despite the name does not address the effects of climate change on Himalayan glaciers or the Indus Basin rivers. Indeed, the word "water" does not appear in the document at all, and there has been very little effort by the two countries to discuss the management of their respective parts of the Indus Basin.

Early 2009 saw a return of water-related tensions between Pakistan and India as both sides began to accuse the other of responsibility for acts of terrorism. "After the Mumbai attacks of November 2008, Pakistani military commentators began to focus on India's violations of the Indus Water Treaty, suggesting that water resources were a latent cause of the perpetuation of the Kashmir conflict."[28] However, it should be noted that one political rather than ecological reason that the government of Pakistan is increasingly blaming India is to divert attention away from disputes between Pakistani provinces over water allocation, as well as the serious inefficiencies in aging irrigation works throughout the country.[29]

By 2010, water was one of the Pakistani government's highest priorities, and water issues became a key component of the Pakistan–United States Strategic Dialogue, as demonstrated by the creation of the Water Working Group that first met in Islamabad on June 17, 2010. At this meeting, Pakistani and U.S. officials discussed different aspects of the water situation in Pakistan, including water shortages, pollution, biodiversity, global warming, and transborder issues. Sardar Muhammad Tariq, executive director of the Pakistan Water Partnership, an environmental nongovernmental organization, placed great emphasis on the need to honor the IWT "in letter and spirit."[30]

It is clear, however, that even if the IWT is observed faithfully by both India and Pakistan, there are "critical transnational issues stemming from the complex hydrologic interconnectivity of Indus Basin waters" that are not covered by the IWT.[31] Neil Padukone has argued that the seriousness of the water situation between China and India suggests that "a broader, effectual treaty with China along the lines of the Indus Waters Treaty, complete with formal, protracted and institutionalised information-sharing and coordinated management institutions, may be required to pre-emptively address any management issues."[32] While such a treaty might indeed be useful, it would address only part of the problem. According to a study by the United Nations Environment Program, "there is a need for more efficient, and integrated, management of the upper Indus Basin. This calls for the involvement of other riparian countries—most important, India and China—along with Afghanistan for the other parts of upper Indus. In the face of a rapidly growing population and associated food requirements, the benefits from managing the upper Indus Basin as a single system would be substantial."[33] Given its deep commitment in the region, there is no way the United States could avoid being involved in such an effort.

## The Indus Waters Treaty

The only agreement guiding the division of the Indus River Basin's water resources is the Indus Waters Treaty, signed in 1960 between India and Pakistan. The IWT was facilitated by the World Bank and has proved to be relatively successful in political terms. The treaty was designed to prevent conflict between India and Pakistan over use of the Indus waters and, despite decades of hostility, both sides still observe its requirements—more or less.[34] For example, the treaty led to the establishment of the permanent Indus Water Commission, which meets regularly to exchange data and discuss ongoing issues, but a neutral expert had to be appointed in 2005 to resolve a dispute over the Baglihar Dam.

Although the IWT has been extensively studied as a political document, it has received much less attention as an ecological document. Past studies have focused on diplomacy, international law, and security questions but have failed to examine the ecological sustainability of water use in the basin as a whole. The IWT has important limitations. Two major flaws of the IWT are that only two of the four countries located in the basin are parties to it and that it does not address the issue of the variation of the total water supply.

In looking at the context of the IWT, it is important to note that it addresses issues that arose from the Partition in 1947. Essentially, the Boundary Commission headed by Sir Cyril Radcliffe did not specifically address the division of river water.[35] As such, canals and irrigation works crisscrossed the new border in a way that left the headworks for a given canal on one side of the border and the area receiving the water on the other side. Disputes between both sides immediately arose over allocation of the water. Although disagreements over the allocation of water between provinces had existed for decades, there was no longer any central authority capable of mediating the disputes. In 1948, the Indian state of East Punjab attempted to shut off the water supply to the Pakistani province of West Punjab, thereby threatening the water supply of Lahore.[36] When the government of Pakistan sought to bring the dispute before the United Nations Security Council, the Indian government quickly restored the water flow through the Inter-Dominion Agreement with Pakistan, but the potential for serious conflict was obvious.[37] Referring to the Chenab River as "the jugular vein of its life-line," Pakistani officials clearly recognized the need to resolve this unfinished part of Partition.[38]

Over the next few years, India and Pakistan negotiated a series of short-term agreements over the division of the Indus water flow but failed to find a more permanent solution. In 1951, the World Bank intervened in the negotiations by offering its good offices as a neutral third party. The three-party negotiations began with a statement of "essential principles" by Eugene Black, then president of the World Bank. Significantly, the first principle was that "the Indus Basin water resources are sufficient to continue all existing uses and to meet the further needs of both countries for water from that source."[39] This may have seemed a reasonable observation in 1951, because at the time more than half of the total volume of river water reached the sea.[40] Greater utilization of the water seemed quite sustainable, and many of Pakistan's development plans assumed that there was "an ultimate steady state" in the supply of water.[41]

However, the IWT takes the division a step further than a simple geographic division by seeking to maintain the same volume of water flow as in 1947. This required Pakistan to construct link canals to supply water from the western rivers to canals that formerly had been supplied by the eastern rivers.[42] As a result, all of the irrigation works used by Pakistan would be located in Pakistan, and the same for India. In Article V of the IWT, India was obligated to pay for the construction of these link canals, although later the World Bank, the United States, Canada, Britain, West Germany, New Zealand, and Australia provided substantial financial support, while Pakistan borrowed more than $200 million from the World Bank.[43] Eventually, eight link canals totaling almost 400 miles in length were built over the next few decades.[44] In support of the IWT, the United States provided financial and technical assistance to Pakistan over the next two decades for numerous projects, including the Mangla and Tarbela dams. The United States also provided aid for Indian projects in the Indus Basin, such as the Beas Dam and the 400-mile-long Indira Gandhi canal, which provides irrigation for over five million acres in the Indian state of Rajasthan.

An important element of the IWT was the creation of the Indus Water Commission in order to "establish and maintain co-operative arrangements for the implementation of [the] Treaty [and] to promote co-operation between the Parties in the development of the waters of the Rivers."[45] The commission is made up of two commissioners, one appointed by each country, and is required to meet at least once per year. The commission is tasked with investigating problems and disagreements between the two countries, but lacks the authority to alter the treaty or arbitrate disputes. The most distinctive aspect of the commission is that it has continued to meet, even during wartime, up to the present.

## The Environmental Costs of the Indus Waters Treaty

Today, much of the lower Indus River Basin (downriver of the Tarbela Dam) is plagued with numerous environmental problems, including groundwater pollution, poor drainage, and soil salinization. In 2009, approximately 25 percent of the irrigated command area of 18 million hectares had rising saline levels, with the problem being more severe in the lower part of the basin in Sindh Province where up to 56 percent of irrigated land is salt affected.[46] The IWT, however, did not create these problems; even before Partition, several regions experienced difficulties with waterlogging and salinization for decades, especially Punjab.[47] The potential for additional problems has been exacerbated by the complexity of the irrigation works throughout pre-Partition Punjab Province. Not only were there multiple dams and canals, but link canals had to be built to ensure adequate water flow in all the rivers in Punjab. These link canals transferred water from one river to another (e.g., from the Chenab to the Ravi). The canals were unlined and suffered a great deal of seepage of up to one-third of the water volume.[48] Moreover, there was widespread sentiment among colonial officials that existing irrigation works were underutilized and that water reaching the sea (known as the "escapage") was literally wasted.[49]

After Partition, both India and Pakistan built increasingly larger dams, canal networks, and irrigation facilities, but these new works were planned independently from each other. Outside agencies like the World Bank hesitated to fund the new works due to uncertainty about ownership and usage rights. Construction was often delayed throughout the 1950s, so most megaprojects were initiated only after the signing of the IWT in 1960. The IWT itself is a technical document that divides the rivers and irrigation works between the two countries with the goal of a permanent division of the rivers rather than joint management of the facilities. The treaty assigns the consumptive usage of the waters of the "eastern rivers" (Sutlej, Beas, and Ravi) to India and the "western rivers" (Indus, Jhelum, and Chenab) to Pakistan.[50]

To implement this assignment of rivers, new barrages, canals, and other irrigation works had to be constructed. The idea was that the irrigation infrastructure of both countries would be completely separated physically so that the international border would no longer divide the headworks from water distribution channels of some of the canals. This direct separation would forestall the need for active joint management of the irrigation works. However, due to cost, most of these new canals in Pakistan were unlined, allowing up to a third of the water to seep into the ground and leading to substantial waterlogging and salinization of the soil, even though a 1964 report had recommended that the canals be lined.[51] By 1984, Pakistan's Water and Power Development Authority determined that 60 percent of the country's irrigated land was affected by waterlogging, while 24 percent had rising saline levels.[52] Another consequence of the unlined canals is that much of the water seeping into the soil has contaminated the groundwater with agricultural runoff and salt on both sides of the border.[53] In addition, silt is reducing the water flow and storage capacities in numerous dams and canals throughout the basin. The Indus River has one of the highest silt loads in the world, carrying twice the volume of silt as the Missouri River and four times as much as the Nile.[54] The live capacity of Pakistan's Mangla Dam declined by 20 percent from 1967 to 2000, while the country's Tarbela Dam lost 40 percent of its capacity from 1975 to 2000.[55] The capacity has continued to decline, as about 0.6 million tons of sediment are deposited at the Tarbela Dam daily.[56] As more groundwater is used to make up for this reduced water flow, the water table has dropped, leading to greater use of contaminated surface water to recharge the aquifer. On both sides of the border in Punjab, anywhere from 50 to 80 percent of the groundwater has been recycled from the surface.[57]

The IWT simply does not address these environmental problems, because the treaty itself represents the last stage of Partition, permanently dividing the water resources in the Indus Basin. The ecological sustainability of water use was not considered during the negotiations, while the purpose of subsequent development projects has been to maximize water use for agriculture and hydroelectric power generation. The IWT does have a provision governing the movement of water pollution between India and Pakistan but does not address pollution solely within either country.[58] Within Pakistan, the Indus River and its tributaries are highly polluted, which has resulted in the contamination of drinking and irrigation water.[59] The volume of pollution has continued to increase such that, "by the early 1990s, Lahore and adjoining areas discharged 200 million gallons of waste water daily into the Ravi River."[60] In 2009, the discharge volume had risen to 270.7 million gallons and included both municipal and industrial waste.[61]

## Continuing Controversies in the Indus River Basin

In the decades after the signing of the IWT, Pakistani officials continued to link control over the waters of the Indus River Basin with the security of the country, despite Indian efforts to discount the connection.[62] In a visit to the White House in 1957, Pakistani prime minister Husein Shaheed Suhrawardy outlined to U.S. president Dwight D. Eisenhower his fear that

India could divert water from Pakistan's irrigation network in response to the conflict in Kashmir.[63] In 1961, in meetings with U.S. president John F. Kennedy, vice president Lyndon Johnson, and ambassador to India John Kenneth Galbraith, Pakistani president Mohammed Ayub Khan explained that part of Pakistan's concern over Kashmir was the potential threat posed by India's control over the headwaters of several of the Indus Basin rivers.[64]

Pakistani concerns were exacerbated in the 1970s, due to a dispute over India's plan to construct a dam on the Chenab River. One of Pakistan's objections was that the proposed dam was too large and could be used to interfere with the flow of water and cause droughts or floods in Pakistan. After three years of negotiations, the two countries were able to conclude an agreement allowing a modified dam to be built. A similar controversy arose in 1985, when Pakistan learned that India had begun constructing a barrage on the Jhelum River the year before. The government of the Pakistani province of Punjab led the criticism of the project, arguing that it would turn 1.3 million acres of farmland into a desert. It was not until 1997 that the two countries were able to work out a compromise.[65]

More recently, some of the technical assumptions made in the IWT have proved to be obsolete. The was made clear in 2005 when Raymond Lafitte was appointed by the World Bank as a "neutral expert," tasked with arbitrating a dispute over India's construction of a hydroelectric dam on the Chenab River. In 2007, Lafitte issued a ruling that addressed technical details such as the height of the dam, dam crest elevation, and maximum pondage. In explaining his ruling, Lafitte observed that the treaty was based on the technology and engineering standards of the 1950s and that its provisions for water flow volume did not take the effects of climate change into account.[66] The IWT as well as numerous hydropower projects assumed that there would be an ultimate steady state in the supply of water, and it is now obvious that this is false.[67] Briscoe has argued that Lafitte's ruling has "gutted the IWT of its essential balance" and that Pakistan and especially India have to take steps to establish a "new regime on the Indus waters."[68]

With the drought of 2009 and the floods of 2010, it is clear that the volume of water in the Indus River Basin can vary a great deal from year to year. It is highly likely that the volume of water will be subject to tremendous disruption over the next half century. The glaciers of the Himalayas are among the most important sources of water in the Indus Basin, especially above the Tarbela Dam. Growing evidence indicates that the glaciers are receding, although the exact rate of retreat is unclear.[69] The floods of 2010 are consistent with the effects of global warming on the

Himalayan glaciers, with current models predicting that runoff will tempo-rarily increase as the glaciers retreat. However, there has been some debate over how to assess the effects of global warming on this particular incident. While some commentators have suggested that the floods are "linked" to global warming, others argue that heavy rains and the dilapidated condition of the flood levees in Pakistan are more to blame.[70]

A decline in the water level of the Indus, resulting from the South Asian drought of 2009, points to the potential for sustained conflict over water. As the water level dropped, a massive controversy emerged within Paki-stan—from January to March 2010—over the cause.[71] Widespread senti-ment quickly blamed India for "water theft," "using water as a weapon," or even "water terrorism." Politicians, journalists, and various civic leaders discussed the dire consequences of India's alleged plan to render Pakistan a desert. General Ashfaq Parvez Kayani, Pakistan's chief of the Army Staff, declared that the Pakistani Army would retain an "India centric" posture, drawing troops away from the fighting along the border with Afghanistan, until issues such as Kashmir and water disputes were resolved. Publica-tions linked to extremist organizations like Lashkar-e-Taiba even raised the prospect of jihad against India over water. It is important to note, though, that by March several commentators in Pakistan questioned the lack of evidence for water theft by India and speculated about the motives of those who made such claims, although the controversy only subsided when floods erupted just a few months later.[72]

This near frenzy in targeting India did not disrupt the regular work of the Indus Water Commission, which maintained its regular schedule of meet-ings. Pakistan's Indus water commissioner, Jamaat Ali Shah, insisted that although India was in technical violation of the treaty, such issues could be resolved through the dispute resolution mechanisms created by the treaty.[73] At a meeting of the commission on July 22, 2010, Pakistan and India agreed to install a water telemetry system in order to generate real-time data that will reduce confusion and disagreement over water flow. They also agreed to conduct joint inspections of recently constructed river embankments on the Ravi River in India and to discuss pollution issues.[74]

The United States was brought into the controversy after politicians and various nongovernmental organizations in Pakistan requested U.S. media-tion of the dispute. The secretary of state, Hillary Clinton, the assistant secretary of state for South and Central Asian affairs, Robert Blake, and the undersecretary of state for democracy and global affairs, Maria Otero, were all obligated to comment as the U.S. government declined to intervene and suggested instead that Pakistan turn to the World Bank, as provided for in the IWT.[75] However, despite the initial reluctance of the State Department to get involved in this specific dispute, the importance placed on this issue by the government of Pakistan motivated the Water Working Group of the United States–Pakistan Strategic Dialogue, co-led by Otero, to identify water management issues "as a key area for increased cooperation."[76]

The political dynamic changed dramatically in the summer of 2010 as the monsoon rains caused massive floods throughout the basin. Beginning in May, the water level in the basin's rivers started to rise, with the first floods occurring in the Indian state of Jammu and Kashmir along the Jhelum River.[77] Then flooding spread to the Beas, Ravi, and Sutlej rivers in the Indian states of Haryana and Punjab, leading to the destruction of nearly 600 villages and 400,000 acres of rice and wheat, losses estimated at over $200 million.[78]

The floods in Pakistan were even worse. Beginning on the Kabul and Swat rivers, the floods rapidly spread to the rest of the Indus Basin and up to a third of the country by July. The full extent of the devastation is still being calculated, but it appears that thousands of people were killed and 20 million (11 percent of the population) were displaced, while at least three million acres of crops and one million houses were destroyed. Reconstruction costs for houses, roads, bridges and irrigation works are projected to exceed $20 billion.[79]

The United States has been very active in relief efforts throughout Pakistan, providing over $400 million in financial assistance and millions more in in-kind aid like 15 million water purification tablets. The United States used at least nineteen aircraft to rescue more than 30,000 people and deliver nearly 22 million pounds of relief supplies.[80] Moreover, numerous high-ranking U.S. officials visited the area, including Admiral Mike Mullen, chairman of the Joint Chiefs of Staff, who marveled that the damage was far worse than depicted in news coverage.[81] The U.S. relief effort has been motivated by more than altruism. The goal of the United States is to improve its reputation in order to prosecute the war against al-Qaeda. According to Richard C. Holbrooke, then U.S. special envoy for Afghanistan and Pakistan, "If we do the right thing, it will be good not only for the people whose lives we save but for the U.S. image in Pakistan."[82] Moreover, the flood damage was so severe that it threatened to destabilize Pakistan and, as noted above, U.S. strategy in the region has been historically devoted to achieving stability as a prerequisite for the advancement of U.S. strategic interests in South Asia.[83] Thus, the consequences of the floods for U.S. security extended throughout the Indus Basin, not just in Pakistan, which suggests that the United States' ad hoc approach that addresses issues like the 2010 floods as isolated events should be replaced by a policy that addresses the basin as an ecological and political whole.

## A New Indus Waters Treaty?

As seen above, the IWT focuses on the two downstream nations while excluding the two upstream ones, which has had serious consequences for the present: Because the treaty is essentially political rather than ecological in design, it lacks the flexibility to accommodate increased water use by Afghanistan and China or a reduction of the total water volume due to climate change. Indeed, it is certain that demand for water will grow in all four countries while the supply is likely to decline. The governments of the four riparian countries have said little publicly about the need for a new IWT, but there has been a debate during the past twenty years over the IWT's continuing usefulness.

Much of the debate over the IWT has focused on the bilateral relationship between India and Pakistan. Numerous authors see the IWT as solely or at least mostly concerned with maintaining the peace between Pakistan and India over water issues and do not consider either the concerns of Afghanistan and China or the changing ecological conditions within the basin. Neda Zawahri, for example, argues that the IWT created the necessary institutions that have "enabled India and Pakistan to manage peacefully their Indus River system for over 40 years" and shows that wars over water are not inevitable.[84] Salman M. A. Salman and Kishor Uprety agree, describing the IWT as "one of the most shining examples of dispute resolution" and should be a model for other countries with water conflicts.[85]

Other authors agree that though it does have some flaws, the IWT has been successful up to now but that institutions alone are not enough. They argue that both India and Pakistan must cooperate in good faith to make the IWT work in the future. Sinha observes that "riparian relations between India and Pakistan over the Indus . . . are at a crossroads," with a serious decline in both the quantity and quality of water in the basin.[86] He then argues that the two parties should cooperatively evaluate whether the treaty has outlived its usefulness and should be renegotiated or replaced.[87] Pakistan's Indus water commissioner, Jamaat Ali Shah, agrees. He argues that although at present the IWT is adequate, problems like global warming will threaten its future viability. He concludes that India and Pakistan "will now have to look beyond the treaty for solutions," but is vague about what that might mean. He implies that this could simply be cooperation on issues not covered by the IWT or the future negotiation of a replacement treaty.[88]

There are, however, authors who recognize that the IWT has limitations that need to be addressed. B. G. Verghese argues that "the Indus Treaty was good as far as it went as a quick and practical water sharing arrangement. It could, however, be optimized to provide improved drainage, more storage, and certainly more energy through what might be called Indus-II."[89] This new treaty would be a supplement rather than a replacement. John Briscoe argues that the IWT is threatened by rapid population growth in Pakistan, poor water management in Pakistan, and a possible reduction in water supply due to global warming. In something of an overstatement, Briscoe asserts that Pakistan and especially India must choose to cooperate and establish a "new regime on the Indus waters" in order to "head off this looming train wreck."[90] While vague about what this new regime should look like, Briscoe sees it as only involving Pakistan and India, even though he acknowledges that the exclusion of Afghanistan from the IWT is a serious weakness of the treaty.

Numerous authors have noted that the IWT involves only two of the four countries in the Indus Basin, but very few of them have examined how to address this problem. It is clear, however, that the potential for conflict over the waters of the Indus is not limited to only India and Pakistan. As Briscoe notes, the absence of Afghanistan from the IWT is a distinct threat to the continued viability of the treaty and it is time to act upon this insight.

There have been serious border disputes between Afghanistan and Pakistan and India and China as well as between Pakistan and India. Although new border wars between these countries seem highly unlikely, future water shortages will certainly exacerbate competition over water access. The IWT can serve as a model for a new four-country treaty in terms of conflict prevention, but a new treaty must also include consideration of water use sustainability and water quality. If the total water supply declines in the future, the allocation of water will need to be adjusted, given that the various Himalayan glaciers are melting at differing rates. An agreement based on a permanent, fixed allocation of water among the four countries may not be possible. They would then be required to actively cooperate in managing the basin. The present treaty was the result of a decade of negotiation, and it is highly probable that a successor treaty will also require many years of diplomacy. It is in the best interests of all the countries involved, including the United States, to begin work on a successor treaty now, in order to be prepared for future disruption of the Indus Basin water supply. The United States was a strong supporter of negotiations between India and Pakistan over water issues in the 1950s, and its support—especially financial assistance—was critical in getting the original IWT signed. As in the 1950s, the United States today views stability in South Asia as an important factor in its national security, and U.S. support of a new Indus treaty can go a long way toward moving the process forward.

## Notes

1. The Indus River Basin includes the Indus and Sutlej rivers, which originate in Tibet; the Kabul and Kurram rivers, which originate in Afghanistan; the Swat River, which originates in Pakistan; the Jhelum River, which originates in Kashmir; and the Chenab, Ravi, and Beas rivers, which originate in Himachel Pradesh. In terms of water flow, the largest tributary of the Indus is the Chenab, followed by the Jhelum, Kabul, Sutlej, Beas, and Ravi rivers.

2. Shaista Tabassum, *River Water Sharing Problem Between India and Pakistan: Case Study of the Indus Waters Treaty* (Colombo: Regional Centre for Strategic Studies, 2004), 19.

3. See Jane Perlez, David E. Sanger, and Eric Schmitt, "Nuclear Fuel Memos Expose Wary Dance with Pakistan," *New York Times*, November 20, 2010; Anatol Lieven, "How the Afghan Counterinsurgency Threatens Pakistan," *The Nation*, January 3, 2011.

4. See U.S. National Intelligence Council, *India: The Impact of Climate Change to 2030: Geopolitical Implications* (Washington, D.C.: National Intelligence Council, 2009).

5. U.S. National Security Council, "The Position of the United States with Respect to South Asia," January 21, 1951, NSC 98/1, in *Foreign Relations of the United States, 1951* (Washington, D.C.: U.S. Government Printing Office, 1977), vol. 6, pt. 2, 1650–52. See also Dennis Merrill, *Bread and the Ballot: The United States and India's Economic Development, 1947–1963* (Chapel Hill: University of North Carolina Press, 1990), 59.

6. U.S. National Security Council, "Position of the United States," 1651–52.

7. Amit Gupta and Kaia Leather, "Kashmir: Recent Developments and U.S. Concerns," Congressional Research Service, June 21, 2002, 2.

8. K. Alan Kronstadt, "Pakistan–U.S. Relations," Congressional Research Service, February 6, 2009, 1.

9. Uttam Kumar Sinha, "India and Pakistan: Introspecting the Indus Treaty," *Strategic Studies* 32, no. 6 (2008), 961.

10. Michael Kugelman, "Introduction," in *Running on Empty: Pakistan's Water Crisis*, edited by Michael Kugelman and Robert M. Hathaway (Washington, D.C.: Woodrow Wilson International Center for Scholars, 2009), 19.

11. Steven Solomon, "Drowning Today, Parched Tomorrow," *New York Times*, August 15, 2010.

12. See "Besieged Neighbors," *Economic and Political Weekly* 45, no. 34 (2010): 8.

13. Ramaswamy R. Iyer, "Water through Pakistani Eyes," *The Hindu*, August 6, 2010.

14. Sinha, "India and Pakistan," 961.

15. D. R. Archer, N. Forsythe, H. J. Fowler, and S.M. Shah, "Sustainability of Water Resources Management in the Indus Basin under Changing Climatic and Socio-Economic Conditions," *Hydrology and Earth System Sciences* 14 (2010), 1677.

16. Biswajit Mukhopadhyay and Aniruddha Dutta, "A Stream Water Availability Model of Upper Indus Basin Based on a Topologic Model and Global Climatic Data-sets," *Water Resource Management* 24 (2010): 4405.

17. Asif Inam, Peter D. Clift, Liviu Giosan, Ali Rashid Tabrez, Muhammad Tahir, Muhammad Moazam Rabbani, and Muhammad Danish, "The Geographical, Geological and Oceanographic Setting of the Indus River," in *Large Rivers: Geomorphology and Management*, edited by A. Gupta (New York: John Wiley & Sons, 2007), 343.

18. Archer et al., "Sustainability of Water Resources Management," 1673. Simi Kamal, "Pakistan's Water Challenges: Entitlement, Access, Efficiency, and Equity," in *Running on Empty*, edited by Kugelman and Hathaway, 29, suggests that the true figure may be 225 kilometers.

19. Archer et al., "Sustainability of Water Resources Management," 1671; "Pakistan: Water Diplomacy," *Friday Times*, March 13, 2010.

20. Walter W. Immerzeel, Ludovicus H. van Beek, and Marc F. Bierkens, "Climate Change Will Affect the Asian Water Towers," *Science* 328 (2010): 1385.

21. G.R. Lashkaripour and S.A. Hussaini, "Water Resource Management in Kabul River Basin, Eastern Afghanistan," *Environmentalist* 28 (2008): 258.

22. Matthew King and Benjamin Sturtewagon, *Making the Most of Afghanistan's River Basins: Opportunities for Regional Cooperation* (New York: EastWest Institute, 2010), 3.

23. King and Sturtewagon, *Making the Most of Afghanistan's River Basins*, 10; "Lala Ji! Mend Your Ways!" *Nawa-i-Waqt*, December 11, 2010 (supplied by BBC Worldwide Monitoring); "Saeed Accuses India of Releasing Waters in Pak Rivers," Press Trust of India, September 5, 2010.

24. John Briscoe, "Troubled Waters: Can a Bridge Be Built over the Indus?" *Economic and Political Weekly* 45, no. 50 (2010): 30.

25. Meixue Yang, Shaoling Wang, Tandong Yao, Xiaohua Gou, Anxin Lu, and Xue-jung Guo, "Desertification and Its Relationship with Permafrost Degradation in Qing-hai-Xizang (Tibet) Plateau," *Cold Regions Science and Technology* 39 (2005): 47–53; Chun-Lai Zhang, Xue-Yong Zou, Hong Cheng, Shuo Yang, Xing-Hui Pan, Yu-Zhang Liu, and Guang-Rong Dong, "Engineering Measures to Control Windblown Sand in Shiquanhe Town, Tibet," *Journal of Wind Engineering and Industrial Aerodynamics* 95 (2007): 53–70.

26. "India, China Likely to Share Hydrological Info on Sutlej," *Financial Express*, March 19, 2005.

27. P. K. Gautam, "Sino-Indian Water Issues," *Strategic Analysis* 32, no. 6 (2008): 971.

28. Asia Society, Leadership Group on Water Security in Asia, *Asia's Next Challenge: Securing the Region's Water Future* (New York: Asia Society, 2009), 18.

29. Sinha, "India and Pakistan," 963; "Punjab, Sindh Inflexible on CJ Canal Issue," *Dawn*, July 12, 2010.

30. Pakistan–U.S. Strategic Dialogue Water Working Group, "Record of Note/ Proceedings on Pakistan–United States Strategic Dialogue Water Working Group Held on June 17, 2010 at Islamabad (Pakistan)," 5, http://www.wapda.gov.pk/pakus/pak-us percent20strategic percent20energy percent20dialogue.pdf.

31. Majed Akhter, "More on the Sharing of the Indus Waters," *Economic and Political Weekly* 45, no. 17 (2010): 100.

32. Neil Padukone, "Climate Change in India: Forgotten Threats, Forgotten Opportunities," *Economic and Political Weekly* 45, no. 22 (2010): 52.

33. Mukand S. Babel and Shahriar M. Wahid, *Freshwater under Threat: South Asia* (New York: United Nations Environment Program, 2008), 21.

34. During the 1965 war, India launched an attack on Pakistan to the southeast of the city of Lahore. There was fighting along the Bedian Link Canal but the canal itself was not targeted. "Telegram from the Embassy Office in Pakistan to the Department of State," September 6, 1965, in *Foreign Relations of the United States, 1964–1968* (Washington, D.C.: U.S. Government Printing Office, 1969), vol. 25, 360–61.

35. Niranjan D. Gulhati, *Indus Waters Treaty: An Exercise in International Mediation* (Bombay: Allied Publishers, 1973), 587; F. J. Fowler, "Some Problems of Water Distribution between East and West Punjab," *Geographical Review* 40, no. 4 (1950), 587.

36. Ian Talbot, *Pakistan: A Modern History* (New York: St. Martin's Press, 1998), 112.

37. "Inter-Dominion Agreement between the Government of India and the Government of Pakistan, on the Canal Water Dispute between East and West Punjab," May 4, 1948, http://www.internationalwaterlaw.org/regionaldocs/punjab-canal.htm.

38. Gulhati, *Indus Waters Treaty*, 140. See also Aloys Arthur Michel, *The Indus Rivers: A Study of the Effects of Partition* (New Haven, Conn.: Yale University Press, 1967), 11.

39. Asit K. Biswas, "Indus Waters Treaty: The Negotiating Process," *Water International* 17 (1992), 205.

40. Gulhati, *Indus Waters Treaty*, 41. See also Michel, *Indus Rivers*, 84.

41. Robert Dorfman, Roger Revelle, and Harold Thomas, "Waterlogging and Salinity in the Indus Plain: Some Basic Considerations," *Quarterly Journal of the Pakistan Institute of Development Economics* 5, no. 3 (1965), 335.

42. "Pakistan–India Indus Waters Treaty," Karachi, September 1960; "Ratifications Exchanged January 12, 1961," *American Journal of International Law* 55 no. 3 (1961), 802.

43. "Pakistan–India Indus Waters Treaty," 804; Tom Roberts, "The Indus: Life-Blood of Pakistan," *Asian Affairs* 36, no. 1 (2005), 4.

44. Salman M. A. Salman, "The Baglihar Difference and Its Resolution Process: A Triumph for the Indus Waters Treaty?" *Water Policy* 10 (2008), 106.

45. "Pakistan–India Indus Waters Treaty," 807.

46. Asad Sarwar Qureshi, Peter G. McCornick, A. Sarwar, and Bharat R. Sharma, "Challenges and Prospects of Sustainable Groundwater Management in the Indus Basin, Pakistan," *Water Resources Management* 24 (2010): 1558–59; Archer et al., "Sustainability of Water Resources Management," 1670.

47. Michel, *Indus Rivers*, 455.

48. Fowler, "Some Problems of Water Distribution," 586.

49. Gulhati, *Indus Waters Treaty*, 41.

50. "Pakistan–India Indus Waters Treaty," 797–802.

51. White House–Department of Interior Panel on Waterlogging and Salinity in West Pakistan, *Report on Land and Water Development in the Indus Plain* (Washington, D.C.: White House, 1964), 15.

52. Roberts, "Indus," 4.

53. Neda A. Zawahri, "India, Pakistan and Cooperation along the Indus River System," *Water Policy* 11 (2009): 6.

54. Binayak Ray, *Water: The Looming Crisis in India* (Lanham, Md.: Lexington Books, 2008), 74.

55. S. Khan, T. Rana, H. F. Gabriel, and Muhammad K. Ullah, "Hydrogeologic Assessment of Escalating Groundwater Exploitation in the Indus Basin, Pakistan," *Hydrogeology Journal* 16 (2008): 1635.

56. Shams Ul Mulk, "Pakistan's Water Economy, The Indus River System and Its Development Infrastructure, and the Relentless Struggle for Sustainability," in *Running on Empty*, edited by Michael Kugelman and Robert M. Hathaway (Washington, D.C.: Woodrow Wilson International Center for Scholars, 2009), 80.

57. Khan et al., "Hydrogeologic Assessment," 1635; Kenneth Pomeranz, "The Great Himalayan Watershed: Agrarian Crisis, Mega-Dams and the Environment," *New Left Review* 58 (2009): 24.

58. "Pakistan–India Indus Waters Treaty," 803.

59. Roberts, "Indus," 5; Rashid Faruqee, "Role of Economic Policies in Protecting the Environment: The Experience of Pakistan," *The Pakistan Development Review* 35, no. 4 (1996): 491–92.

60. Talbot, *Pakistan*, 44.

61. Jamaluddin Jamali, "Sewage Endangers Aquatic Life in Ravi," *The Nation*, December 8, 2009.

62. Saleem H. Ali, "Water Politics in South Asia: Technocratic Cooperation and Lasting Security in the Indus Basin and Beyond," *Journal of International Affairs* 61, no. 2 (2008): 171–72; Rakesh Ankit, "1948: The Crucial Year in the History of Jammu and Kashmir," *Economic and Political Weekly* 45, no. 11 (2010): 51–55.

63. Dennis Kux, *The United States and Pakistan, 1947–2000* (Washington, D.C., and Baltimore: Woodrow Wilson Center Press and Johns Hopkins University Press, 2001), 90.

64. "Memorandum of Conversation, May 20, 1961," in *Foreign Relations of the United States, 1961–1963* (Washington, D.C.: U.S. Government Printing Office, 1995), vol. 19, 50; "Memorandum of Conversation," in *Foreign Relations of the United States, 1961–1963*, vol. 19, 69; "Telegram from the Embassy in Pakistan to the Department of State, December 13, 1961," in *Foreign Relations of the United States, 1961–1963*, vol. 19, 159.

65. Tabassum, *River Water Sharing Problem*, 36–42; Salamat Ali, "Propaganda Barrage," *Far Eastern Economic Review* 146, no. 51 (1989): 51.

66. Salman, "Baglihar Difference," 114–15.

67. Pavan Nair, "Distressed Neighbors," *Economic and Political Weekly* 45, no. 15 (2010): 76.

68. Briscoe, "Troubled Waters," 28.

69. Anil V. Kulkarni, I. M. Bahuguna, B. Rathore, S. K. Singh, S. S. Randhawa, R. K. Sood, and Sunil Dhar, "Glacial Retreat in Himalaya Using Indian Remote Sensing Satellite Data," *Current Science* 92, no. 1 (2007): 73; H. J. Fowler and D. R. Archer, "Conflicting Signals of Climatic Change in the Upper Indus Basin," *Journal of Climate*

19 (2006): 4291; Tandong Yao, Jianchen Pu, Anxin Lu, Youqing Wang, and Wusheng Yu, "Recent Glacial Retreat and Its Impact on Hydrological Processes on the Tibetan Plateau, China, and Surrounding Regions," *Arctic, Antarctic, and Alpine Research* 39, no. 4 (2007): 642.

70. Julian Hunt, "Deluges after the Deluge," *The Guardian*, August 24, 2010; Alister Doyle, "Pakistan Floods, Russia Heat Fit Climate Trend," Reuters, August 9, 2010; Khaleeq Kiani, "Poorly Built Levees Main Cause of Devastation," *Dawn*, August 23, 2010.

71. This is not the first public controversy to occur in Pakistan over Indian river projects. For a discussion of a "panic" in 1954, see Tabassum, *River Water Sharing Problem*, 20.

72. "Pak Army to Remain 'India Centric' Unless Issues like Kashmir Resolved: Kayani," *Hindustan Times*, February 4, 2010; "MNAs Slam India for Blocking Pakistan's Share of Water," *Daily Times*, February 13, 2010; "POL: Closure of Water by India, Inhuman Act: HRM Leaders," Pakistan Newswire, February 11, 2010; G. Parthasarathy and Naveen Kapoor, "Pakistan Water Cry against India: Charade or Real?" *Hindustan Times*, March 10, 2010; Kuldip Nayar, "Enough Is Enough," *Dawn*, April 16, 2010; "Pakistan: Troubled Waters," *Friday Times*, April 11, 2010; Irfan Husain, "The Great Water Debate," *Dawn*, May 1, 2010; "Water Row," *Dawn*, May 4, 2010.

73. "Distrust Complicates India–Pakistan River Row," *Dawn*, February 24, 2010; Amber Rahim Shamsi, "We Will Have to Look Beyond the Indus Water Treaty," *Dawn*, March 3, 2010; "Violations of Indus Waters Treaty by India Never Go Unnoticed," *Business Recorder*, March 23, 2010.

74. "Pakistan and India Agree to Install Telemetry System," *Dawn*, July 23, 2010.

75. "COM: PWF Gives Presentation to U.S. Consulate Over Use of Water by India as Weapon," Pakistan Newswire, February 5, 2010; "U.S., China and U.K. Briefed about Indian Water Terrorism," *Business Recorder*, Lalit K. Jha, "U.S. Refuses Mediation in Indo-Pak Water Dispute," Press Trust of India, April 2, 2010; "Pakistan Asks U.S. to Help Bridge Gulf With India," *Dawn*, May 26, 2010.

76. Embassy of the United States in Pakistan, Joint U.S.-Pakistan Press Statement: Pakistan–United States Strategic Dialogue Water Working Group," June 17, 2010, http://islamabad.usembassy.gov/pr-10061705.html.

77. "Flood Alert in Kashmir as Rivers Cross Danger Mark," United News of India, May 29, 2010.

78. "Rs 1300cr Flood Loss in Haryana, Punjab," *Times of India*, July 11, 2010; "Flood Waters Recede in Punjab, Haryana: Epidemics Loom," United News of India; "Ignoring Flood Warnings, Punjab, Haryana Engage in Blame-Game," *Times of India*, July 21, 2010.

79. Ahmed Rashid, "Last Chance for Pakistan," *New York Review of Books*, August 16, 2010; "150 Major Irrigation Structures Damaged by Floods," *Dawn*, August 27, 2010; "Asian Development Bank Loans to Help Flood Victims," *Dawn*, September 20, 2010. However, controversy over the damage figures has begun as the governments of Sindh and Punjab provinces have been accused of inflating the numbers in order to receive greater financial compensation. "KP to Challenge Flood Damage Figures of Punjab, Sindh," *Dawn*, September 2, 2010.

80. "Operational Aspects of Ongoing U.S. Military Relief Effort," *Daily Times*, August 15, 2010; "Pakistan Floods: 'When the Children Come Running, It Makes My Heart Drop,'" *The Guardian*, October 1, 2010; "Fact Sheet: U.S. Response to Pakistan's

Flooding Disaster," Embassy of the United States in Pakistan, November 7, 2010, http://islamabad.usembassy.gov/pr-10110701.html.

81. Anwar Iqbal, "Flood Loss Worse Than Depicted: Mullen," *Dawn*, September 4, 2010.

82. Eric Schmitt, "U.S. Offers Aid to Rescue Pakistanis and Reclaim Image," *New York Times*, August 14, 2010.

83. Carlotta Gall, "Floods in Pakistan Carry the Seeds of Upheaval," *New York Times*, September 5, 2010.

84. Zawahri, "India, Pakistan and Cooperation," 17.

85. Salman M. A. Salman and Kishor Uprety, *Conflict and Cooperation on South Asia's International Rivers: A Legal Perspective* (Washington, D.C.: World Bank, 2002), 58.

86. Sinha, "India and Pakistan," 961.

87. Ibid., 962.

88. Amber Rahim Shamsi, "We Will Have to Look beyond the Indus Water Treaty," *Dawn*, March 3, 2010.

89. B. G. Verghese, "Water Conflicts in South Asia," *Studies in Conflict and Terrorism* 20 (1997): 194.

90. Briscoe, "Troubled Waters," 32.

# Chapter 5

# Marine Fisheries in Crisis: Improving Fisheries Management in Southeast Asia

*Robert S. Pomeroy*

The coastal waters of Southeast Asia are among the most productive and biologically diverse in the world. As a consequence, they are critical both for global economic and food security and as a conservation priority. Sixty percent of global fish production takes place in Asia, including 34 percent of the world's exports of fish and employing a staggering 87 percent of all fishery and aquaculture workers. The members of the Association of Southeast Asian Nations (ASEAN)—Indonesia, Malaysia, the Philippines, Singapore, Thailand, Brunei, Vietnam, Laos, Myanmar, and Cambodia—are themselves responsible for one-quarter of global production, 21 million tons of fish products, every year. Southeast Asians rely more heavily on fish as a primary source of dietary protein and income generation than any other people in the world.[1] Furthermore, fish consumption continues to increase across the region, ensuring that the role of fisheries in providing livelihoods, trade, and food security to Southeast Asia will continue to grow.

High rates of population growth and rapidly increasing food needs are putting enormous pressures on the region's coastal and marine resources, as

are uneven levels of economic development, resource use, and technological change. It is now almost universally accepted that most of the nearshore
fisheries in Southeast Asia are overfished and that fishing overcapacity is
one of the leading causes of this overfishing.[2] Consequently, these waters
are now experiencing increased levels of conflict and social unrest, affecting both regional security and environmental sustainability.[3]

Overfishing, overcapacity, and the multiple sources of fishing pressure
in Southeast Asian coastal waters have resulted in the reduction or collapse
of important fishery populations and high levels of conflict over remaining
stocks.[4] This situation has, in turn, created a complex, negative feedback
cycle. Rapid population growth, combined with fewer economic opportunities and access to land, increases the number of coastal people dependent on fishery resources and thus the number of fishers. Increased fishing
pressure results in fish population declines, stock collapses, and increased
resource competition, both between fishers and between different scales
of fishing operation (e.g., small vs. commercial).[5] Such competition is not
always passive in nature, as armed conflict and violence are increasingly
being reported.[6] The result of increasing competition is reduced income
and food security, increased poverty, and a lower overall standard of living
and national welfare.[7] This desperation, then, drives users to employ more
destructive and overefficient fishing technologies in the "rush" to catch
what remains, thereby further depleting fishery populations. These factors
lead to further increased user competition, and thus higher rates and probabilities of human conflict over remaining stocks, restarting this destructive
cycle and leading to a pattern of self-reinforcing "fish wars" with deterio-
rating social and environmental consequences.

Decreasing fish stocks combined with increasing conflict are driving
some people out of fishing. This is leading to increasing unemployment
in many rural areas. This added level of instability contributes to national
levels of social unrest and political instability, thereby acting as a powerful and destabilizing risk factor to regional and global security concerns.
The imperative of immediately reconciling the compounding needs for
improving the ecological sustainability of fisheries consumption while
also improving food security and reducing overcapacity and resource
conflicts has recently begun to be widely acknowledged by the Southeast
Asian community.[8]

If managed more effectively, capture fisheries can provide economic
benefits to the countries of Southeast Asia. Better management can also
avoid the continuing collapse of aquatic and marine ecosystems and the

loss of associated biodiversity occurring throughout the region's oceans and aquatic environments.[9] The importance of fisheries' future contributions to livelihoods, food security, and regional relationships in Southeast Asia cannot be underestimated. Because of the globalized nature of markets, the huge economic stakes, and the weakness of international and regional institutions for cooperation and sustainable fishery management, there is currently limited optimism concerning the fate of the region's marine fisheries resources.[10] Past failure to address the multiple drivers of change facing marine fisheries in Southeast Asia has had significant social consequences, including economic losses for millions of people living in fishing communities, and is severely affecting associated ecosystem resilience and biodiversity. These problems will only worsen if national governments and international donors continue to give low priority to capture fisheries issues. While often politically difficult, there is a growing suite of proven strategies that provide opportunities for the United States to support significant reform that can generate real and tangible social and economic benefits.

## The Importance of Marine Capture Fisheries in Southeast Asia

Several ASEAN member countries are among the world's major producers of marine capture fish (i.e., captured wild fish or shellfish).[11] Indonesia is the third-largest fish producer in the world, followed by Thailand, the Philippines, and Vietnam. (China and India are numbers one and two, respectively.) Indonesia annually produces 4.7 million tons, while Thailand produces 2.8 million tons, and the Philippines produces 2.2 million tons. Myanmar, Malaysia, and Vietnam all produce more than 1 million tons annually.

Approximately 70 percent of the overall capture fishery production comes from waters distributed over 80,000 kilometers of coastline, about 4 million square kilometers of known shelf area, and more than 20 million square kilometers of actual or potential exclusive economic zone. These marine fish resources are concentrated in the South China Sea and the west-central Pacific Ocean.

Trade in fish represents a significant source of foreign currency earnings in Southeast Asia. Regional trade in fisheries products is also growing, in part as a result of the removal of tariffs and quotas. Nontariff barriers—food safety regulations, and quality standards—are becoming major factors affecting regional trade.

In terms of share of gross domestic product, the contributions of fisheries range up to approximately 10 percent in Southeast Asian countries, as they do in Indonesia and Vietnam. However, these figures are frequently underestimated due to poor reporting. The share of fish exports in total agricultural exports was high for Vietnam, at 52 percent. For the rest of the countries in the region, this share was up to 38 percent.

The proportion of people employed in fishery-related jobs in Asia has doubled since the 1970s. There are estimated to be more than 30 million fishers in the ASEAN nations. With average fishing households numbering five individuals, the segment of the population directly dependent on fisheries for food and income can be roughly estimated at 150 million people. Another 60 million people work in associated industries such as boat building, manufacture of fishing gear, bait preparation, marketing, and processing. Women constitute a large proportion of such workers, employed mostly in processing. In the Philippines, fisheries provide employment to roughly 12 percent of the labor force working in agriculture, fisheries, and forestry and to about 5 percent of the country's total labor force.

The importance of fisheries to food security within the region cannot be overestimated. The countries of Southeast Asia—Brunei, Cambodia, Indonesia, Laos, Malaysia, Myanmar, Philippines, Singapore, Thailand, and Vietnam—have a total population of more than 540 million, of whom approximately 35 percent live below the poverty line. Approximately half of the people in the Southeast Asian region get more than 20 percent of their animal protein from fish. This figure rises to more than 50 percent in such countries as Cambodia and Indonesia. The average fish consumption for the region is relatively high at 22 kilograms per capita per year and is higher in coastal communities. In some countries and fishing communities, fish provides the main source of animal protein. In the Philippines, where per capita fish consumption was estimated at 26.8 kilograms per year, fish contributes 12.3 percent of total food intake, 22.4 percent of protein intake, and 56 percent of animal protein intake. In addition, fishing and the extraction of aquatic resources provide the main livelihood for millions of families.[12]

It is estimated that the demand for food fish in 2010, calculated at a constant per capita consumption rate of 22 kilograms a year, would be 18 to 19 million metric tons.[13] Per capita consumption of fish in the Southeast Asian region is expected to increase by an additional 2 percent per year until 2020.

Marine capture fisheries production is not expected to keep pace with demand, creating concerns for food security in Asia. Fish are becoming less available and relatively more expensive than other food items. The increasing demand for fish from the expanding population will create more stress on the already depleted coastal and inshore fishery resources targeted by small-scale fishers. Some researchers estimate that overfishing in South and Southeast Asia has depleted coastal fish stocks by 5 to 30 percent of their unexploited levels.[14] Among the overexploited stocks are coastal demersal (bottom-dwelling) and small pelagic (non–bottom-dwelling) species in the Java Sea and the waters between Indonesia and the Philippines, demersal and small pelagic species and prawns in the Gulf of Thailand, and green mussels and pearl oysters off the coast of Vietnam.

This trend, which disproportionately affects poor people, is likely to continue. Access to or exclusion from fisheries resources may influence the vulnerability of people to both poverty and food insecurity. Production from coastal capture fisheries in the region will decline over the next ten to twenty years unless excess fishing capacity and fishing effort are greatly reduced. Prospects for increasing catches are further dimmed by some fishing methods involving the use of cyanide and explosives, methods that have had a devastating impact on coastal fisheries, fish habitats, and the health and welfare of fishing households. Although male fishers are most often the ones maimed by explosives and disabled as a result of gearless diving, the women of these households are left to shoulder the burden of these men's care and increase their own income-earning activities to replace that previously earned by the men.

## Drivers of Change in Southeast Asian Fisheries

A range of forces is compounding the already complex challenge of overfishing and overcapacity facing Southeast Asian fisheries, and these forces can be broadly categorized as weak governance, socioeconomic conditions, and ecosystem change.[15]

### Weak Governance

Weak governance is one of the main causes of the present poor condition of fisheries. Factors characterizing weak governance in fisheries in the region include (but are not limited to) corruption, lack of stakeholder participation, poor enforcement, weak institutional capacity, overcapacity of fishing fleets, inadequate information, and illegal fishing.

*Corruption.* There is anecdotal information on corrupt practices in the fisheries sector in a number of Southeast Asian countries. Demands for illegal payments for fishing licenses, permits, or access rights by politicians and public servants are probably the most pervasive form of alleged corruption in the fishery sector. Many corrupt situations are common, including politicians and permitting officers having vested interests in fishing companies, demanding bribes from fish market vendors, and allowing illegal fishing practices, such as commercial boats operating in nearshore waters.

*Lack of participation in governance and management.* The centralized administrative fisheries management approach used by Southeast Asian countries involves little effective consultation with resource users. This approach is not well suited to countries with limited financial means and expertise attempting to manage fisheries resources in widely dispersed fishing grounds because the government cannot effectively undertake monitoring, surveillance, or enforcement operations. A fishery cannot be effectively managed without the cooperation of fishers and other stakeholders—including both men and women—to help the laws and regulations function effectively. For example, in the Philippines, Vietnam, and Indonesia, fisher participation in co-management has led to a decrease in fisheries conflicts.[16]

*Poor enforcement.* The inability to enforce regulations that have been centrally promulgated—with little stakeholder involvement—has been the downfall of many fisheries management projects. Small-scale fishers and traders are often among the poorest people in society. Therefore, the political and judicial will to enforce regulations on them is often absent, especially when the action is seen as taking food from the fishers' families. Furthermore, in most Southeast Asian countries, the judicial systems are bogged down with cases that the courts perceive as more important than enforcement of fishery regulations, thus providing limited incentives to stop illegal fishing practices.

*Weak institutional capacity.* In Southeast Asia, institutional weaknesses and constraints are pervasive in the fisheries resource management sector. Legal, policy, and institutional frameworks are not crafted to suit the unique features of fisheries, and this has resulted in mismatches and overlaps. For example, the national fisheries policy of Vietnam contains conflicting statements concerning both conservation of fisheries resources and increasing production from fisheries. A recent study has concluded that overlapping mandates, institutional confusion, and conflict have become the dominant features in the administration of fisheries resources in the region.[17]

*Overcapacity of fishing fleets.* For most Southeast Asian countries, small-scale fisheries are systematically overfished—defined as the action of fishing beyond the level at which fish stocks can replenish themselves through natural reproduction—due to high levels of overcapacity (fishing capacity greater than some optimal or desired level, in terms of catch and corresponding fleet size).

*Inadequate information.* One of the greatest obstacles to decisions and policymaking with regard to fisheries is the lack of reliable data and information about various facets of the sector. Currently available statistics are often highly inaccurate and minimally useful. In Vietnam, for example, the actual number of fishing vessels is still unknown.

*Illegal fishing.* Illegal fishing involves such practices as the use of explosives, chemicals, and small-mesh nets. In many countries in the region, illegal fishing by large-scale vessels, including those from other countries operating without licenses, is widespread. Such boats often come into conflict with small-scale fishers by encroaching on inshore waters, increasing competition for resources, and leaving such areas depleted and habitats degraded. For example, in the Philippines small trawlers are often falsely registered with municipalities as 2.99 gross tons, in order to be classified as a municipal fishing gear (under 3 gross tons). Illegal practices by small-scale fishers themselves are difficult to regulate, particularly in view of their scattered nature and the generally poor monitoring, control, and surveillance systems in most Southeast Asian countries.

### Socioeconomic Conditions

A number of socioeconomic factors—including poverty, globalization of trade and market access, technological advances, population growth, health, marginalization, and gender inequity—both constrain improved fisheries management and are root causes of some overfishing problems in the region.

*Poverty.* Poverty among many fishing communities and households often leads to or reinforces unsustainable fishing practices. Pulling fishing households out of poverty is, in itself, constrained by few livelihood options and by high population growth rates in shoreline and coastal communities. Many rural communities have a low priority in national economic development planning and thus have been left behind as economic development has progressed in other parts of the country. Consequently, rural fishing communities generally have a higher percentage of people living below the poverty line than the national average.[18] Other factors contributing to the poverty of these rural fishing villages include limited access to land, unsustainable land use practices and development, competition and conflicts over resources, health burdens, and civil strife. These rural, highly resource-dependent fishing communities become even more vulnerable as resource conditions change and decline.

*Globalization of trade and market access.* The globalization of trade creates both opportunities and risks for the fishers of Southeast Asia. In some cases, it puts the decision-making beyond the fisher and those involved in other fishing activities. For example, in Indonesia, the high demand for live reef food fish such as grouper encourages fishers to utilize illegal fishing methods such as cyanide. The market both provides and restricts livelihood opportunities for small-scale fishers and traders. The constraints to market access for fishers in the region include weak bargaining power, poor marketing strategies, monopolies among wholesalers, poor product-holding infrastructure, difficulties meeting quality standards, and a lack of market information. For example, fishers' dependency on intermediaries for access to credit, such as under the *suki* system in the Philippines, forces fishers to engage in unsustainable fishing practices such as catching undersized fish.

*Technological advances.* Technological changes such as the introduction of motorization, monofilament nets, cell phones, and global positioning systems have enabled fishers to exploit inshore as well as offshore fisheries more intensively than was ever imagined a few decades ago. In the Philippines, cell phones are used by fishers to inform each other about patrol boats and obtain real-time fish price information in order to target higher-value species. These technology advances have led to increased conflict between large and small fishers, as larger boats using more advanced technology can overfish nearshore waters.

*Population growth.* In common with other poor rural populations, a fisher's socioeconomic status is usually conducive to high fertility. The population of the ten ASEAN member countries is expected to reach 650 million by the year 2020. Rapid population growth, including both intrinsic population growth and immigration to coastal areas, contributes to the increasing overexploitation of natural resources and degradation of the local environment.

*Poor health infrastructure and vulnerability to HIV/AIDS.* Due to their physical and socioeconomic isolation, many fishing communities often lack adequate sanitation, clean water, and health care. The rates of HIV infection in fishing communities in Southeast Asia can be five to ten times higher than those in the general population. In Thailand, 20 percent of workers employed on fishing boats are HIV-positive, while the general rate in the population is 1.5 percent. Premature death robs fishing communities of the knowledge gained by experience and reduces incentives for longer-term and intergenerational stewardship of resources.

*Political and economic marginalization.* Small-scale fisheries have been systematically ignored and marginalized over the years. In most cases, this was not deliberate but the result of an accumulation of policies and development decisions to "modernize" fisheries. Many rural coastal communities have been left behind as economic development has progressed in other parts of the country, furthering economic marginalization. In part, the problem is related to the low priority of rural fishing communities in national economic development planning. For example, in Vietnam, poverty reduction in coastal communities was not a clear goal for the government until late 2003, when the Comprehensive Poverty Reduction and Growth Strategy elaborated the general objectives, institutional arrangements, policies, and solutions of a ten-year strategy and five-year plan into detailed, specific action plans.

*Gender inequality.* There is significant gender differentiation in the ways men and women utilize and perceive fisheries resources. Failure to fully understand gender roles, inequalities, and perspectives have confounded many well-intended fisheries development and conservation initiatives. For example, Bugis and Christian women in the same and neighboring communities in coastal North Sulawesi Province (Indonesia) appear to differ significantly in their level and type of engagement in fishing. In general, gender issues related to fisheries include gender division of labor and income, gendered access to decision making (representation and advocacy), gender-based rights to natural and other resources, and gender-based access to markets, market information, and trade.

Women are, as a result, denied access to institutional and state support, as well as capacity-building interventions. They cannot avail themselves of development resources and programs. There is little regulation of labor conditions in fish processing work, even though such labor tends to be poorly compensated and exploitative. Finally, fisherwomen tend to be excluded from decision-making processes and governance at family, community, and state levels. This lack of recognition for women's contributions in the sector also diminishes the ability of women fishworkers to organize, access and control livelihood resources, and negotiate with various actors in the sector.

## Ecosystem Change

Unsustainable fishing practices result in direct changes to the structure and composition of aquatic and marine ecosystems, changes that make them less resilient and less able to produce food for millions of people in Southeast Asia. However, there are also a number of indirect human activities that affect the biodiversity and productivity of fisheries ecosystems. These include pollution from land-based sources, as well as habitat degradation and destruction. From a longer-term perspective, anthropogenic climate change is expected to have significant effects as well, with several Southeast Asian nations, such as Vietnam and Indonesia, likely to face particularly heavy effects.

*Habitat loss, degradation, and pollution.* Coastal ecosystems (coral reefs, mangroves, sea grass, wetlands), upon which many fish species depend for at least part of their life cycle, are degraded and increasingly threatened by human activities ranging from coastal development and destructive fishing practices to overexploitation of resources, marine pollution, runoff from inland deforestation and farming, mining, and oil exploration. In Southeast Asia, it is estimated that 64 percent of the region's coral reefs are threatened by overfishing and 56 percent are threatened by destructive fishing techniques.[19]

*Climate change.* One likely result of climate change is worsening conditions for marine fish stocks resulting from lower rainfall, increased sea surface temperatures, acidification, and sea level rise. A climate change vulnerability assessment of the capture fisheries of 132 countries identified two in Southeast Asia, Cambodia, and Vietnam, as the most vulnerable.[20] Small-scale fishers, who lack mobility and alternatives and are often the most dependent on specific fisheries, will suffer disproportionately from such changes.

## Overfishing and Overcapacity

Of all the forces negatively affecting the fisheries in Southeast Asia, the most pervasive may be overcapacity. As stated in the introduction, it is now almost universally accepted that most of the nearshore fisheries in Southeast Asia are overfished. It is also accepted that overcapacity is one of the leading causes of this overfishing. Although the problem of overcapacity is well recognized and relatively easy to analyze, it remains one of the most intractable problems in fisheries management.

The term "overcapacity" conveys the fact that fishing capacity is greater than some optimal or desired level, in terms of catch and corresponding fleet size. Overcapacity is a long-term concept, in that there are excessive levels of capacity over the longer term in relation to some target level of yield or capital (boats, gear, fishers) used in the fishery. In simple terms, overcapacity refers to the fact that there are "too many fishers chasing too few fish" in the long term. The objective of capacity management is to identify the desired level of capacity and bring existing capacity in line with this target level.[21]

Overcapacity in a fishery tends to develop as a result of some market imperfection, such as the absence of clear property rights, and leads to several problems, including:[22]

- overinvestment in fishing boats and gear,
- too many fishers (captains and crew),
- reduced profit and decline in quality of life of fishers and their families,
- increasing conflict in the fishery, and
- political strife in the management process.[23]

Overfishing has also reduced the contribution of coastal fisheries to employment, export revenue, food security, and rural social stability.[24] Unless remedial action is taken, resource declines, increasing poverty, and impaired contribution to national development are expected to worsen as coastal populations increase.

The problem of reducing overcapacity in small-scale fisheries in developing countries is much more complex than that of reducing overcapacity in industrial fleets. Because the capital and labor employed in small-scale fisheries are generally not easily mobilized for other economic uses, their exit is often difficult and painfully slow. Many small-scale fishers exist at the subsistence level and have a short-run survival strategy of taking care of themselves and their family that day.[25] Such fishers, due to limited mobility and lack of alternative employment, utilize whatever resources are available (technology, skill, capital) to harvest as much fish as possible before others do so. The fisher living at the subsistence level has a high discount rate concerning use of the resource; that is, profits and food are preferred today rather than a continual flow into perpetuity. Under such conditions, as long as small-scale fishers can obtain a positive return, they will continue fishing and try to circumvent any command and control regulatory measures, such as gear limitations, closure of fishing areas, and other means.

Issues of overcapacity and unsustainable resource use cannot be isolated from poverty, unemployment, and declining quality of life in fishing communities, because overfishing most directly affects highly resource-dependent populations such as fishing households. The main brunt of such economic and social distress is borne by women, children, and unskilled fishers, as well as by unskilled people who are directly and indirectly dependent on fishing. Silvestre and colleagues state that

> the results of overfishing in South and Southeast Asia are that coastal fish stocks have been severely depleted. Resources have been fished down to 5–30 percent of their unexploited levels. Such declines have increased poverty among coastal fishers who are already among the poorest of the poor in developing Asian countries. Overfishing has also reduced the contribution of coastal fisheries to employment, export revenue, food security, and rural social stability in these nations. The trends (resource decline, increasing poverty and impaired contribution to national development) are expected to worsen as coastal populations increase, unless remedial action is undertaken.[26]

Other articles have echoed these concerns. Stobutzki, Silvestre, and Garces state that "there is an urgent need to reduce fishing capacity in the region";[27] and Sugiyama, Staples, and Funge-Smith predict that, "based on current trends, production from capture fisheries in the Asia-Pacific region will decline over the next 10–20 years unless overcapacity and fishing effort are greatly reduced."[28]

The excess capacity of Indonesia in the Java Sea is estimated at between 86 and 207 percent, whereas that of the Philippines is between 120 to 130 percent. More specifically, in the Philippines, the total number of vessels in the municipal fishery sector was estimated at 20,000 units in the whole country in 1948, of which 83 percent were nonmotorized. This grew to an estimated 500,000 units during the next forty years with a higher percentage of motorized boats.[29] The total number and tonnage of commercial fishing boats rose from 3,265 and 150,260 tons, respectively, in 1988, to 4,014 and 216,090 tons (increases of 23 percent and 44 percent, respectively) in 1994.[30] Catch per unit effort (measured in tons per horsepower), for the total small pelagic fish catch from municipal (small-scale) fisheries in the Philippines, has declined from 2.9 in 1948 to an estimated 0.2 in 2000.[31]

The Lingayen Gulf, a major fishing ground in northern Luzon, Philippines, reached its maximum sustainable yield more than twenty years ago.[32] It is estimated that the fishery now has four times the needed fishing effort for the available fish stocks. Catch rates in Lingayen Gulf are five times smaller that they were in 1990. In 1983, Pomeroy estimated that there were 767 full-time fishers using twenty-five different fishing gear types in the ten coastal *barangays* (villages) of the Municipality of Matalom, Leyte, in the central Visayas region of the Philippines.[33] Subsequent visits in 1993 and 2001 found an increase in the number of full-time fishers to 923 and 1087, respectively. Daily fish catch for line fishers had declined from 2.1 kilograms in 1983 to 0.5 kilogram in 1993; for fish trap fishers, from 13.5 to 5.4 kilograms; and for gillnet fishers, from 23.7 to 8.3 kilograms.[34] Research conducted by the WorldFish Center on coastal fish stocks in the Philippines found that, overall, "the level of fishing in the grossly modified stock is 30 percent higher than it should be (i.e., fish are being harvested at a level 30 percent more than they are capable of producing)."[35] The same general pattern of overfishing and overcapacity likely holds true for other small-scale fisheries in Southeast Asia.

An expert on the management of fishing capacity in the Southeast Asian region concluded that the "improvement of fishery management could not be done without addressing the issue of management of fishing capacity." In addition, it was noted that "no aggregated data exist on fishing capacity at national/regional level, however, the information is available in more site-specific and projects related forms," and though "national policy and plans exist for management of fishing capacity, . . . in most countries there is not any proper management system in place."[36]

*The Role of Southeast Asian Governments in Addressing Overcapacity*

Morgan, Staples, and Funge-Smith, in a review of fishing capacity management in Asia, state that "there is an increase in awareness of, and actions to address, fishing capacity issues by member countries." Despite this, however, *actual* fishing capacity in the largest fisheries of the region continued to increase within the period 2002–5, particularly in small-scale fisheries. Over the same time period, there was also a parallel reduction in catches from the vast majority of these fisheries, which together account for more than 80 percent of total catches in the region. They further state:

While there has been an increase in the use of capacity reduction programmes in small-scale fisheries in countries of the region within the past few years, this has not occurred to the same extent in industrial fisheries. This parallels the increase in activity related to measurement of fishing capacity in small-scale fisheries, but not industrial fisheries.[37]

Morgan and colleagues report that national plans of action on fishing capacity in the region are now more common and that some progress has been reported in attempting to assess fishing capacity in major fisheries, particularly small-scale fisheries. In addition, the number of specific capacity reduction programs undertaken in the region has been increasing, again with the emphasis on small-scale fisheries. However, the effectiveness, on a regional scale, of these initiatives is not yet apparent because fishing capacity in both industrial-scale and small-scale fisheries has continued to rise.[38] Clearly, the impact of capacity reduction programs undertaken to date has been small when considered in a regional context, and countries themselves have reported that these programs have rarely achieved their original objectives. A lack of policy and operational tools in the region was identified by many countries, with only 50 percent of the major fisheries having management plans. Methods for measuring fishing capacity—such as vessel licensing systems, census data, and fishery statistical systems—are often being poorly developed, and monitoring, control, and surveillance capabilities (i.e., the ability to implement a fisheries plan or strategy) are generally inadequate.

Although many of the fishing capacity issues of the region are demonstrably national issues and lie within the jurisdiction and responsibility of individual states, there is a clear need for a regionally coordinated approach. There is a dearth of effective international and regional institutions for cooperation in sustainable fishery management, especially in capacity reduction programs. Regional fisheries institutions—such as the Food and Agriculture Organization of the United Nations (FAO), the Southeast Asian Fisheries Development Center, the Asia-Pacific Economic Cooperation forum, and the Asia-Pacific Fishery Commission—have held several meetings to discuss the issue of fishing capacity. However, none of these organizations has provided clear leadership to address the issue, with the sole exception of FAO's national plans of action on fishing capacity under the Code of Conduct for Responsible Fisheries, which sets out principles and international standards of behavior for fishing practices.[39]

Many countries in Southeast Asia have not effectively addressed the management of fishing capacity. Management plans for specific fisheries that could provide the policy guidance for capacity management are still not in place for all fisheries, although this is improving. A recent study of capacity management measures in Cambodia, the Philippines, and Thailand found that some management measures are acceptable to the fishers, while others are not.[40] Overall, measures concerning effort reduction are not acceptable. Although most measures involving gear, area, and temporal restrictions are acceptable, there is certain ambivalence toward closed seasons, which are sometimes imposed during the breeding period of harvested species in the belief that this will achieve greater reproductive output. Measures that seek to provide alternative and supplemental livelihoods were well accepted in all three countries.

Management measures tend to be used in isolation. In Southeast Asia, boat/gear restrictions and space/time restrictions are the most common measures used to reduce overcapacity in small-scale fisheries. Social support programs to get fishers to leave fishing are also used in many countries. While there may be an increase in regional awareness of overcapacity, there is no quantitative confirmation that capacity-reduction measures in small-scale fisheries have brought about any substantive improvements in either the fisheries resource or the lives of people. Morgan and colleagues report, however, that these programs are "being implemented without parallel programs to achieve real fishing capacity reduction" and that "capacity reduction programs in the region to date have not been successful in limiting or reducing fishing capacity."[41]

## Finding a Solution:
## An Integrated Approach to Reducing Overcapacity

Fisheries managers in Southeast Asia have become increasingly aware of the need to develop appropriate policies to facilitate the exit of capital and labor from overexploited fisheries. Due to the complexities inherent in small-scale fisheries, countries are unlikely to prepare effective plans to address overcapacity in this subsector without support to analyze the problem and generate new policy options. As mentioned above, actions taken to date by resource managers, such as command and control regulation and vessel and gear buyback, have not been effective. Unless the core issues of overcapacity are addressed—by implementing access control, defined property or user rights, and facilitating the exit of labor and capital from the fishery—any regulatory measures or other management strategy, such as establishing marine protected areas, will simply be a stopgap measure, because more people will continue to enter the fishery.

There is no simple solution to the overcapacity problem facing small-scale fisheries in Southeast Asia. Any single approach for reducing overcapacity, when used in isolation, is rendered ineffective by the complexities of small-scale fisheries (such as those described as "drivers of change" above). The only effective solution will be one based on a coordinated and integrated approach involving resource management (fishing rights and access control measures in combination with conventional fisheries management measures), resource restoration and conservation (marine protected areas and restoration of marine habitats such as coral reefs, mangroves, sea grass, and wetlands), livelihood, economic, and community development (providing supplemental and alternative livelihoods alongside public services and infrastructure), and restructured governance arrangements (co-management).[42] The reduction of overcapacity implies an increased focus on human solutions involving participation, livelihoods, rights, and communities rather than on purely technological solutions. The foundation of such an approach should be a plan that has been developed and agreed upon through a participatory process, and which identifies goals and objectives, management and development strategies and actions, and the roles and responsibilities of all partners. This plan should be structured around the key components of resource management, capability development, community and economic development, livelihood development, resource restoration and conservation, and institutional development.

This approach recognizes that solutions involve targeting not just the individual fisher but the whole household and its broader economic livelihood strategies. To be effective, solutions must address not only resource and technical issues of overcapacity but the underlying non–resource-related issues of poverty, vulnerability, and marginalization in coastal households and communities. The strategy needs to address multiple challenges, including food security, employment, income generation, livelihoods, health, improved quality of life, social development, community services, and infrastructure. This approach finds solutions to the problem of overcapacity in both the fishery sector and nonfishery economic sectors. This calls for a broader vision of the fisheries system as a whole, going beyond fisheries sector–specific policies to the vast array of seemingly unrelated policies that may have beneficial side effects for the fisheries sector. The broader policy context is justified by the understanding and development of linkages between fisheries resource management, social and community development, coastal community economies, and regional and national economies. The departments or agencies responsible for fisheries cannot undertake this approach alone. There will be a need to reach out and coordinate with other government ministries or departments with expertise in economic and social development, for example, and across different levels of government from national to local.

It may take a long period of time to reduce overcapacity in small-scale fisheries, because the mobility of labor and capital is limited. The timing and sequencing of interventions and actions are critical. For example, rather than trying to remove fishers all at once, it may make more sense to phase in reduction in order to reduce social and economic disruption. Supplemental and alternative livelihoods need to be in place before access-control measures are implemented. Gear restrictions, for example, should still allow fishers to have a livelihood while reducing overall fishing effort.

## Implications for the United States: A Strategic Opportunity— Improved Fisheries Management in Southeast Asia

Overfishing and overcapacity in Southeast Asian waters have direct implications for U.S. trade and security interests. The United States is dependent on Southeast Asian fisheries for imported edible and nonedible fishery products. In 2009, more than 30 percent of United States imports of these products came from Southeast Asian countries.[43] Sustainable fisheries management in Southeast Asia will result in a continued source of fishery products for U.S. markets and employment for thousands of people in the U.S. seafood marketing industry.

Southeast Asian waters are now experiencing increased levels of conflict and social unrest. This decrease in security in coastal fishing communities and waters has several implications for U.S. interests in the region. Since the exclusive economic zones were established in the 1970s, disputes over fishing rights and resources have become more frequent and more violent. Foreign boats or migrant fishermen from neighboring regions are frequently expelled by force. Vessels are boarded and crew members imprisoned. Occasionally, violence occurs and people are killed. In the Philippines and Thailand, competition over fishing rights and resources between small and large fishers regularly leads to violence, and even fatalities. International disputes have also arisen between Vietnam and Cambodia and between the Philippines and China over access to territorial waters. On a global scale, the total number of reported piracy attacks reached 276 in 2005, with the majority of attacks occurring in the waters of Indonesia, Malacca Straits, Bangladesh, and India. Many of the pirates are believed to be from rural fishing communities. In addition, illegal smuggling of many products in the region, including people, is carried out by fishers.

For the Southeast Asian region, sustainable fisheries management will result in economic growth that provides jobs and food and preserves cultural values over the long term. Sustainable fisheries management will reduce humanitarian crises, provide for increased security, and provide opportunities for those nations emerging from conflict and poverty.

The United States can play an important and essential role in helping build and sustain more democratic, well-governed marine fisheries management systems that responsively address critical needs of thousands of fishing communities in Southeast Asia in an environmentally sustainable manner. The Coastal Resources Center has recommended that the U.S. government, through agencies such as the U.S. Agency for International Development, make a strong organizational commitment to attack several critical issues for fisheries management at this time. In particular, it should focus its attention on (1) strengthening governance, and (2) reducing excess fishing capacity, with the main goal to achieve economically and politically secure fishing communities by building and strengthening sustainable fisheries resources management systems.[44] This strategy seems well suited to the overall goal of the U.S. framework for foreign assistance.[45]

The United States is already strategically positioned to promote more sustainable fisheries management in Southeast Asia. The U.S. government has supported improved fisheries and coastal resources management in Southeast Asia through bilateral programs from the U.S. Agency for International Development in Indonesia and the Philippines since the 1980s. An example of current U.S. support for fisheries in the region is the U.S. Coral Triangle Initiative. The Coral Triangle is an area encompassing almost 4 million square miles of ocean and coastal waters in Southeast Asia and the Pacific surrounding Indonesia, Malaysia, Papua New Guinea, the Philippines, Timor-Leste, and the Solomon Islands. The Coral Triangle countries are also home to some 363 million people and encompasses economic zones in which each country has exclusive rights to marine resources. Recognized as the global center of marine biological diversity, the region serves as the spawning and juvenile growth areas for five species of tuna, comprising the largest tuna fisheries in the world. The biological resources of the Coral Triangle directly sustain the lives of more than 120 million people living within this area, and benefit millions more worldwide.

Recognizing the potential of the Coral Triangle Initiative to be a truly transformative regional initiative with far-reaching environmental and economic benefits, the United States, working with the six Coral Triangle countries, has offered considerable financial, political, and technical support through both bilateral and multilateral channels. The U.S. Coral Triangle Initiative's Support Program is guided by an overall vision: improved management of biologically and economically important coastal and marine resources and its associated ecosystems that support the livelihoods of peoples and economies in the Coral Triangle.

Improved marine fisheries management in Southeast Asia will have direct implications for U.S. trade and security interests and will result in economic growth that provides jobs and food in Southeast Asia. Failure to address the issues surrounding marine fisheries has already resulted in significant social and economic consequences for millions of people living in fishing communities and for marine and coastal ecosystem resilience and biodiversity in Southeast Asia. These problems will only worsen if national governments and international donors continue to give low priority to capture fisheries issues. The United States cannot expect to address all of these issues alone, but partnering with national governments, nongovernmental organizations, other donors, and the private sector to address these challenges in a strategic, multifaceted, and coordinated manner can help build and sustain more democratic, well-governed marine fisheries management systems that responsively address the critical needs of thousands of fishing communities in an environmentally sustainable manner.

## Notes

1. International Center for Living Aquatic Resources Management (ICLARM), *Aquatic Resources in Developing Countries: Data and Evaluation by Region and Resource System*, ICLARM Working Document 4 (Manila: ICLARM, 1999); Food and Agriculture Organization of the United Nations (FAO), edited by *The State of World Fisheries and Aquaculture* (Rome: FAO, 2001).

2. S. Garcia and I. De Leiva Moreno, "Trends in World Fisheries and Their Resources," in *The State of the World Fisheries and Aquaculture* (Rome: FAO, 2000); L. Burke, E. Selig, and M. Spalding, *Reefs at Risk in Southeast Asia* (Washington, D.C.: World Resources Institute, 2002).

3. M. Williams, *The Transition in the Contribution of Living Aquatic Resources to Food Security* (Washington, D.C.: International Food Policy Research Institute, 1996).

4. D. Pauly, "On Malthusian Overfishing," *NAGA: ICLARM Quarterly* 13, no. 1 (1990): 3–4.

5. I. Stobutzki, G. Silvestre, and L. Garces, "Key Issues in Coastal Fisheries in South and Southeast Asia, Outcomes of a Regional Initiative," *Fisheries Research* 78 (2006): 109–18.

6. R. Pomeroy, J. Parks, R. Pollnac, T. Campson, E. Genio, C. Marlessy, E. Holle, M. Pido, A. Nissapa, S. Boromthanarat, and Nguyen Thu Hue, "Fish Wars: Conflict and Collaboration in Fisheries Management in Southeast Asia," *Marine Policy* 31, no. 6 (2007): 645–56.

7. S. Sugiyama, D. Staples, and S. J. Funge-Smith, *Status and Potential of Fisheries and Aquaculture in Asia and the Pacific*, RAP Publication 2004/25 (Bangkok: FAO Regional Office for Asia and the Pacific, 2004); Asian Development Bank (ADB), *ADB Fisheries Policy*, Operations Evaluation Department (Manila: ADB, 2006).

8. G. Morgan, D. Staples, and S. Funge-Smith, *Fishing Capacity Management and IUU Fishing in Asia*, RAP Publication 2007/16, Asia-Pacific Fishery Organization (Bangkok: FAO Regional Office for Asia and the Pacific, 2007).

9. F. Berkes, R. Mahon, P. McConney, R. Pollnac, and R. Pomeroy, *Managing Small-Scale Fisheries: Alternative Directions and Methods* (Ottawa: International Development Research Center, 2001).

10. S. Garcia and C. Newton, "Current Situation, Trends and Prospects in World Capture Fisheries," in *Global Trends: Fisheries Management*, American Fisheries Society Symposium 20, edited by E. K. Pikitch, D. D. Huppert, and M. P. Sissenwine (Bethesda, Md.: American Fisheries Society, 1997), 3–27.

11. Sugiyama, Staples, and Funge-Smith, *Status and Potential*.

12. ADB, *ADB Fisheries Policy*.

13. C. Delgado, N. Wada, M. Rosegrant, S. Meijer, and M. Ahmed, *Fish to 2020: Supply and Demand in Changing Global Markets* (Washington, D.C., and Penang: International Food Policy Research Institute and WorldFish Center, 2003).

14. Stobutzki, Silvestre, and Garces, "Key Issues."

15. Coastal Resources Center at the University of Rhode Island and Florida International University, *Fisheries Opportunities Assessment* (Kingston and Miami: Coastal Resources Center at the University of Rhode Island and Florida International University, 2006); ADB, *ADB Fisheries Policy*.

16. Pomeroy et al., "Fish Wars."

17. M. Torell and A. M. Salamanca, *Institutional Issues and Perspectives in the Management of Fisheries and Coastal Resources in Southeast Asia* (Penang: ICLARM, 2002).

18. E. Whittingham, J. Campbell, and P. Townsley, *Poverty and Reefs* (Paris: UNESCO, 2003).

19. Burke, Selig, and Spalding, *Reefs at Risk*.

20. E. Allison, A.L. Perry, M.-C. Badjeck, W. Neil Adger, K. Brown, D. Conway, A. S. Halls, G. M. Pilling, J. D. Reynolds, N. L. Andrew, and N. K. Dulvy, "Vulnerability of National Economies to the Impacts of Climate Change on Fisheries," *Fish and Fisheries* 10 (2009): 173–96.

21. J. M. Ward, J. E. Kirkley, R. Metzner, and S. Pascoe, *Measuring and Assessing Capacity in Fisheries: Basic Concepts and Management Options*, FAO Fisheries Technical Paper 433/1 (Rome: FAO, 2004).

22. D. Gréboval and G. Munro, "Overcapitalization and Excess Capacity in World Fisheries: Underlying Economics and Methods of Control," in *Managing Fishing Capacity: Selected Papers on Underlying Concepts and Issues*, FAO Fisheries Technical Paper 386, edited by D. Gréboval (Rome: FAO, 1999), 1–48.

23. R. Metzner and J. M. Ward, *Report of the Expert Consultation on Catalysing the Transition Away from Overcapacity in Marine Capture Fisheries, Rome, 15–18 October, 2002*, FAO Fisheries Report 691 (Rome: FAO, 2002).

24. Ward et al., *Measuring and Assessing Capacity.*

25. R. S. Pomeroy, "Small-Scale Fisheries Management and Development: Towards a Community-Based Approach," *Marine Policy* 15 (1991): 39–48.

26. G. Silvestre, L. Garces, I. Stobutzki, C. Luna, M. Ahmed, R. A. Valmonte-Santos, L. Lachica-Alino, Munro, V. Christensen, and D. Pauly, eds., *Assessment, Management, and Future Directions for Coastal Fisheries in Asian Countries*, WorldFish Center Conference Proceedings 67 (Penang: WorldFish Center, 2003).

27. Stobutzki, Silvestre, and Garces, "Key Issues."

28. Sugiyama, Staples, and Funge-Smith, *Status and Potential.*

29. Dalzell and Corpuz, "The Present Status of Small Pelagic Fisheries in the Philippines," in *Philippine Tuna and Small Pelagic Fisheries: Status and Prospects for Development*, Book Series 07 (Laguna: Philippine Council for Aquatic and Marine Research and Development, 1990), 25–51.

30. C. Courtney, J. A. Atchuee, M. Carreon, A. T. White, R. Pestano-Smith, E. Deguit, R. Sievert, and R. Navarro, "Coastal Resource Management for Food Security," Coastal Resources Management Project, Cebu, Philippines, 1998, http://oneocean.org/download/db_files/food_security.pdf.

31. S. J. Green, A. T. White, J. O. Flores, M. Carreon, and A. E. Sia, "Philippine Fisheries in Crisis: A Framework for Management," Coastal Resource Management Project, Cebu, Philippines, 2003, http://oneocean.org/download/db_files/philippine_fisheries_in_crisis.pdf.

32. Ibid.

33. R. S. Pomeroy, "Monitoring and Evaluation of Fishery and Agriculture Projects: A Case Study and Discussion of Issues," in *Monitoring and Evaluating the Impacts of Small-Scale Fishery Projects*, edited by R. B. Pollnac (Kingston: International Center for Marine Resource Development at the University of Rhode Island, 1989), 41–55.

34. Pomeroy, personal observation.

35. WorldFish Center, *Strategies and Options for Increasing and Sustaining Fisheries and Aquaculture Production to Benefit Poorer Households in Asia*, Project Completion Report ADB-RETA 5945 (Penang: WorldFish Center, 2002).

36. Southeast Asian Fisheries Development Center, *Regional Technical Consultation on Management of Fishing Capacity and Human Resource Development in Support of Fisheries Management in Southeast Asia, 19–22 September 2006, Phuket, Thailand* (Bangkok: Southeast Asian Fisheries Development Center, 2006).

37. G. Morgan, D. Staples, and S. Funge-Smith, *Fishing Capacity Management and IUU Fishing in Asia*, RAP Publication 2007/16, Asia-Pacific Fishery Organization (Bangkok: FAO Regional Office for Asia and the Pacific, 2007).

38. Ibid.

39. FAO, "Progress on the Implementation of the International Plan of Action for the Management of Fishing Capacity: Technical Consultation to Review Progress and Promote the Full Implementation of the IPOA to Prevent, Deter and Eliminate IUU Fishing

and the IPOA for the Management of Fishing Capacity, Rome, June 24–29, 2004"; D. Gréboval, *The FAO International Plan of Action for the Management of Fishing Capacity* (Rome: FAO, 2000).

40. N. Salayo, L. Garces, M. Pido, K. Viswanathan, R. Pomeroy, M. Ahmed, I. Siason, K. Seng, and A. Masae, "Managing Excess Capacity in Small-Scale Fisheries: Perspectives from Stakeholders in Three Southeast Asian Countries," *Marine Policy* 32 (2008): 692–700.

41. Morgan, Staples, and Funge-Smith, *Fishing Capacity Management*.

42. R. S. Pomeroy and R. Rivera-Guieb, *Fishery Co-Management: A Practical Handbook* (Wallingford, U.K.: International Development Centre and CABI Publishing, 2006).

43. National Marine Fisheries Service, *Fisheries of the United States 2009, Current Fishery Statistics 2009* (Silver Spring, Md.: National Oceanic and Atmospheric Administration, 2010).

44. Coastal Resources Center at the University of Rhode Island and Florida International University, *Fisheries Opportunities Assessment*.

45. U.S. Agency for International Development, *Policy Framework for Bilateral Foreign Aid*, Report PD-ACG-244 (Washington, D.C.: U.S. Agency for International Development, 2006).

# Chapter 6

# The 2009 H1N1 Flu Pandemic and the Policy Response in East Asia

*Yanzhong Huang*

The 2009 flu pandemic, commonly referred to as "swine flu," was caused by a strain of H1N1 influenza virus that had never been encountered before 2009. The first observation of this new strain was recorded in April 2009 in Mexico. After early outbreaks in North America, the virus quickly spread to all regions of the world. The World Health Organization (WHO) raised its alert level to Phase 5 within one week of the first report, suggesting an "imminent" threat of a pandemic. Although the WHO had pronounced the virus a full-blown pandemic on June 11, it had in fact reached the criteria to be categorized at this highest alert level by May 8. The pandemic reached its peak in North America by November 2009, but a steep decline in the number of the cases did not occur worldwide until May 2010. On August 10, 2010, the WHO declared an end to the pandemic.[1] By then, most countries had confirmed infections from the virus, which led to more than 18,000 laboratory-confirmed deaths worldwide.[2]

Although the virus has run its course for now, health experts and policymakers alike have begun pondering the effectiveness of existing anti-H1N1 strategies. Given the divergent regional response toward the H1N1 virus, an assessment of government response measures in East Asia may shed some critical light on the preparation for the next infectious disease outbreak. This chapter will first give an overview of the region's response to the 2009 H1N1 pandemic. Next, it will provide an assessment of the pandemic prevention and control efforts in the region, followed by an analysis of the rationale behind East Asia's heavy reliance on the containment approach. It concludes with an examination of the policy implications for U.S. global health security.

## An Overview of East Asia's Pandemic Response

As the H1N1 influenza virus spread rapidly to all parts of the globe, countries sought to combat the virus by intensifying their efforts to safeguard public health and minimize any potential impact on society and economy.[3] Countries employed a diverse range of policy responses in attempts to manage initial cases and prevent further transmission of the virus.[4] The WHO's Global Influenza Preparedness Plan, released in April 2009, prescribes different policy responses based on the phases of pandemic alert.[5] In Phase 4, sustained human-to-human transmission, an important goal is "to contain the new virus within a limited area or delay its spread to gain time to implement interventions, including the use of vaccines."[6] This can be achieved by active case finding and confirmation, extensive contact tracing, treatment of all infections, and/or quarantine of contacts.[7] In contrast, beyond Phase 4, when the human-to-human transmission causes community-level outbreaks, containment measures are no longer recommended. Instead, the WHO advises member states to implement a mitigation strategy, aiming to slow down the spread of the virus in the community and minimize the societal and economic impact of the pandemic. This involves rapidly identifying cases, treating those who are severely ill or patients with a higher risk of complications (e.g., pregnant women, people with certain chronic conditions), and limiting the use of prophylaxis to protect those with a higher risk of contracting severe diseases.[8]

However, in 2009, given the rapid transmission of the virus, the feasibility of a containment strategy was called into question. Further, when the WHO declared Phase 4 on April 27, the organization made it clear that the outbreak had surpassed the criteria for containment, suggesting the need for mitigation.[9] Countries in North America adhered to WHO advice, taking the approach of mitigation from the start of the outbreak. This approach involves managing H1N1 cases and outbreaks with methods similar to those utilized for the regulation of seasonal influenza. In Europe, despite initial attempts at containment—the foremost example being the United Kingdom—most countries quickly focused their energy and resources on preparing to treat increasing number of cases and preparing for mass vaccination.[10]

Compared with countries in Europe and North America, many East Asian countries implemented strict containment measures to halt the spread of the virus. By the end of April 2009, governments across the region had stepped up checks at airports and seaports in a bid to ward off the new flu threat. Almost all countries in the region instituted thermal scanners to screen people with high temperatures. China, Japan, and Taiwan took this screening a step further by conducting onboard inspections on flights coming from North America. Despite the WHO statement that pork products handled in a hygienic way were not a source of the H1N1 virus and would be safe to consume, China, South Korea, Thailand, the Philippines, and Indonesia all instituted a ban on fresh pork and/or pork products.[11] Indeed, Indonesia did not officially lift its ban until March 2010. Countries in the region also implemented strict quarantine inspection measures. On May 2, 2009, right after East Asia's first known case was identified in Hong Kong, the territorial government ordered a full quarantine on all the three hundred guests and staff members of the hotel where the patient stayed, the first imposition of an involuntary quarantine to contain the virus.[12] Similar, albeit less drastic, quarantine measures were implemented by most countries in the region.[13] On May 5, Brunei quarantined about two hundred British military personnel who arrived on a chartered flight from London after three of the passengers were found to have fevers, despite subsequent tests showing that none of them had the H1N1 virus.[14]

Among these countries, China's response was the most aggressive. For example, on May 1, 2009, the Chinese government immediately halted all direct flights from Mexico to Shanghai after it was discovered in Hong Kong that a Mexican passenger who had transited through Shanghai had H1N1. Additionally, the Chinese authorities sought to quarantine all passengers who were on the flight, resulting in a nationwide manhunt. On May 22, in an effort to identify and treat every H1N1 patient, China began tests on every inbound international flight. Masked health inspectors, draped from head to toe in biohazard suits, boarded planes and checked each passenger for fever with a thermal forehead scanner. Through the end of May, an entire flight could be quarantined and all passengers could be placed under medical observation if just one passenger on board had a temperature above 37.5 degrees Celsius; suspect cases were taken to government-designated hotels or hospitals via negative-pressure ambulances. Even after clearing customs, if it was discovered that someone had close contact with a suspect case, that person could still be tracked down and held in a government-designated facility. One day after his arrival in Shanghai in early June, New Orleans mayor Ray Nagin was held in quarantine simply because a passenger in the row ahead of him exhibited flu-like symptoms.[15]

Despite the prominence of containment policies in East Asia, responses were still heterogeneous across the region. By the end of May 2009, some countries began to scale down their response measures after obtaining more information about the H1N1 virus. On May 15, the Singaporean Ministry of Health no longer required passengers returning from Mexico to be subject to enforced self-quarantine.[16] One week later, Japan began to ease measures aimed at controlling the spread of swine flu, including phasing out onboard quarantine inspections.[17] By the end of June, even Hong Kong, known for its stringent containment policy, ceased the practice of tracking down people who had close contact with confirmed cases and instead placed priority on treating severe cases.[18] Paradoxically, during this same period, China stepped up its efforts to contain H1N1, throwing tens of thousands of people into government quarantine facilities and tracking down suspected cases in an almost Orwellian approach to public health. Guangzhou's local Center for Disease Control (CDC) managed to locate the taxi taken by a suspect case through the use of the Global Positioning System, accessing the person's public transportation record, and mobilizing local residents to come forward with information that led to his "capture." The climate of fear and pressure was so intense that the father of China's second confirmed H1N1 case made a public apology for his son's illness on local television.

## Assessing East Asia's Virus-Containment Efforts

On the surface, the region's virus-containment efforts were quite a success. By July 6, 2009, fewer than 10,000 confirmed cases, or only 10 percent of the world total, were found in East Asia (Southeast Asia and Northeast Asia combined), even though nearly one-third of the world's population lives in the region.[19] Furthermore, many Southeast Asian countries instituted containment measures with the hope to "contain the disease for as long as possible."[20] By decreasing the effective reproduction number (*R*), this aggressive approach delayed the inevitable acceleration of the pandemic until autumn. For example, it took Vietnam nearly two months to experience community-level outbreaks after its first H1N1 case was detected on May 31.[21] This could potentially buy more time for preparation and for vaccines to be developed and licensed. The epidemiologic data in China appear to support the role of government intervention in slowing down transmission. A sharp increase of the cases occurred only after September 2009, when China abandoned the containment-based strategy and became the first country in the world to mass-produce H1N1 vaccine.[22]

Even so, these containment measures were less successful in preventing the sustained spread of the virus in the communities. Sustained community transmission began to be observed in Japan as early as mid-May 2009.[23] China fared better, with community-level outbreaks occurring in Guangdong Province on June 19.[24] Similar outbreaks were identified in Singapore in late June.[25] The Singapore case is illuminating because, with a small geographical area and a highly trained and efficient health-care service, the country was in a much better position than its neighbors to trace contact and enforce quarantine. Only a relatively isolated society could potentially stem the spread of such a highly contagious disease, but even in Singapore containment was not ultimately successful at preventing outbreaks.

China took additional measures, employing other containment techniques such as entry point and border screening measures. However, according to the WHO, border screening measures can be an effective monitoring technique, but they are not an effective way of identifying cases or preventing transmission. A 2010 study by Huang and Smith found that about 1 per 100,000 visitors checked from late April to mid-July in China were confirmed to have H1N1 flu.[26] If the total number of confirmed cases by July 15, 2009, is taken into account, fewer than one-third of the cases were identified through the stringent border screening measures.[27] Other countries that undertook border screening measures faced similar problems. According to a study conducted by researchers at the University of Tokyo, the number of people infected with the virus who passed undetected through airport temperature screening during April and May 2009 was about fourteen times the number of infected who were stopped at the airports.[28] According to a medical scientist at the National Taiwan University Hospital, 30 percent of the patients who carried H1N1 were asymptomatic, while another 15 percent came down with mild signs that did not include fever.[29] As such, a large proportion of infected people were not picked up by temperature screening at borders. Worse, border screening may have generated a false sense of security, with infected people assuming that they were well because of their lack of symptoms.[30]

By the same token, there is no indication that rounding up apparently healthy individuals and confining them to government-designated hotels worked as an effective method of disease control. China only identified twenty-three cases by June 18, 2009, through involuntary quarantine. Including the H1N1 cases discovered through border screening, over 60 percent of the identified cases came from self-reporting.[31] Home quarantine measures, too, turned out not as effective as expected. In Malaysia, the director-general of health admitted that, among the more than a thousand people placed under home quarantine, none of them had developed flu symptoms.[32]

In a statement issued on May 1, 2009, the WHO made it clear that both scientific research and historical records indicated that restricting travel would have limited or no benefit in stopping the spread of disease.[33] According-ing to a study published by *Tropical Medicine and International Health* in November 2009, while China's anti–severe acute respiratory syndrome (SARS) measures (e.g., quarantine and social distancing) might have played a role in speeding up the disappearance of SARS or preventing the outbreak in yet unaffected regions, they "contributed little to the factual containment of the SARS epidemic."[34] In late May 2009, health ministers from thirteen East Asian countries (the members of the Association of Southeast Asian Nations, plus China, Japan, and South Korea) had a meeting in Malaysia, where they agreed to comply with recommendations of the WHO on international travel in order to prevent social and economic disruption.[35] Still, many countries in East Asia looked to a centuries-old approach to "contain" the rapid spread of H1N1. In that sense, Asia's response to the 2009 H1N1 flu pandemic is also a testimony to the international community's inability to harness a disease that is symptomatic of globalization.

Although the aggressive government response measures were not that effective, the cost of implementing such measures was immensely high. Singapore was said to have used up half of its stockpile of face masks in the first three weeks of the pandemic.[36] In China, it was estimated that by early July, at least tens of millions of yuan had already been spent just on enforc-ing quarantine measures, not including other expenses.[37] Fear-mongering and self-serving protectionism hurt the country's domestic pork industry, discouraged tourism and international trade, and even spoiled China's relations with other countries such as Mexico and Canada.[38] By July 2009, even though the country had only been engaged in combat with H1N1 for eight weeks, signs of fatigue and resource depletion had already set in. According to a senior health official, the free treatment and strict quarantine policy had put a strain on the government's economic and human resources. As Laurie Garrett of the Council on Foreign Relations noted, it was worth considering just how much *more* fatigue, financial pain, and organizational energy would be expended were this virus to transform into a far more lethal, yet still highly contagious, form.[39]

The main issues surrounding the debate on the efficacy of mitigation versus containment (delaying) concerned the opportunity costs of aggressive case finding, contact tracing, and management. As Nicoll and Coulombier have noted, the question was whether there was enough manpower to deliver the necessary response seven days a week and what could not be achieved once the limited resources were fully committed to case finding, contact tracing, testing, and treating.[40] For example, there were only eighty quarantine officials at Japan's Narita Airport to conduct quarantine inspections of thirty-five flights each day. Due to the shortage of quarantine officers, the inspections sometimes took nearly two hours to complete.[41] As the officials were preoccupied with keeping up with quarantining passengers and flights on a day-to-day basis, they were unable to provide speedy update of the lists of passengers subject to follow-up checks by local governments.[42] In China, CDCs at each level were forced to remain on call twenty-four hours a day, every day. In contrast to regular day-to-day activities, CDC officials saw their workloads double as a result of the pandemic, with new responsibilities such as inspecting quarantined people and conducting epidemiologic studies. The government agency charged with facilitating quarantine and border screening—the General Administration of Quality Supervision, Inspection, and Quarantine—did not have enough staff members to conduct temperature checking, and as a consequence, the government was forced to bring in military personnel to assist. At the same time, because the H1N1 prevention and containment strategy sucked up most of China's public health resources, other public health concerns were neglected. For example, between March and May 2009, China witnessed 400,000 cases and 155 deaths from hand, foot, and mouth disease.[43] The Indonesian Ministry of Health also noted that the H1N1 pandemic distracted health workers from dealing with dengue fever in Southeast Asia.[44] In Malaysia, H1N1 led to 13,000 confirmed cases and 81 fatalities over the course of 2009, while dengue fever caused about 14,000 cases and 47 fatalities in less than four months (between January 1 and April 10) in 2010.[45]

There is no denying that the aggressive government responses might have contributed to the delayed spread of the virus in the spring and summer of 2009. Nevertheless, it is worthwhile to pursue a delaying strategy only if a vaccine is produced and distributed in sufficient quantities to meet the needs of a meaningful percentage of a country's population. By February 2010, no Asian country was able to achieve that objective. The highest vaccination rate was found in Taiwan, where—thanks to a series of aggressive vaccination campaigns—24 percent of the population was immunized by late January.[46] Mainland China was the first to mass-produce the vaccine, but by February 19, 2010, it had only manufactured and distributed 122 million doses, barely enough to cover 10 percent of the population. For the poor countries in the region that did not have vaccine development capabilities or could not afford to order vaccines from overseas manufacturers, access to the vaccine had to be made possible through the WHO-coordinated donation, which turned out to be too little, too late. Limited availability—lasting until the autumn/winter viral wave had nearly peaked—contributed to low vaccine coverage in the region. As table 6.1 shows, none of the five recipient countries in East Asia (Laos, Mongolia, Myanmar, Cambodia, and North Korea) had a coverage rate higher than 15 percent, and Myanmar and North Korea had only 2 percent of their population covered by the vaccine. Indeed, the WHO was still planning vaccine deliveries to some of these countries days before it officially declared the end of the pandemic.

Countries that adopted a mitigation-oriented strategy relatively early in the outbreak were able to minimize problems related to vaccine access, as a large proportion of the population was exposed to a mild form of the virus in the spring, and as such, had a natural immunity. However, countries that engaged in a sustained containment strategy had a different experience. As a result of the limited vaccination coverage, these countries did not have "firewall" protection, and H1N1 was able to easily spread across the population. Worse, the extended employment of a containment strategy may have also, prior to the fall, unintentionally resulted in shielding a large percentage of people from the relatively "benign" virus. This compromised "herd immunity," because the limited vaccination failed to provide a measure of protection for the majority of the population who have not developed immunity.[47] This problem was recognized by a senior Chinese health official, who invoked a nationwide serum survey to suggest that an absolute majority of the population was susceptible to H1N1.[48] An epidemiologic survey conducted in the spring of 2010 also demonstrated that no more than one-quarter of the population in China was immune to the virus. The

*Table 6.1. The World Health Organization's Delivery of Vaccines
to East Asian Countries, 2010*

| Country | Completed Vaccine Deliveries, January 1–August 1 | | | Planned Vaccine Deliveries, August 2–31 (No. of doses) |
| | No. of doses | Arrival | Coverage (%) | |
| --- | --- | --- | --- | --- |
| Laos | 600,600 | February 25 | 9.7 | 400,000 |
| Mongolia | 270,000 | March 29 | 9.3 | 300,000 |
| Myanmar | 972,000 | April 4 | 2.0 | |
| Cambodia | 1,800,000 | May 3 | 12.4 | 212,900 |
| North Korea | 476,500 | May 26 | 2.0 | 1,899,000 |

*Source:* World Health Organization, "Pandemic (H1N1) 2009 Vaccine Deployment Update–02 August 2010."

belated spread of the virus in the spring/summer therefore could have been responsible for the dramatic increase in the documented cases in the fall.[49]

In addition, countries moving away from the containment approach had to wrestle with a major communication problem: how to convince the public that the policy shift was absolutely necessary. It was argued that once decisionmakers adopt delaying or containment as a formal policy rather than an operational practice, "it can be especially difficult to change policy in a timely manner."[50] The initial containment strategy, when implemented in the H1N1 outbreak, presumed the spread of a highly dangerous virus. Yet, the H1N1 virus has proven to be a relatively "benign" one. The virulence of H1N1, measured by case fatality rate (CFR), was lower than that of the routine seasonal influenza, and well below that of the dreaded 1918 pandemic virus or SARS. Its transmissibility was higher than that of seasonal influenza, but not a terrifying level of contagion compared with the 2002 SARS outbreak. Most patients recovered without needing medical treatment, which led a health expert to call the 2009 pandemic "the mildest pandemic on record."[51] The containment strategy hence mobilized tremendous resources to address a disease even after its mildness was already well known (i.e., treating everyone who was infected or suspected to be infected). When that strategy failed to work or was no longer sustainable, it had to give way to a mitigation strategy under which antivirals or vaccines were only offered to those in high-risk groups. Explaining this to the public was not easy. Not surprisingly, among countries (regions) in East Asia, only the Philippines, Malaysia, Hong Kong, Singapore, and Japan officially announced the shift toward a mitigation strategy. Countries such as China that did not have a very clear exit strategy approached the shift to mitigation strategy without any communication or explanation of the policy change to their public. The government consequently sent mixed signals to the public. On the one hand, seemingly in attempt to quell public fear, the government told the people that H1N1 virus was "preventable, controllable and treatable."[52] On the other hand, the government invoked the memory of SARS as a justification for its extreme response measures, such as when a Ministry of Health spokesman announced that a "large-scale breakout would be fatal for China."[53] Difficulties surrounding the effectiveness of risk communication, as well as the quick-moving nature of H1N1, encouraged panic that further complicated surge response capabilities in China. In Chongqing municipality, the hospital system was overwhelmed in October 2009 when parents rushed to hospitals seeking care for their children who exhibited flu symptoms. For a time, the city's Children's Hospital received a record high of over 5,300 patients each day.[54] In that sense, the aggressive approach also undermined a country's ability to handle the second-wave attack in autumn 2009. The argument here is consistent with the findings of an international conference held in Singapore in March 2010. A consensus among the participants—including public health experts and WHO officials—was that most of the nonmedical response measures implemented in the 2009 H1N1 outbreak were ineffective, if not excessive.[55]

## Explaining East Asia's Policy Response

Why did countries in this region pursue a costly but largely ineffective strategy in handling a very mild pandemic? Panic certainly played a role. Fear is humankind's natural response to an unknown novel disease agent. Indeed, "we respond to the likelihood of death in the event the disease is contracted, rather than the compound probability of contracting the disease and succumbing to its effects."[56] During the pandemic, the public fear and anxiety over the flu were whipped up by various media reports as well as by the predictions that millions were going to die when the virus mutated. In South Korea, for example, a media report quoted medical experts that the H1N1 virus appeared to have a fatality rate "exceeding 5 percent"—twice the total fatality rate of the 1918 Spanish flu.[57] Politicians are not exempt from panic, either. Very often, the political and economic stakes are so high that policymakers choose to err on the side of caution. Indeed, what was seen during the 2009 pandemic was not media panic but "official panic, inconsistent information and rapid policy changes that seem inspired by political demands, not medical need."[58] As the Hong Kong secretary of health suggested, even though the current risk for the disease was not too high, "we must be alert and prepare for the worst."[59]

East Asia was not the only region where governments made misguided attempts to quell popular fears. The Egyptian government ordered that pigs be slaughtered, even though the country did not have a single case of H1N1, Ukraine quarantined several provinces and shut down parliament, and Slovakia closed most of its border crossings with Ukraine.[60] Like China, Argentina, Cuba, Ecuador, and Peru suspended flights to Mexico, leading Mexican president Felipe Calderón to lash out at countries he said were "acting out of ignorance and disinformation" and taking "repressive, discriminatory measures."[61] Again, decisionmakers sometimes can be so overwhelmed by the consequences of being wrong that they may not be able to tell the difference between consequences and likelihood, leading them to overreact in preparing for disease outbreaks.

However, compared with countries in other regions, many East Asian countries did implement a more aggressive, drastic, and sometimes draconian approach to the H1N1 pandemic, as evidenced by the more frequent and prolonged use of quarantine measures. As early as June 12, 2009, the WHO representative for China recommended that the priority be on diagnosis and treatment of patients instead of containing the disease.[62] However, it was not until early July that the Ministry of Health relaxed some of the quarantine and treatment measures.[63] Stringent border screening and temperature checks remained in place until the end of that month. Indeed, it was only in September 2009 that the country formally abandoned the containment-centered strategy in favor of a more measured, mitigation-based approach. Similarly, Malaysia began its switch from containment to mitigation in August 2009, but was still quarantining students with H1N1 symptoms until mid-April 2010.[64] East Asia's stringent reaction to the flu pandemic reflected the painful lessons regional governments drew from the SARS epidemic in 2003 and the deadly H5N1 outbreak in 2005. Public policy literature suggests that previous policy experience can play a crucial role in policy learning. In studying the Swedish and British welfare states, Heclo suggests that a technique, once adopted, tends to be readopted, to be considered the "natural" policy response for seemingly similar policy challenges.[65] In other words, decisionmakers facing uncertain problems tend to lean heavily on preexisting policy frameworks, adjusting only at the margins to accommodate distinctive features of new situations. It is thus no surprise that many Southeast Asian countries built their pandemic preparedness plans on how to rapidly contain the highly pathogenic avian influenza virus (i.e., H5N1) arising in their backyard. As observed by a Japanese virologist, most of the flu plans of Southeast Asian countries focused on "how to cull chickens."[66] They were not fully prepared for a virus that emerged from overseas and was different from H5N1 in terms of severity and contagiousness.[67] In the same vein, on May 1, 2009, China's Ministry of Health presented an official framework on H1N1 prevention and control that plainly targeted a SARS-like virus.

Many East Asian countries' heavy reliance on containment-based strategies was also due to the lack of core surveillance and response capabilities (e.g., planning, communications, routine influenza surveillance, epidemiologic and laboratory capabilities, resources for containment) to address health threats. As Fidler has noted, while both state and nonstate actors shape responses to transnational health threats, building and maintaining public health infrastructure still remain predominantly a national government function.[68] Even though the 2005 International Health Regulations require "states parties" to develop minimum core surveillance and response capacities, many countries in the region failed to build and sustain public health capabilities locally and nationally. In certain respects, the increasingly demanding international health rules and norms regarding pandemic response merely serve to highlight and exacerbate the capacity gap in East Asia. By June 2009, for example, Thailand had only 5 percent of the population covered by government antiviral stockpiles, while South Korea had 11 percent, both of which were lower than the United States (25 percent) and United Kingdom (50 percent) and below the recommended stockpile (covering 20 percent of the population).[69] Most other Asian countries had only 1 percent of their population covered.[70] Lack of access to pandemic vaccines was another major concern in this region, where most countries do not have advanced biotech capabilities. Indonesian officials admitted that it would take the country two years to develop a vaccine that Western pharmaceutical firms could develop in four to six months.[71] The arrival of an unexpected virus from overseas and the inadequacy of medical surge-capacity building (in terms of hospital beds, emergency rooms, intensive care units, health care workers, and other medical facilities) led many nations in the region to turn to nonmedical response measures, such as travel and trade restrictions, with the hope of containing the spread of the virus. In China, because forceful measures, such as enforced quarantines and travel restrictions, were widely credited with helping stop the spread of SARS, such measures became thought of as silver bullets for defeating all infectious diseases.

Of course, there are no silver bullets for combating a novel virus. But even if the sustained, excessive government response was not scientifically justified, it made perfect political sense. Each health threat intertwines with political, economic, social, and diplomatic factors to shape how it emerges and spreads. In taking these kinds of "social determinants of health" into account, public health solutions must address nonhealth issues, such as politics. In a *New York Times* op-ed piece published after the suspension of the U.S. swine flu program in 1976, Harry Schwartz questioned the ability of government officials to "put biological reality before political expediency."[72] The danger is that when health is placed in the realm of realpolitik, it runs the risk of "being dependent on the logic of such politics"—which is "not based on science and not subject to public deliberation and peer review, but on the Machiavellian instincts of those in power."[73] Because the H1N1 virus emerged in tandem with the global financial crisis, a major disease outbreak would give politicians an opportunity to defuse public discontent with their (mis)handling of the economic crisis.[74] Rather than getting the blame for failure in managing the economy, they would be credited for launching a high-profile battle against the virus. Measures such as the ban on pork imports are clearly nonsensical methods of disease control, because the H1N1 virus is not transmitted through pigs or pork products. Policymakers were aware of that, but as a South Korean health official admitted, the measures were in place primarily to settle public anxiety toward the virus.[75] In the Philippines, political pressure from hog farmers led the government to impose a ban on pork products from North America.[76]

Compared with their East Asian counterparts, Chinese leaders had even stronger political incentives to pursue an excessive approach not informed by epidemiology. In 2009, Chinese officials worked to reverse the negative image they generated after their initial mismanagement of the 2003 SARS crisis, by seeking to create the impression that they were acting differently with H1N1, and that they truly cared about people's health and well-being. Indeed, strong government action against H1N1 seemed to garner support for regime legitimacy, on the eve of the twentieth anniversary of Tiananmen Square and through the months leading up to sixtieth anniversary of the People's Republic. According to a survey conducted by *China Youth Daily*, 85 percent of respondents approved of the draconian government measures.[77] Further, a leading and independently minded economics magazine, *Caijing*, indicated that preserving social and economic stability was of primary concern to government officials, whereas the cost borne by public health personnel, H1N1 patients, and others affected by the virus was considered secondary.[78] The unique political factors explained why China implemented sustained and extreme intervention measures in containing the spread of H1N1. Interestingly, there was little public criticism of the government's containment strategy in most Asian countries. Few epidemiologists, politicians, or civil society leaders voiced their opposition to the stringent government actions.[79] On the contrary, there was strong popular support of the government's response. Some Chinese Netizens even criticized the U.S. approach for not doing enough in containing the spread of the virus.[80]

## Pandemics and Security: Implications for the United States

Infectious disease outbreaks today are increasingly seen as a threat to national and international security.[81] However, the securitization of infectious disease is not a new phenomenon. Historically, quarantinist ideologies mandated harsh laws that frequently inflamed tensions between state and society.[82] For example, when the bubonic plague engulfed Europe in the fourteenth and fifteenth centuries, rulers in Milan and Mantua did not hesitate to implement draconian disease prevention and control measures, including inspecting travelers, quarantining ships, and instituting the *lazaretto* (quarantine hospitals) to treat contagious patients. Indeed, the word "quarantine" is derived from the Italian *quarantina*, meaning "about forty," the number of days in isolation imposed by the City of Venice. In those days, military forces were employed to enforce disease control measures, and those who sought to slip through the military *cordon sanitaire*, the quarantine line, were routinely executed.[83] Later, the French Revolution affirmed that the state had a responsibility to preserve the health of the citizens and therefore ought to legislate and impose changes when necessary. But as attention and commitment were increasingly redirected toward the goal of enhancing the welfare of population, older forms of sovereign and disciplinary power were giving way to new mechanisms of rule in managing infectious diseases.[84] As a result, not only was health no longer treated as an individual responsibility, but public health campaigns and sanitary institutions were increasingly focusing on domestic reforms. Interestingly, the security aspect of health was forgotten in this endeavor to promote *population* health and welfare.

It was not until after the end of the Cold War that health was "rediscovered" as a "nontraditional" security challenge. More recently, Japan has invested substantially in health-related human security issues. In reviewing the anti-H1N1 measures, Japan's health, labor, and welfare minister reportedly said that "how we fight infectious diseases is a matter of national security."[85] In the aftermath of the SARS debacle, Chinese president Hu Jintao also made it clear that "health security is part of national security."[86] In a June 2009 speech, he juxtaposed energy security, food security, and public health security as three major nontraditional security challenges.[87] In the United States, since the 2001 anthrax attacks, an unanticipated microbial catastrophe has increasingly displaced nuclear winter as a defining security anxiety. In addition to its negative impact on economic prosperity and sociopolitical stability,[88] a major disease outbreak could generate dynamics that directly threaten U.S. national security. As a scholar at the U.S. Naval War College has pointed out, the U.S. military cannot afford to be immobilized by pandemic influenza in light of its substantial global responsibilities, but the extensive deployment of U.S. forces and the sheer scope of U.S. military operations also increased the likelihood for a pandemic influenza to compromise the operational capabilities of U.S. forces by infecting troops, civilians, and dependents.[89]

Unlike the health-security nexus of earlier times, countries today recognize that an infectious disease outbreak is more than a *national* security threat. Globalization enables diseases to travel swiftly and far. Indeed, virtually any city in the United States today can be reached by commercial flight within thirty-six hours, less than the incubation period for most infectious diseases. In 2005, against the background of the looming avian flu pandemic, two members of the U.S. Senate Foreign Relations Committee, Barack Obama and Richard Lugar, coauthored an opinion piece that began: "An outbreak could cause millions of deaths, destabilize Southeast Asia . . . and threaten the security of governments around the world."[90] This is echoed in the 2010 U.S. National Security Strategy Report: "An epidemic that begins in a single community can quickly evolve into a multinational health crisis that causes millions to suffer, as well as spark major disruptions to travel and trade."[91] For this reason, traditional, state-centered approaches may not be fully effective in addressing transborder public health threats such as pandemics. The U.S. National Security Strategy under both the

Bush and Obama administrations has clearly emphasized the importance of international cooperation in addressing the threat of contagious disease. In that sense, the lack of core surveillance and response capabilities in under-resourced developing countries—which are at special risk during influenza pandemics—poses a threat to U.S. national security, but it also presents an opportunity for the United States to burnish its international image through strengthening core public health surveillance and intervention capabilities in those countries. In its 2009 report submitted to President Obama, the President's Council of Advisors on Science and Technology recommended that the U.S. government take action to "produce, purchase, or redirect vaccines, antiviral drugs, antibiotics, and medical material to developing countries in need of such support."[92]

To be fair, the United States has taken some important steps to support global pandemic preparedness in areas of information sharing and capacity building.[93] In June 2009, the U.S. Centers for Disease Control and Prevention provided seed samples of the virus to China and other countries so that they could start developing the vaccine immediately. In September, a United States–led group of twelve industrial nations pledged to make 10 percent of their stocks of H1N1 vaccine available to the WHO for distribution to about 100 developing countries. Kathleen Sebelius, the secretary of health and human services, then indicated that the donation would be triggered after 40 million doses were procured by the United States.[94]

However, a closer look at its response toward the pandemic suggests that while the United States recognizes that solutions to global health problems necessitate strategies of cooperation over disease prevention and control, its actions on global health problems are still justified from the lens of national interests. Even though underlying health conditions make populations in the developing world particularly vulnerable, the United States and other Western governments donated little funding for international capacity building. By August 2009, the lion's share of the H1N1 vaccine had been reserved by industrial countries, where most global vaccine production was located. According to the WHO, about 1 billion doses of H1N1 vaccine were ordered worldwide, and one-quarter of the order went to the United States. Moreover, in view of the delay in the vaccine production and strong domestic pressures, the United States modified its plan on donating vaccines to the WHO and emphasized instead the need to meet domestic vaccine demands as the first priority. At the end of October, Secretary Sebelius implied that the United States would not donate the vaccine to poor countries until 150 million at-risk Americans had been inoculated against the virus.[95] As a result, the first WHO shipments of vaccine did not arrive in the developing world until early January 2010, and they were donated by drug manufacturers, not Western governments. By April 2010, when the pandemic had almost run its course, less than half of the 229 million ordered doses of vaccine had been administered in the United States, which means that an estimated 71.5 million doses would soon expire and have to be discarded.[96] By contrast, only twenty-six of ninety-four poor countries in need of the vaccine had received it by then.[97]

The existence of this "vaccine apartheid" sent a chilling message to the developing world. Countries in Southeast Asia had already entertained deep-seated grudges against industrialized countries over the discrepancy between obligatory information sharing and voluntary benefit sharing. Prior to the H1N1 outbreak, Indonesian health minister Siti Fadilah Supari (who coined the term "viral sovereignty") had refused to share H5N1 samples with the WHO, arguing that big pharmaceutical companies in industrialized nations would develop vaccines using the samples the country provided free of charge, yet market the vaccine with prices too high for sufficient distribution in Indonesia. The continuous failure of the United States and other industrialized nations to adequately address concerns of such countries during the H1N1 outbreak will only encourage widespread noncompliance with the WHO's International Health Regulations and undermine past efforts to protect public health globally.[98]

## Conclusion

As the first officially designated pandemic in the twenty-first century, the 2009 H1N1 influenza presented a litmus test of humankind's ability to handle major disease outbreaks in the era of globalization. Paradoxically, while pandemics are firmly part of the globalized era, state responses to the spread of H1N1 are not.[99] In contrast to the responses of countries in Europe and North America, many East Asian countries adopted a containment-centered approach in combating the H1N1 virus. They did so against the WHO's advice, and for some countries, even after the mildness of the virus was already well known. As this study demonstrates, the containment measures were very costly to implement and sustain and were only of limited benefit in stopping the spread of the virus. While panic and previous policy experiences were certainly to blame, the lack of core response capacity and domestic political dynamics intertwined to make a scientifically uninformed, costly, and ineffective approach more appealing to decisionmakers in the region. The East Asian countries' response to H1N1 thus lends further support to the argument that as health is transformed from a humanitarian, technical, "low politics" issue to one that features prominently on the security agenda, states' responses to public health are increasingly subordinate to political deliberations and interventions. The growing politicization of public health problems can lead a country to pursue a political agenda that does not address the needs or concerns of others—as evidenced in the China-Mexico diplomatic row—and that eventually undercuts trust and goodwill among states.

But East Asian countries are not the only ones that failed the globalization test. Despite the presence of a global threat and the recognition of urgency for international collaboration and cooperation to cope with the pandemic, the United States did not demonstrate a strong commitment to supporting developing countries in East Asia and other regions in terms of vaccine access and capacity building. The continued heavy reliance on a state-centric approach intensified the North-South capacity gap during the pandemic and encouraged the use of the containment strategies in East Asia. Moreover, by contributing to the "vaccine apartheid" between industrial nations and the developing world, the state-centric approach makes U.S. calls for global cooperation on international health emergencies sound hypocritical and disingenuous. This could compromise the ability of the United States to project its "smart power" abroad, and, by making obligatory information sharing and international cooperation more difficult to justify, increase the risk to U.S. national security. In short, policymakers need to update their thinking about the threats posed by diseases and the effective strategies for responding to these threats.

## Notes

1. World Health Organization, Media Centre, "H1N1 in Post-Pandemic Period," August 10, 2010, http://www.who.int/mediacentre/news/statements/2010/h1n1_vpc_20100810/en/index.html.

2. World Health Organization, "Pandemic (H1N1) 2009: Update 112," August 6, 2010, http://www.who.int/csr/don/2010_08_06/en/index.html. A recent study suggested that the death toll for the pandemic might be higher than the initial estimate. See Sharon Begley, "2009 Swine Flu Outbreak Was 15 Times Deadlier: Study," Reuters, June 26, 2012, http://www.reuters.com/article/2012/06/26/us-swineflu-idUSBRE85O1DF20120626.

3. See Gabriel M. Leung and Angus Nicoll, "Reflections on Pandemic (H1N1) 2009 and the International Response," *PLoS Medicine* 7, no. 10 (2010): 1–6.

4. Gabor D. Kelen and Melissa L. McCarthy, "The Science of Surge," *American Academy of Emergency Medicine* 13, no. 11 (2006): 1089–94.

5. World Health Organization, "Pandemic Influenza Preparedness and Response," WHO guidance document, April 2009, http://www.who.int/influenza/resources/documents/pandemic_guidance_04_2009/en/.

6. Ibid.

7. A. Nicoll and D. Coulombier, "Europe's Initial Experience with Pandemic (H1N1) 2009: Mitigation and Delaying Policies and Practices," *Euro Surveillance* 29, no. 14 (23 July 2009): 1–6, available at www.eurosurveillance.org.

8. Ibid.

9. World Health Organization, Media Centre, "Swine Influenza," April 27, 2009, http://www.who.int/mediacentre/news/statements/2009/h1n1_20090427/en/index.html.

10. Nicoll and Coulombier, "Europe's Initial Experience."

11. "Background Information: A List of Countries Banning Imports of U.S. Pork Products," Reuters, April 30, 2009, http://cn.reuters.com/article/idCNChina-4373120090430.

12. Jonathan Cheng, Juliet Ye, and Peter Stein, "The Flu Outbreak: Hong Kong Orders Quarantine of Hotel," *Wall Street Journal*, May 2, 2009.

13. Peter Stein, "Flu Lockdown Spurs Quarantine Debate," *Wall Street Journal*, May 7, 2009.

14. "Brunei Quarantines about 200 British Military Personnel," *BBC Monitoring Asia Pacific*, May 5, 2009.

15. "New Orleans Mayor Ray Nagin, Wife Quarantined in China Amid Flu Fears," Associated Press, June 8, 2009, http://www.foxnews.com/story/0,2933,525347,00.html.

16. "Ministry of Health of Singapore Abolished Self-Quarantine Measures," May 16, 2009, http://www.sinchew-i.com/node/93465?tid=12.

17. Sharon Otterman, "Flu Spreads, but Some Countries Ease Measures," *New York Times*, May 23, 2009; "Japan to Phase Out Onboard New-Flu Quarantine Inspections," *BBC Monitoring Asia Pacific*, May 19, 2009.

18. Patsy Moy, "Virus Victims May Get Home Stay," *The Standard*, June 25, 2009.

19. After July 6, 2009, countries were no longer required to test and report individual cases to the World Health Organization.

20. Annie Freeda Cruez, "Warning of Community Outbreak," *New Straits Times* (Malaysia), August 2009.

21. "Vietnamese Report Highlights Shortcomings in Flu Prevention," *BBC Monitoring Asia Pacific*, June 2, 2009; "Vietnamese Health Minister Confirms Spread of H1N1 Flu at Community Level," *BBC Monitoring Asia Pacific*, 22 July 2009.

22. Yanzhong Huang and Christopher J. Smith, "China's Response to Pandemics: From Inaction to Overreaction," *Eurasian Geography and Economics* 51, no. 2 (March–April 2010): 162–83.

23. Dennis Normile, "H1N1 Rocks Japan, But WHO Says It's Still No Pandemic," *ScienceInsider*, May 18, 2009.

24. "Mainland Officials Concede They Can't Contain Swine Flu," *South China Morning Post*, June 30, 2009.

25. Pei Pei Chan et al., "Outbreak of Novel Influenza A (H1N1-2009) Linked to a Dance Club," *Annals of the Academy of Medicine* (Singapore) 39, no. 4 ( 2010): 299–302.

26. Huang and Smith, "China's Response to Pandemics."

27. Ibid.

28. "Quarantine at Ports Found Ineffective against New Flu," *Daily Yomiuri*, January 8, 2010.

29. "Experts: 45% of H1N1 Cases Asymptomatic," *China Post*, September 2, 2009, http://www.chinapost.com.tw/taiwan/national/national-news/2009/09/02/222953/Experts-45.htm.

30. Lee Wei Long, "Let It in While Benign to Develop Herd Immunity," *Straits Times*, May 15, 2009.

31. Huang and Smith, "China's Response to Pandemics."

32. "Malaysia Discharges 239 H1N1 Flu Patients from Hospital Nationwide," *BBC Monitoring Asia Pacific*, July 6, 2009.

33. World Health Organization, Global Alert and Response (GAR), "No Rationale for Travel Restrictions," May 1, 2009, http://www.who.int/csr/disease/swineflu/guidance/public_health/travel_advice/en/index.html.

34. Sake J. de Vlas, Dan Feng, Ben S. Cooper, Li-Qun Fang, Wu-Chun Cao, and Jan Hendrik Richardus, "The Impact of Public Health Control Measures during the SARS Epidemic in Mainland China," *Tropical Medicine and International Health* 14, no. S1 (2009): 101–4.

35. "Plan to Share Supplies in 13 Countries," *New Straits Times*, May 22, 2009.

36. Author's communication with John Wong, East Asian Institute of Singapore, August 2010.

37. Ren Bo et al., "Yu 'Jialiu' Gongcun" (Coexist with A/H5N1 Flu), *Caijing* (Finance and Economics), no. 14, July 6, 2009.

38. According to a survey conducted in six cities in early August 2009, 20 percent of the respondents believed that eating pork could lead to infections with H1N1 virus; Reuters, September 4, 2009, http://cn.reuters.com/article/idCNCHINA-541920090904. For the impact of China's response on its foreign relations, see Yanzhong Huang, "Pursuing Health as Foreign Policy: The Case of China," *Indiana Journal of Global Legal Studies* 17, no. 1 (2010): 105–46.

39. Council on Foreign Relations, "Global Health Update," June 30, 2009.

40. Nicoll and Coulombier, "Europe's Initial Experience."

41. "Quarantine Checks Taking 2 Hrs," *Daily Yomiuri*, April 30, 2009.

42. "Local Governments Struggle with Flu Checkups," *Daily Yomiuri*, May 5, 2009.

43. Ren Bo et al., "Yu 'Jialiu' Gongcun" (Coexist with A/H5N1 Flu).

44. Dessy Sagita, "Swine Flu the Biggest Challenge for Indonesia Health Ministry in 2009," *JakartaGlobe*, December 22, 2009.

45. "Combating Complacency," *New Straits Times*, April 16, 2010.

46. "CDC to Enforce 2nd National Vaccination Campaign," *China Post*, January 20, 2010.

47. See T. Jacob John and Reuben, "Herd Immunity and Herd Effect: New Insights and Definitions," *European Journal of Epidemiology* 16, no. 7 (2000): 601–6.

48. "A Decline in the Intensity of H1N1 Spread in Beijing," *Beijing Evening News*, December 19, 2009, http://beijing.qianlong.com/3825/2009/12/19/135@5366187.htm.

49. "Certain Level of Immunity Has Been Built among Our Country's Mainland Population." Xinhua, September 10, 2010, http://news.sciencenet.cn/htmlnews/2010/9/237359.shtm.

50. Nicoll and Coulombier, "Europe's Initial Experience."

51. Rob Stein, "Flu Pandemic Could Be Mild," *Washington Post*, December 8, 2009.

52. See the Web page of XinhuaNews. net, http://www.xinhuanet.com/politics/yfzlg/.

53. Simeon Bennett, "They Shoot Frequent Fliers, Don't They? Only in China's Flu Era," Bloomberg, June 21, 2009, http://www.bloomberg.com/apps/news?pid=news archive&sid=a3hHFvo8NN1k.

54. See "Chongqing Children's Hospital Received 5,300 Patients in One Day," October 27, 2009, http://news.39.net/shwx/0910/27/1042291.html.

55. Conference on Strengthening Health and Non-Health Response Systems in Asia: A Sustained Approach for Responding to Global Infectious Disease Crises, organized by the RSIS Centre for Non-Traditional Security (NTS) Studies, Nanyang Technological University, March 18–19, 2010, Singapore.

56. Jessica Stern, "Dreaded Risks and the Control of Biological Weapons," *International Security* 27, no. 3 (Winter 2002–3): 105.

57. See "Korea Moves to Prevent Swine Flu Outbreak," *Korea Herald*, April 28, 2009.

58. Anne Applebaum, "Playing Politics with a Pandemic," *Washington Post*, November 17, 2009.

59. Ng Yuk-Hang, "HK Well Equipped for Outbreak after SARS, Health Secretary Says," *South China Morning Post*, April 27, 2009.

60. Applebaum, "Playing Politics with a Pandemic."

61. Marc Lacey and Andrew Jacobs, "Even as Fears of Flu Ebb, Mexicans Feel Stigma," *New York Times*, May 4, 2009.

62. Joint Press Conference of the Ministry of Health and the World Health Organization, June 12, 2009, http://www.sinotf.com/GB/News/1005/2009-06-13/1NMDAwMDAyOTI1NQ.html.

63. Yin Pumin, "Changing Battle Plans," *Beijing Review*, July 23, 2009.

64. "Warning of Community Outbreak," *New Straits Times*, August 2009; Malaysian National News Agency, "24 Students with H1N1 Symptoms Quarantined," April 15, 2010, http://www.bernama.com/bernama/v5/newsgeneral.php?id=490902.

65. Hugh Heclo, *Modern Social Politics in Britain and Sweden* (New Haven, Conn.: Yale University Press, 1974), 316.

66. "Avian Influenza Aided Readiness for Swine Flu," *Nature* 459 (2009): 757, http://www.nature.com/news/2009/090610/full/459756a.html.

67. T. Kamigaki and H. Oshitani, "Influenza Pandemic Preparedness and Severity Assessment of Pandemic (H1N1) 2009 in South-East Asia," *Public Health* 124 (2010): 5–9.

68. David Fidler, "Architecture amidst Anarchy: Global Health's Quest for Governance," *Global Health Governance* 1, no. 1 (Spring 2007).

69. "How to Contain Flu," *Korea Times*, August 24, 2009; "Avian Influenza Aided Readiness for Swine Flu," 756.

70. "Avian Influenza Aided Readiness for Swine Flu."

71. "Asia Worries about the Capacity Gap in Producing New Flu Vaccine," Reuters, May 19, 2009, http://cn.reuters.com/article/idCNChina-4524520090519.

72. Harry Schwartz, "Swine Flu Fiasco," *New York Times*, December 21, 1976.

73. Konrad Obemann, "Global Health and Foreign Policy," *Lancet*, 2007, 1688.

74. "Political Animal," *South China Morning Post*, May 14, 2009.

75. Bae Ji-sook, "Quarantine Starts against Swine Flu," *Korea Times*, April 26, 2009.

76. "Rising Pandemic Fear Prompts Heightened Alert," *BusinessWorld*, April 27, 2009, S1/1.

77. "Survey Shows 85 Percent of the Public Were Satisfied with China's Anti-H1N1 Measures" (in Chinese), *China Youth Daily*, May 26, 2009, http://news.anhuinews.com/system/2009/05/26/002261874.shtml.

78. "Coexist with H1N1/A" (in Chinese), *Caijing*, July 6, 2009.

79. See Jeremy Au Yong, "Better to Err on Side of Caution," *Straits Times*, July 3, 2009; "China Criticised for Overreacting to Swine Flu," Agence France-Presse, May 14, 2009, http://www.asiaone.com/print/News/Latest%2BNews/Asia/Story/A1Story20090514-141409.html.

80. *Global Times* (Huanqiu shibao), May 19, 2009, http://news.cctv.com/china/20090519/102464.shtml.

81. See, e.g., Jennifer Blower and Peter Chalk, *The Global Threat of New and Reemerging Infectious Diseases: Reconciling U.S. National Security with Public Health Policy* (Santa Monica, Calif.: RAND Corporation, 2003).

82. Price-Smith, *Contagion and Conflict*, 43.

83. R. S. Bray, *Armies of Pestilence: The Effects of Pandemics on History* (Cambridge: James Clarke, 2004), 70.

84. Elbe, *Virus Alert*.

85. "Now Is the Time to Rethink New Flu Tack," *Daily Yomiuri*, April 17, 2010.

86. Quoted by Shao Yiming in an interview with CCTV, http://vote.cctv.com/news/china/20031129/100267_2.shtml.

87. "Hu Jintao: Make Efforts to Be the First to Recover from the International Financial Crisis," June 17, 2009, http://finance.cctv.com/20090617/100939.shtml.

88. Yanzhong Huang, "In-Flew-Enza: Pandemic Flu and Its Security Implications," in *Innovation in Global Health Governance: Critical Cases*, edited by Andrew F. Cooper and John J. Kirton (London: Ashgate, 2009), 127–50.

89. Andrew Erickson, "Combating a Collective Threat: Prospects for Sino-American Cooperation against Avian Influenza," *Global Health Governance* 1, no. 1 (Spring 2007), www.ghgj.org.

90. Barack Obama and Richard Lugar, "Grounding a Pandemic," *New York Times*, June 6, 2005.

91. Barack H. Obama, "National Security Strategy," May 2010, 49, http://www.whitehouse.gov/sites/default/files/rss_viewer/national_security_strategy.pdf.

92. President's Council of Advisors on Science and Technology, "PCAST Report to the President on U.S. Preparations for 2009-H1N1 Influenza," Office of Science and Technology Policy, August 24, 2009, 44.

93. Ibid.

94. Chris Neefus, "Sebelius Says U.S. Will Donate Part of H1N1 Vaccine Supply to Foreign Nations before Meeting This Nation's Demand," CNSNews.com, October 21, 2009, http://www.cnsnews.com/news/article/55907.

95. "Americans Get Priority," Agence France-Presse, October 30, 2010, http://www.thedailystar.net/story.php?nid=111928.

96. Rob Stein, "Millions of H1N1 Vaccine Doses May Have to Be Discarded," *Washington Post*, April 1, 2010.

97. Richard Wenzel, "What We Learned from H1N1's First Year," *New York Times*, April 13, 2010.

98. This "vaccine apartheid" further bolstered the Indonesian's "viral sovereignty" thesis, discouraging the sharing of samples of avian influenza, even threatening vaccine production and public health preparedness. Not surprisingly, when the H1N1 pandemic hit Indonesia, the country's minister of health ramped up the rhetoric by accusing the United States of genetically engineering H1N1 and H5N1 as biological weapons and threatening with severe punishment any Indonesian scientists caught collaborating with NAMRU-2, the U.S. Naval Medical Research Unit in Jakarta. See, e.g., Delthisa Ricks, "Flu Wars," *Discover* 30, no. 11 (December 2009).

99. Yanzhong Huang, "The H1N1 Virus: Varied Local Responses to a Global Spread," *YaleGlobal Online*, September 1, 2009.

# Chapter 7

# Effectively Responding to Pandemics: Adapting Responses to Differing Institutional Circumstances in the United States and China

*Jonathan Schwartz and Rachel D. Schwartz*

Scientists have long argued that epidemics and pandemics caused by emerging infectious diseases are not rare exceptions, but rather recurring crises that can be expected to arise at least once per generation.[1] This pattern is exemplified by the 1918–19 Spanish influenza catastrophe that killed 50 to 100 million people and the horrific Asian influenza outbreak of 1957–58 that caused 2 million deaths worldwide.[2] Severe pandemics can be described as nontraditional security threats with the potential to cause serious social and political upheaval on a global level. During the past ten years, outbreaks of severe acute respiratory syndrome (SARS), H5N1 (avian influenza), and H1N1 (swine influenza) have raised awareness of the need for global and local pandemic preparedness among health-care providers, public health officials, and the general public. As a result of these emerging infections, international bodies concerned with global health issues have had to focus on developing effective tools for pandemic preparedness and response. These efforts are evident in ongoing initiatives that follow the continuing mutation and spread of H5N1 and H1N1 (in

2009), and also in the emphasis placed on global pandemic response and preparation policies. Scientists agree on the inevitable emergence of a devastating pandemic that is severe and easily transmissible between humans. How should we prepare for this type of nontraditional security threat?

In preliminary research published in *Global Health Governance* (2010), we examined preparedness levels in the United States and China. We sought to draw lessons about effective pandemic preparedness and response from the general preparedness and past experiences of these two countries. As might be expected when comparing such dissimilar countries, a number of major differences distinguish their social and political systems, making the direct adoption of foreign models extremely difficult. Nonetheless, this examination allowed us to identify four spheres that proved crucial to effective pandemic preparedness and response in both China and the United States:

1. the role of the state bureaucracy,
2. the nature of relations between state and nonstate actors,
3. the role of the media and their relationship with the state, and
4. relations between the state and international community regarding pandemic response.

In this chapter we draw on these four spheres to identify policy-relevant recommendations for achieving effective pandemic preparedness and response, while addressing cultural obstacles to adopting these recommendations. The chapter opens with a brief discussion of the pandemic threat before engaging in a historical review and comparison of response capabilities in the United States and China. We then examine the four spheres we have identified as crucial to effective pandemic response. We begin with the role of the state bureaucracy, and then consider state-nonstate actor relations, the role of the media, and finally, relations between the state and the international community in pandemic preparedness and response. We then present the ramifications of the aforementioned differences for pandemic response capabilities. Though both countries have had some success in pandemic preparedness and response, the political, social, and cultural differences between the countries are such that successful strategies are not directly adoptable. On the basis of our analyses, we develop policy recommendations that take these differences into account. We argue that these recommendations can promote the translation of successful practices between countries despite political, social, and cultural differences. Finally, we consider the implications of differing values on United States–China cooperation in pandemic response.

## The Pandemic Threat

Global pandemics have long been a threat to humanity, appearing at regular intervals three to four times a century. Certain attributes of expanding globalization—such as the movement of goods, services, and people across the planet in ever-increasing numbers—have exacerbated human vulnerability to pandemics.[3] As a result, the public health community has generally accepted that a novel or reemerging highly virulent and easily transmissible virus is both inevitable and long overdue.[4] Indeed, the World Economic Forum's 2006 *Global Risks Report* ranked pandemics among the gravest risks confronting the world.[5]

Past examples of serious pandemics include the 1348–51 Black Death, which resulted in between 20 million and 40 million deaths worldwide; the 1918–19 Spanish influenza, which infected approximately one-third of the world's population, killing between 50 million and 100 million people; and the 1957–58 Asian influenza, which killed 2 million people worldwide.[6] More recently, in 2002–3 the SARS pandemic caused fewer than one thousand deaths, with economic costs of between $40 billion and $60 billion.[7]

The impact of 2009 H1N1 (swine flu) cannot yet be fully calculated. According to Margaret Chan, director-general of the World Health Organization (WHO), between 20 and 40 percent of the world's population was infected with H1N1, and, in responding to this pandemic, "we have been aided by pure good luck. The virus did not mutate during the pandemic to a more lethal form," and vaccines proved effective and safe.[8] Nevertheless, the speed with which the virus spread, reaching more than 214 countries and overseas territories as of August 1, 2010, left leaders pondering the implications for humanity should a similarly easily spreading disease, but one with a higher fatality rate, develop.[9]

One likely candidate for a dangerous pandemic is highly pathogenic avian influenza, H5N1. According to the WHO, the H5N1 fatality rate among humans is over 50 percent, but the disease does not spread easily between humans. If this were to change through mutation, the results could be disastrous. As of September 2010, there were 507 confirmed cases of human infection, including 302 deaths, and the numbers continue to rise.[10] A WHO study predicts on the basis of past pandemics that human-to-human transmissible influenza could result in 1.5 billion people seeking medical attention, with fatalities ranging between 2 and 7 million people. In a 2005 study, the World Bank estimates the economic cost of a severe influenza pandemic at $800 billion, with tens of millions of fatalities.[11] The U.S. Centers for Disease Control and Prevention (USCDC) estimates 207,000 U.S. deaths from a pandemic, while the Department of Health and Human Services suggests 1.9 million, with initial economic costs of between $166 billion and $200 billion.[12]

Although one response to a pandemic will be the rapid development of antivirals and vaccines, these cannot arrest the spread nor fully protect the global population. Notably, combined global vaccine production capacity is approximately 300 million doses per year—clearly insufficient to meet demand. Perhaps the most important response to a future pandemic is global cooperation. As the USCDC asserts, "The scope and intensity of global health challenges ensures that no single country or agency can work alone to meet them."[13] Stohr describes the need for global cooperation including international coordinated responses, cooperation on domestic pandemic plan development, institutionalized cross-border information sharing, and collaboration on novel and reemerging viral infections.[14]

Faced with an inevitable pandemic, it is essential for the international community to prepare by drawing on existing best practices from around the world while also developing strong cooperative relations.

## Pandemic Response Capabilities

The SARS outbreak originated in China in 2002. At the time of the outbreak, China's public health system was weaker than it had been in the prereform era under Mao Zedong.[15] This weakness was the result of the shift from a past emphasis on preventive care to a new emphasis on curative care. This shift occurred as a result of China's move away from state-provided health care to a system more similar to that found in the United States. However, the shift left China's health care system underresourced and unprepared to respond effectively to a pandemic. The initial Chinese response to SARS reflected this lack of preparedness as the disease spread rapidly, yet information about it was restricted and resources to contain and treat SARS were unavailable. However, despite wide recognition that China's initial response was poor, the international community eventually came to regard China's SARS response to be relatively effective.[16]

The United States, unlike China, was essentially untouched by SARS. This has largely been attributed to good fortune. Whereas China and other SARS-affected countries had "superspreaders" in their midst, the United States had none. These superspreaders, defined as people who infected at least ten other people, were key to the rapid spread of SARS. Thus, it would be inappropriate to refer to U.S. "success" in battling SARS, or to evaluate U.S. pandemic response capabilities using SARS alone as a benchmark. In fact, whereas China can be viewed as having developed an effective pandemic response in the face of SARS, the United States was bypassed by the disease, and therefore did not have to develop a sophisticated pandemic response.

Whereas U.S. capabilities were never tested in response to SARS, the same cannot be said with regard to 2009 H1N1. In this case, the United States was forced to cope with a rapidly spreading, potentially deadly disease outbreak that was only recognized after it had already begun infecting citizens. The first case was officially diagnosed in mid-April 2009 by the USCDC and is believed to have been imported from Mexico.[17] The first identified case of H1N1 in China was imported from the United States and reported on May 11, 2009.[18] Thus, in contrast to the U.S. experience of H1N1, and unlike the case of SARS, China enjoyed the luxury of a window of time to prepare a response to this rapidly spreading novel disease. The Chinese government took advantage of the time to take some dramatic steps, occasionally exceeding the World Health Organization's recommendations, in an effort to stop or at least slow the spread of H1N1 into and across the country.

Four factors are key to understanding the difference between the U.S. and Chinese responses. Let us briefly consider each one.

*The Role of the State Bureaucracy*

In the United States, the public health bureaucracy is highly decentralized. The state-level public health authorities oversee local public health agencies (LPHAs), but response occurs mostly at the local level, varying according to the personalities and relationships of elected and bureaucratic leaders. Clear, institutionalized lines of control do not exist between state and federal levels, among different states, or even within individual states (figure 7.1).[19] State public health agencies and local public health departments set their own policies and priorities, based on idiosyncratic political and legal interests. Thus, in the event of an emerging infection pandemic,

*Figure 7.1. Simplified Structure of U.S. Federal, State, and Local Public Health System Operations*

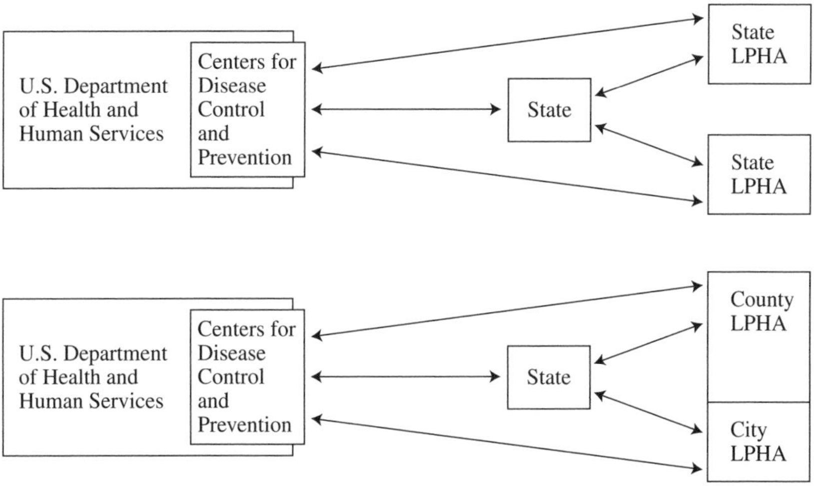


*Note:* LPHA = local public health agency. For a more detailed description of the Department of Health and Human Services and how public health fits into it, see http://www.hhs.gov/about/orgchart/.

"it is possible for federal, state, and local health authorities simultaneously to have separate but concurrent legal quarantine power."[20] In addition, LPHAs—which are already underfunded and understaffed—frequently decide that they cannot cope with preparing plans for pandemic response and choose not to do so. For example, when federal funding was provided to states for H5N1 pandemic preparedness, some LPHAs refused their share of it, arguing that the requirements attached to the funding made implementation impossible, given their already strained infrastructure, without compromising their mission to provide basic public health services.

These differences in priorities, as well as the dominance of states' rights, can prompt the federal government to overrule local and state governments in the case of a pandemic. However, it is difficult for federal agencies—led by the USCDC—to direct a coordinated response to pandemic outbreaks. The USCDC lacks the authority and personnel to require or enforce the recommendations and guidelines it establishes. Instead, it must be invited by the states to investigate disease outbreaks. Given that each state has different response capabilities and priorities, and often waits to request the USCDC's assistance, there is no standard strategy for the USCDC to follow, especially because the outbreak may already be well established by the time the USCDC is contacted.

Pandemic response is further constrained by the lack of clear and flexible legal mechanisms that would allow the federal government to adjust laws and regulations in order to better combat novel pandemics. In the United States, the legal authority and responsibility for public health are constitutionally placed in the hands of the states, each of which oversees multiple LPHAs. Each LPHA is structured differently according to the resources and needs of its community.

Although the U.S. president, as head of the executive branch, has authority to issue executive orders with the force of law, he is constrained by statute and constitutional authority. Any order that might restrict civil liberties would likely face a constitutional challenge. Experts have argued that laws regarding public health are antiquated and even obstructionist.[21] Multiple reports dating back to the mid–twentieth century have sought to address the confusion caused by the arrangement of public health response powers, including the federalization of public health, but there has been little success in adopting or implementing them.[22]

In the event of a pandemic, the federal government derives its authority for isolation and quarantine from the commerce clause of the U.S. Constitution. Consequently, the focus tends to be on preventing transmission from foreign nationals and on interstate commerce of animals. Diseases must appear on a federal list if quarantine and isolation orders are to be given. Because the authority for carrying out these functions on a daily basis has been delegated to the USCDC and, as we have seen, their enforcement ability is virtually nonexistent, this creates another roadblock to the centralization of response.[23] Instead, as noted above, the primary responsibility and authority for such declarations reside at the state and local level. The last use of federal quarantine powers occurred during the Spanish influenza pandemic of 1918–19.[24]

In the wake of economic reforms initiated in the late 1970s, China's public health bureaucracy also became quite decentralized, as publicly provided health services were shifted to governments at or below the prefectural level. However, this transfer of responsibilities was not accompanied by an adequate transfer of resources. Thus, by some estimates, prefectural, county, and township governments on average expend 55 percent of their budgets on health care and other public services, a percentage far exceeding the average of less developed countries (13 percent) or developed countries (35 percent).[25] However, in making this investment, these governments

*Figure 7.2. The Chinese Disease Prevention System*

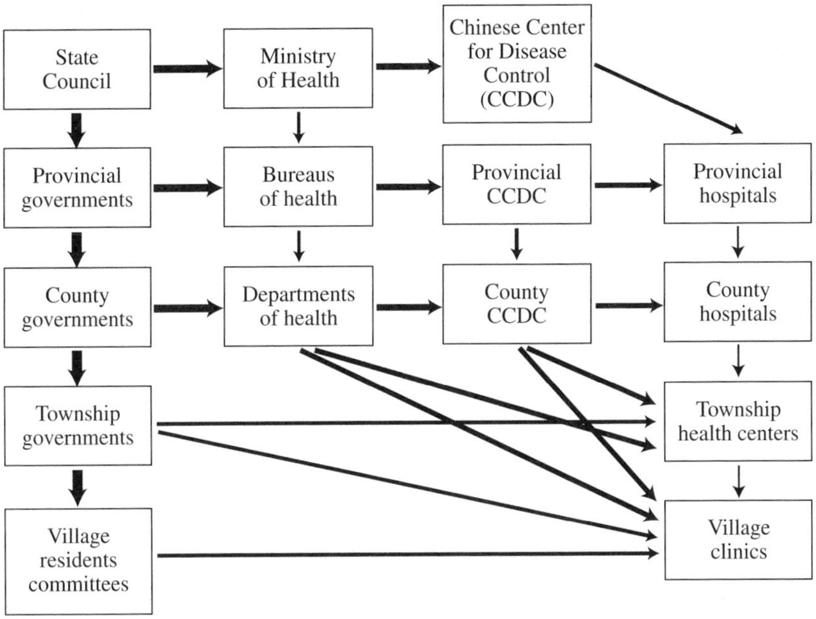

*Note:* Arrows indicate bureaucratic lines of control. Thickness of arrow implies strength of relationship.
*Sources:* Jonathan Schwartz, R. Gregory Evans, and Sarah Greenberg, "Evolution of Health Provision in Pre-SARS China: The Changing Nature of Disease Prevention," *China Review* 7, no. 1 (Spring 2007): 94.

face the danger of failing to meet the central government's benchmarks for economic growth. Given the centrality of economic growth as a criterion for professional advancement in the government and party hierarchies, local officials naturally focus their energy on the economy, deemphasizing and underinvesting in public health, which after all represents a drain on budgets rather than a wealth contributor. The result is that the quality of public health provision in China has deteriorated.

However, while power has shifted to the provincial level and below, and government investment in public health declined, the bureaucratic lines of control running from the central government to the lowest, village level remain intact (figure 7.2).[26] Direction of arrows in figure indicate bureaucratic control and thickness of arrows implies strength of relationship. Within this hierarchy, the Chinese Centers for Disease Control (CCDC) network was established as part of the Ministry of Health's bureaucracy, running from the national level (the national CCDC in Beijing) to the township level. At the national level, the CCDC provides technical supervision and makes recommendations. The national CCDC represents an effort by the central government to establish a center of expertise, though one that is subordinate to the Ministry of Health. The national CCDC receives notification of possible infectious disease outbreaks from hospitals around the country that report outpatient surveillance data for influenza-like illnesses. The CCDC analyzes and interprets these data before sending analyses and response recommendations to the Ministry of Health.[27] Below the national level, approximately 3,000 CCDC units reach to the township level, though they vary dramatically in resources and the quality of training. Local CCDC responsibilities include reporting disease outbreaks, taking disease control measures, conducting limited research, and providing limited health education services.

When China's central leadership realized the gravity of the public health crisis represented by SARS, it was able to undertake a response that differed enormously from that which is possible for the U.S. government. The Chinese leadership declared SARS a high priority, recentralized powers, enacted clear top-down regulations that were forced on lower-level officials both in the public health bureaucracy and across relevant bureaucracies in general, and allocated significant resources to pandemic response.[28]

When initial reports on H1N1 estimated the fatality rates at 10 to 20 percent, the Chinese government again recentralized powers, imposing drastic quarantine and isolation policies, canceling flights to and from Mexico, and initiating temperature checks for passengers on incoming flights. In addition, the third-ranking leader in the State Council (China's Cabinet) visited the national CCDC—the first such visit since the SARS outbreak. While at the CCDC, he committed the Chinese government to providing anything that was required to combat H1N1. Observers confirm that the government provided seemingly unlimited resources, spending tens of millions of dollars in preparation for and response to H1N1. This included massive increases in funding to enhance surveillance capabilities, as well as increasing the number of hospitals prepared to handle pandemic victims and the number of laboratories with the facilities and trained personnel to test for influenza-like illnesses. For uninsured people who contracted these illnesses, as with SARS, the central government committed to covering hospitalization and quarantine costs. This commitment was maintained until new information proved that H1N1 was less dangerous than originally believed.[29]

The central government also established an interagency office called the "mechanism for joint defense and control" (*lianfang liankong jizhi*), which brought together a variety of ministries—such as the Ministry of Health, the Ministry of Finance, the National Research Development Commission, the Administration of Quarantine and Isolation, and the Ministry of Education—to coordinate initiatives such as vaccine production and distribution, and antiviral drug stockpiling and distribution.[30] Intraministerial teams were also established to address issues such as surveillance, logistics, and the media.[31]

In May, data showed a revised fatality rate of less than 1 percent; but the Chinese response remained almost unchanged until September. Central government CCDC officials noted that initial drastic measures such as the quarantine and isolation of incoming potentially ill passengers could be reduced. For the most part, however, local officials maintained existing measures. This behavior reflects the political nature of pandemic response in China. Local leaders sought to retain the immense support and goodwill displayed by the public for the government's strong response to H1N1, while at the same time avoiding inevitable censure by higher-ranking officials should a further outbreak occur.[32]

Thus, the Chinese response to pandemics is not limited to activating the general capabilities of the public health system, but also includes the ability and will of the central government to ramp up response capabilities in the event of a pandemic. The question is not whether the public health system has the capacity to effectively respond to a pandemic but, rather, whether the central government has both the capacity and the will to activate and coordinate a broad coalition of forces in response to a pandemic. The responses to SARS and H1N1 illustrate that the Chinese system exhibits this latter capability. By contrast, the U.S. system, constrained by fragmentation and decentralization, does not.

### Relations between State and Nonstate Actors

Another difference between the U.S. and Chinese systems is the role played by nonstate actors. In China, perhaps the most relevant nonstate actor in terms of pandemic response—the residents committee—is difficult to categorize, given that in some senses it can actually be viewed as a state actor. On the one hand, residents committees represent the interests of the state vis-à-vis the local community; on the other hand, however, they have little coercive power and limited resources. Described as "straddler groups" because they straddle the line between traditional roles played by state and nonstate actors, they facilitate neighborhood activities as well as organizing gatherings, and offer a means to pressure the state.[33] During the SARS outbreak, these committees played an important role by organizing volunteers to provide supplies to quarantined individuals. They also distributed thermometers and face masks, and kept tabs on the comings and goings of strangers in the neighborhoods.[34] Volunteers organized by the residents committees were trained by local CCDCs. Such organizations provide essential support to local public health officials.

Comparably engageable nonstate actors in the United States do not exist. Independent but allied volunteer and corporate organizations such as the American National Red Cross play an important role in any disaster response through their local and national presence in communities. Indeed, surveys found that government aid accounted for only 25 percent of assistance received by victims of Hurricane Katrina, with the remainder provided by the nonstate sector.[35] However, despite their large contributions, it is difficult to place nonstate organizations within the regular response system, as their approaches vary depending upon the type of disaster, the agency requesting assistance, and numerous other political and social factors.[36]

## The Role of the Media

In China, the media are becoming increasingly commercialized and competitive and are providing more investigative reporting. In 2006, China had more than 2,000 newspapers, 8,000 magazines, 374 television stations,[37] and approximately 380 million Internet users.[38] Yet, although the Chinese Constitution guarantees free speech and press, only state agencies may own media outlets. Furthermore, a constitutional requirement to defend the honor, security, and interests of the country offsets the guarantees of free press and speech. The vague wording of the constitutional requirement—coupled with the power of the state to declare published information to be a state secret—means that journalists are under constant threat of prosecution. Many journalists self-censor in order to avoid losing their jobs or face possible imprisonment.[39]

Official censorship is the province of the Communist Party's Central Propaganda Department (CPD). It is charged with ensuring that all content promotes and is consistent with party doctrine. The CPD directs the media on politically sensitive issues such as Taiwan, Tibet, natural disasters, protests, and—of special importance here—health crises. Reflecting the power and centrality of the CPD, its current director, Li Changchun, is a member of the Communist Party's central decisionmaking body, the Politburo Standing Committee. The CPD's reach extends through the party, state, and military bureaucracies from the central level down to the district level. It is responsible for organizing and monitoring the news, broadcasting, television, and publishing to ensure that they effectively promote the Communist Party's guiding principles, current line, and policies.[40] The CPD can hire and fire all senior personnel in the media sector down to the municipality level and must approve all programming by China Central Television, China National Radio, China Radio International, and all print media. According to Brady, "every means of communication and form of organized social interaction in China is ultimately under the supervision of the CPD and its minions."[41]

In the public health sector, the CPD cooperates with the Ministry of Health in organizing such public health campaigns as eliminating pests and educating the population about causes of disease. The link between the propaganda and health systems is the Council for Patriotic Health Campaigns, which has offices at the central, provincial, local, and district government levels. During SARS, these offices guided information releases by the Ministry of Health and ordered neighborhood cleanups and education campaigns.[42] During the H1N1 pandemic, they took advantage of government control over the media to tell members of the public how to avoid infection, for example, how to sneeze correctly and how to maintain personal hygiene. This approach ensured a clear and unified message accepted by the Chinese public; however, it did not admit to errors. In fact, because there was little risk that the public could discover misstatements, the government successfully misinformed the public about the extent of the threat that H1N1 constituted. This Chinese use of the media stands in stark contrast to USCDC interaction with the U.S. media and the numerous reports that the USCDC provided in response to H1N1.

The media in the United States operate on a competitive model and therefore respond more to audience interests than to government interests.[43] Relief efforts draw larger audiences than preparedness efforts because they are more visible and dramatic. At the same time, the media have an interest in providing the most authoritative information they can, so they give airtime to experts such as the head of the USCDC and other response officials. Vasterman, Yzermans, and Dirkzwager argue that the media may have both positive and negative effects during disasters. On the positive side, the media may inform, instruct, and educate the public, lowering general anxiety levels. On the negative side, the media may expose the public to too much coverage of disasters or emergencies and thereby raise anxiety levels.[44] The inability of the United States—in contrast to the Chinese government—to ensure that the media messages relating to a disaster are unified and consistent is problematic. In the case of H1N1, USCDC updates and sometimes contradictory statements occurred as it reported changes in the status of the disease and responses to it as transparently as events would allow.[45] The consumer-driven nature of the media also tends to distort actual levels of risk, sensationalizing disaster coverage and confusing the consumer. However, the relative transparency of the U.S. system forces decisionmakers, responders, and those who deliver the messages at every level to be more accountable to the public than is the case in China.

### Relations between the State and International Community

When SARS broke out in China, the local and later central governments responded by attempting to hide and, later, downplay the outbreak. Local officials hesitated to disclose the novel infection to the center, and the center hesitated to disclose the disease to the international community. The hesitation reflected real concerns at both the local and central levels regarding the impact of a novel, potentially fatal disease on economic growth and development. Because the promise of ongoing economic growth and development has become the basis for the Communist Party's continued rule, news that might potentially threaten economic growth had to be suppressed. The party's preference was to suppress this news until its own officials discovered a solution to the disease that could then be trumpeted to the world as a Chinese success story—adding to the party's legitimacy to rule. Only after SARS had spread to Hong Kong did the Chinese government acknowledge the disease's presence and recognize the need for global cooperation. The Chinese hesitation to reach out to the international community forced Chinese health officials to make do without the expertise, technology, and resources available from organizations like the WHO and the USCDC. If the Chinese government had turned to the international community for assistance early on in the SARS outbreak, the result might have been far better, both for China and the rest of the world.

China's failure to report the status of SARS in 2003 and other failures of international reporting led to an updating of the International Health

Regulations (IHR) in 2005. The new regulations include a requirement that all countries notify the WHO of potential threats to international health and that they give the WHO authority to issue temporary and standing recommendations regarding such international health concerns as travel advisories and requirements for vaccinating travelers.[46] China signed on to the 2005 IHR following its experience with SARS.[47] It then began to share information and staff with the WHO and other public health organizations. Indeed, the CCDC now conducts weekly meetings with the USCDC and the WHO where they share technical data, interpretations, and recommendations.[48]

This cooperative approach carried through to the H1N1 response. China quickly provided information to the WHO and collaborated effectively with the WHO and USCDC, exchanging information, seeking advice on best practices, and obtaining virus strains for vaccine development. This improved level of cooperation can be seen in a 2005 memorandum of understanding signed between the U.S. Department of Health and Human Services and the Chinese Ministry of Health. The memorandum provides for cooperation on emerging and reemerging infectious diseases, and includes ministry-level information sharing as well as establishment of a China-based Field Training Epidemiology Program. The USCDC and CCDC also share offices and personnel, and officials from both sides meet regularly and are even temporarily stationed in each others' offices. This approach has led to a growth of formal and informal relationships between the agencies. Thus, when Feng Zejian, director of emergency response in the CCDC, was at the USCDC in Atlanta during the H1N1 outbreak, he participated in USCDC meetings as it grappled with the disease.[49]

These expanding, institutionalized, interstate relationships have contributed to greater Chinese openness and cooperation on infectious disease responses. Some argue that a major contributor to China's openness was the fact that H1N1, unlike SARS, originated outside China.[50] Consequently, China could not be faulted for the spreading pandemic. Had H1N1 originated in China, the Chinese leadership's response to it would likely have mirrored its response to SARS more closely. Furthermore, even should China seek to maintain secrecy, the constraints on secrecy in the 2005 IHR—that came into force in 2007—made it difficult to maintain a level of secrecy similar to that seen during SARS.[51] Notably, when asked if China sought to hide data on H1N1 cases, a USCDC official based in China asserted unequivocally, "No, absolutely not."[52] The WHO focal point representative in China noted that China actually provided more information than required during H1N1.[53]

Two sources gave a boost to international and WHO negotiations over the new IHR; concern over the 2003 SARS crisis and recognition that biological, chemical, and nuclear terrorism were worldwide problems requiring a global response. Reforms to the IHR had to overcome several obstacles.[54] These included participating countries' concerns over conflicts with international laws, agencies, and treaties regarding health risks, application of IHR to terrorist attacks, and interference with travel and trade. China as well as most major countries operating under federalist systems agreed to adopt the new IHR without reservations. Interestingly, the United States agreed to sign on with the stipulation that it would implement the IHR "in a manner consistent with American federalism," expressing concern that the revised IHR might interfere with states' rights and other elements of the federalist system.[55] Though the practical effects of this stipulation have yet to be seen, they could possibly take the form of further fragmentation and therefore weakening of response as different states take their own approach to the IHR. A failure of cooperation or consistent response would be highly problematic in a pandemic, leading to confusion and inefficiency.

## The Role of Cultural Values

What are cultural values? For cross-cultural theorists, cultural values refer to the widely shared, abstract ideas in a society about what is good, right, and desirable, what is considered desirable and worthy.[56] These values underlie and serve to justify the ways in which the institutions of the society function. They represent the goals that members of the collective are encouraged to pursue, and they serve to justify actions taken in pursuit of these goals.[57] Moreover, cultural values change very slowly, over decades rather than years.[58]

Of particular interest for understanding differences between U.S. and Chinese responses to pandemics is the cultural value dimension of egalitarianism versus hierarchy. In societies with highly egalitarian cultures, people are socialized to feel concern for one another's welfare and to cooperate voluntarily, thus ensuring responsible, productive behavior. In societies with highly hierarchical cultures, on the other hand, people are expected to show deference to superiors and to demand deference from subordinates.[59] Through fulfilling role expectations, people ensure the responsible, productive, cooperative behavior needed to get the work of society done. The unequal distribution of power, roles, and resources is taken for granted and considered legitimate and even desirable.

*Table 7.1. Scores for China and the United States on Cultural Hierarchy and Egalitarianism Compared with International Mean Scores*

| Country or Measure | Cultural Hierarchy | Cultural Egalitarianism |
|---|---|---|
| China | 3.49 | 4.23 |
| United States | 2.37 | 4.68 |
| International mean | 2.33 | 4.70 |
| Standard deviation (across 77 countries) | 0.45 | 0.27 |

*Source:* Data generated by the authors.

Table 7.1 presents the scores for China and the United States on cultural hierarchy and egalitarianism compared with seventy-seven cultural groups from around the world. China scores highest on hierarchy among all the countries surveyed and second lowest on egalitarianism, whereas the United States sits close to the mean for both.[60] China's very high hierarchy and low egalitarianism provide the cultural underpinnings for its ability to centralize power and effectively mobilize the mass media and the public.[61] Consequently, China's population is culturally more amenable to a state-led, top-down, centralized response to crises than is the U.S. population.

Responses to several questions in the World Values Survey complement these findings on cultural value orientations. This survey has been administered in eighty countries around the world in five waves since 1981.[62] Table 7.2 presents the percentage of the population in the United States and in China that expressed a great deal or quite a lot of confidence in various institutions that are relevant to pandemic response: the central government, political parties, the civil services, parliament, charitable or humanitarian organizations, and the press.

The vast majority of China's population—92.7 percent—express substantial confidence in the central government, compared to only 38.2 percent of the U.S. population. The Chinese also express far more confidence in other government-related institutions, such as political parties (the Communist Party), parliament (the National People's Congress), and the civil service (the State Council and its various ministries). These high levels of confidence enable the government to induce the Chinese population to accept its directives and to cooperate with its initiatives in combating a pandemic, because citizens are likely to accept that higher authorities know what is best. In contrast, the lack of confidence exhibited by U.S. citizens in their governmental institutions makes it much more difficult to gain public

*Table 7.2. Percentage of the Population Responding That They Have a "Great Deal" or "Quite a Lot" of Confidence in Various Institutions*

| Institution | United States | Year of Survey | China | Year of Survey |
|---|---|---|---|---|
| Parliament | 38.1 | 1999 | 94.8 | 2001 |
| Political parties | 15.4 | 2006 | 87.8 | 2007 |
| Central government | 38.2 | 2006 | 92.7 | 2007 |
| Civil services | 41.5 | 2006 | 85.8 | 2007 |
| Charitable or humanitarian organizations | 63.9 | 2006 | 75.7 | 2007 |
| Press | 26.7 | 1999 | 69.2 | 2001 |

*Source:* World Values Survey 2010, May 25, 2010, available at www.worldvaluessurvey.org.

cooperation with government initiatives. Suspicion rather than trust of government makes it necessary to persuade citizens that the government knows best and merits their cooperation. These findings can partly explain why a similar government-led response to a pandemic in China and in the United States is more likely to succeed in China.

The media are another important source of information for the public in both the United States and China. However, the primary media that the two governments might find most useful for disaster communication differ somewhat. Daily newspapers are read by 64 percent of Americans but only by 23 percent of Chinese. The percentages using television and radio news on a weekly basis are more similar—87 versus 75 percent.[63] For the governments of both countries, however, the media can serve as key avenues of outreach to inform the public about potential pandemics and desired responses to them. Different attitudes toward the media in the two countries may affect their usefulness in responses to disasters. The 2009 Press Freedom Index, as measured by Reporters without Borders, ranked the United States 20th and China 168th among 175 participating countries. Nonetheless, only 27 percent of Americans express "quite a lot" or "a great deal" of confidence in the press compared with 69 percent of Chinese (see table 7.2).[64] The substantial lack of trust in the press in the United States may make it more difficult for the United States than for the Chinese government to use the media as an effective aid to communicate with the public.

However, the picture of an effective Chinese response that we have drawn may not continue into the future. Despite the fact that China's hierarchical culture is unlikely to change rapidly, the Chinese leadership may not be able to exploit this culture as successfully in years to come. This is due to what the WHO and numerous interviewed scholars, academics, and Chinese public health officials describe as the overreaction of the government to the pandemic.[65] Interviewees repeatedly claimed that the state had been too drastic in its actions. They asserted that Chinese society was becoming increasingly resistant to such state-led, top-down excessive actions, regardless of how effective the actions might be in the short term. If so, the Chinese model, although enjoying some notable successes in the past, may encounter increasing difficulties in the future.

## Conclusion

Pandemics are clear examples of nontraditional security threats that have global ramifications. Because all countries are vulnerable to pandemics, and there is a widespread expectation that it is only a matter of time before future pandemics occur, governments must recognize the benefit of cooperation and learning from each other's experiences. As our research has indicated, national pandemic preparedness and response are highly complex and depend on different institutional circumstances. The United States and China, not unexpectedly, have distinct strengths and weaknesses. Although their respective strengths are not easily transferable from one culture system to another, we argue that lessons learned from the successes and failures of different countries may—with careful consideration of values and institutions—be adapted to the benefit of all stakeholders.

Although this research has focused on two countries, it is crucial that such research continue with the participation of multiple countries. The results can then be adapted for global application. The goal of our research is to contribute to this learning process by conducting a cross-country comparative study and proposing broadly applicable recommendations for effective pandemic responses.

*Mobilizing the State Bureaucracy*

In China's experiences of the SARS and H1N1 pandemics, the response was controlled, top-down, and fairly uniform, with the more or less full cooperation of the state bureaucracy and the public. In the United States, conversely, the long history of states' rights continues to play out in an unwillingness of states to subsume their powers to the federal government, even in emergency situations. Research also indicates that during times of heightened threat, the public was only slightly more likely to support state and federal intervention.[66]

To overcome this challenge, the United States must focus as much as possible on preparedness and advance planning so as to avoid power struggles between federal and local actors. The Pandemics and All Hazards Act (S. 3678), which was passed under President George W. Bush in 2006, lays some of the necessary organizational and legal groundwork for cooperation between federal and local responders; however, experience during the recent H1N1 pandemic indicates that this legislation is inadequate to the task.[67] U.S. officials, faced with resistance to a hierarchical system, must compensate by emphasizing the need for strong and responsible political leadership, particularly at the local level.

Local and state leaders must clearly understand their roles and responsibilities as well as legal challenges during a pandemic event. Because most responses will, at least initially, be local, these leaders must develop cooperative relations with local responders and determine what will trigger requests for involvement of state and federal actors. Moreover, they should assume that definitive diagnosis of diseases will be delayed and that they will have to make decisions based on limited information.[68] In order to mount a successful response to any disaster, public health officials will need to cooperate with and support elected leaders, and those leaders will need to support the efforts of public health officials.[69]

## Mobilizing Nonstate Actors

As we have shown, a key to successful pandemic response in China was the state's ability to effectively mobilize nonstate actors and the general public, particularly in the form of the residents committees. In the United States, by contrast, relatively high egalitarian values—coupled with the public's low levels of trust for the central government, political parties, and politicians in general—make a similarly valuable success in mobilizing nonstate actors and the public unlikely.

Although confidence in government organizations is low in the United States, there is relatively high confidence in nonstate social organizations. Whereas in China the state mobilizes or collaborates closely with nonstate actors, often in the United States, corporations like Walmart and Home Depot mobilize independently, responding quickly and effectively during disasters. This is in part because of their local connections; their access to a market-based feedback loop that provides immediate information on the needs of the community being served; and their "incentives, knowledge, and superior organizational routines that emerge through private ownership and competitive markets."[70] Furthermore, the freedom to act outside the political arena may strengthen their credibility in a country where government actions are so often suspect. This stands in contrast to the Chinese system, in which the government is the main mobilizing force for nonstate organizations.

Another approach to mobilizing nonstate actors in the United States is focusing on faith-based community and national organizations. Faith-based organizations like the Salvation Army and the Southern Baptist Men—as well as individual churches, synagogues, and other places of worship—count disaster response as part of their missions.[71] Many have also become involved in health-based initiatives. However, direct governmental funding or involvement with these organizations is problematic because of issues of separation of church and state.[72] Other community institutions like the American Legion and the Veterans of Foreign Wars, fraternal organizations like the Lions and the Elks, and other clubs might also serve as disaster responders if they were to receive appropriate training.

### Mobilizing the Media

As shown in the Chinese case, a unified message, clearly sent via all media outlets, is a powerful tool in counteracting potential chaos and managing response to a pandemic. This extremely important tool is not available to the U.S. government, nor is this likely to change, given the U.S. Constitution and the freedom of the press in America. Given these conditions, one possible approach to disseminating necessary emergency information is the creation of an alternative media outlet devoted solely to reporting during emergencies. Such an emergency outlet could operate on television, radio, and social networking and other Web-based resources. It would only be used when triggered by a predetermined threshold of disaster (e.g., a declared Level 4 pandemic). In order to ensure a focused message, information would be based on CCDC reports (and possibly WHO reports as well) that were regularly updated.

An important element in building trust and confidence in the emergency outlet would be the appointment of a well-known, trusted, apolitical spokesperson who would serve as the point person for all messaging. This spokesperson would avoid speculative statements, relying instead on the best evidence-based information available, and would emphasize that responding to disasters (especially in the event of disease outbreaks) is an ongoing process requiring flexibility. The spokesperson would also need to make clear that contradictions or changes in recommendations are part of the process of an ongoing pandemic response and do not indicate unreliable information. At the same time, the outlet would make this spokesperson (and a few other, carefully chosen spokespeople) available for interviews and discussions in the standard media. These might be accompanied by the requirement that any editing of actual recommendations or pandemic-specific information be cleared with the outlet to ensure that information was not taken out of context.

For such an outlet to be successful, it would need to be proactive in its reporting, rather than reactive. The focus would need to be on creating headlines in the form of statements based on verifiable facts and scientific evidence, rather than on responding to sensationalism reported in other media outlets, or serving as the mouthpiece of the government. This would require careful timing and excellent coordination between the CCDC (and possibly the WHO) and broadcasters, a sophisticated approach to marketing and technology, and an ability to adjust quickly to the needs of the public.

*Cooperating with the International Community*

We have seen that cooperation with the international community is a key to effective pandemic response. Historically, China has been less open than the United States to interaction with international counterparts at the WHO and other foreign health institutions. Even where public health expertise can be found in China—for example, at the Ministry of Health and the national CCDC—there exists a "poor culture and practice of public health."[73] The Chinese public health culture is not open and innovative, failing to involve inclusive discussion coupled with analytical approaches to data. Although China's public health institutions collect data, they often fail to analyze the data or utilize them to develop innovative solutions. In large part, this lack of innovation is to be expected in a culture that values hierarchy— the desire to avoid challenging superiors in the bureaucracy. Furthermore, the risk of arriving at mistaken conclusions may result in punishment by officials higher up in the bureaucracy. The risk to an official of "getting it wrong" is significant, and the Ministry of Health is likely to quash reports, papers, and studies with which it is unhappy, regardless of the quality of the research and the veracity of the conclusions.[74]

In contrast, in the United States there is a greater atmosphere of engagement and idea sharing. This more egalitarian system is more open to accepting mistakes or necessary changes in information based on new developments in pandemic realities. Those who research and present this information are less likely than their counterparts in China to lose their jobs, where researchers are more likely to maintain their initial opinions without a basis in scientific evidence. The benefits of the more egalitarian U.S. system are obvious. As a highly ranked Chinese Ministry of Health official noted, the United States seems to enjoy a more rational, clear, and professional decisionmaking system based on dialogue and exchange of ideas, resulting in better policy than is arrived at in China.[75]

However, as we have seen, low hierarchy values and high egalitarian values in the United States leave a highly fragmented public health system that lacks the leadership or power to elicit appropriate public response. Thus, even now, when it might seem an obvious step to require, legal battles are being fought over whether health professionals can or should be required by their employers to be vaccinated for diseases like H1N1.[76] No attempt has been made to require flu vaccination of the general population. Even vaccinations for diseases like polio, diphtheria, and pertussis cannot be mandated for children.

The difference in value orientations and institutions necessitates creative approaches to building fruitful cooperation between China and the United States. Since the SARS episode, China has become more open to interaction with foreign institutions. As we have seen, there are ongoing exchanges of personnel, ideas, and data between the CCDC, the USCDC, and the WHO. Chinese officials spend time at the USCDC in Atlanta, attending meetings and observing practices, while U.S. officials play the same role in China. Both the United States and China send officials not only to each other, but also to the WHO. This multisided exchange acknowledges strengths in both systems, rather than favoring one over the other and creating barriers to cooperation. It also allows lessons learned abroad to be presented at home by local representatives, rather than appearing to be imported inappropriately from foreign countries.

In addition, the rising level of trust between the countries, based in large part on the relatively transparent Chinese response to H1N1, opens the door to more productive and transparent scientific collaboration, such as in the development of vaccines and treatment protocols. Ongoing expanded international interactions will further strengthen opportunities for cooperation and exchange of information.

# Notes

1. Derek Blum, "Catastrophic Event Management: Preparing for Extremes," *Society of Actuaries*, July 12, 2010, http://www.soa.org/files/pdf/hspring07-047bk.pdf.

2. "1957 Asian Flu Pandemic," *Global Security*, July 15, 2010, http://www.globalsecurity.org/security/ops/hsc-scen-3_pandemic-1957.htm.

3. Jennifer Brower and Peter Chalk, *The Global Threat of New and Reemerging Infectious Diseases: Reconciling U.S. National Security and Public Health Policies* (Santa Monica, Calif.: RAND Corporation, 2003), 14.

4. Rachel Schwartz and Jonathan Schwartz, "Confronting Global Pandemics: Lessons from China and the U.S.," *Global Health Governance* 3, no. 2 (Spring 2010);World Bank, "Spread of Avian Flu Could Affect Next Year's Economic Outlook," *East Asia Update: Countering Global Shocks* (Washington, D.C.: World Bank, 2005).

5. Mely Caballero-Anthony, "Non-Traditional Security and Infectious Diseases in Asia: The Need for a Global Approach for Health and Human Security," 2007, http://ideas.berkeley.edu/events/pdf/2007.03.08-mely-caballero-anthony.pdf. The often-popular distinction between traditional and nontraditional security seeks to expand our view of nontraditional issues as security threats. Taking this approach, pandemics are nontraditional security threats. However, by taking this approach, pandemics enjoy elevated importance and thus enter the sphere of high politics—an arena where compromise becomes difficult.

6. Case fatality rate is usually expressed as the percentage of persons diagnosed as having a specified disease who die as a result of that illness within a given period. Jeffery K. Taubenberger and David M. Morens, "1918 Influenza: Mother of All Pandemics," *Emerging Infectious Diseases* 12, no. 1 (2006); Laurie Garrett, "The Next Pandemic," *Foreign Affairs* 84, no 4 (July/August 2005).

7. Erik Bloom et al., *Potential Economic Impact of an Avian Flu Pandemic in Asia*, ERD Policy Brief 42 (Manila: Asia Development Bank, 2005).

8. Margaret Chan, "H1N1 in Post-Pandemic Period," World Health Organization, Media Centre, August 10, 2010, http://www.who.int/mediacentre/news/statements/2010/h1n1_vpc_20100810/en/index.html.

9. ProMED-mail, International Society for Infectious Diseases, H1N1 update 112, August 6, 2010, http://www.promedmail.org/pls/apex/f?p=2400:1001:4176923836234668::::F2400_P1001_BACK_PAGE,F2400_P1001_ARCHIVE_NUMBER,F2400_P1001_USE_ARCHIVE:1001,20100807.2680,Y; N. Wilson and M. G. Baker, "The Emerging Influenza Pandemic: Estimating the Case Fatality Ratio," *Eurosurveillance* 14, no. 26 (July 2, 2009), http://www.eurosurveillance.org/ViewArticle.aspx?ArticleId=19255.

10. World Health Organization, Global Alert and Response, "Disease Outbreak News [edited], Avian Influenza, Human (57): Indonesia, WHO Update 4," http://www.who.int/csr/don/2010_10_18/en/index.html.

11. Milan Brahmbhatt, *Avian Influenza: Economic and Social Impacts* (Washington, D.C.: World Bank, September 2005).

12. Garrett, "Next Pandemic."

13. U.S. Centers for Disease Control and Prevention, Global Health Partnerships, October 20, 2010, http://www.cdc.gov/globalhealth/partnerships.htm.

14. Klaus Stohr, "The Global Agenda on Influenza Surveillance and Control," *Vaccine* 21 (2003): 1745, 1747.

15. Jonathan Schwartz, R. Gregory Evans, and Sarah Greenberg, "Evolution of Health Provision in Pre-SARS China: The Changing Nature of Disease Prevention," *China Review* 7, no. 1 (Spring 2007): 81–104.

16. Jonathan Schwartz and R. Gregory Evans, "Causes of Effective Policy Implementation: China's Public Health Response to SARS," *Journal of Contemporary China* 16, no. 51 (2007): 195–213.

17. Centers for Disease Control and Prevention, "2009 H1N1 Early Outbreak and Disease Characteristics," July 12, 2010, http://www.cdc.gov/h1n1flu/surveillanceqa.htm.

18. Chen Yi-Chu et al., "Quarantine Methods and Prevention of Secondary Outbreak of Pandemic (H1N1) 2009," *Emerging Infectious Diseases* 16, no. 8 (2010), http://www.cdc.gov/eid/content/16/8/1300.htm.

19. For a more detailed description of the Department of Health and Human Services and where public health fits into it, see http://www.hhs.gov/about/orgchart/.

20. Centers for Disease Control and Prevention, "Practical Steps for SARS Legal Preparedness: Fact Sheet," September 26, 2003, http://www2a.cdc.gov/phlp/docs/SARSLegalPlanningFactsheetFinal.9.26.03.htm.

21. L. O. Gostin, S. Burris, and Z. Lazzarini, "The Law and the Public's Health: A Study of Infectious Disease Law in the United States," *Columbia Law Review* 99 (1999): 59–128.

22. N. Lurie, "Local Variation in Public Health Preparedness: Lessons from California," *Health Affairs* (Millwood), S1 Web Exclusives (2004), 341–53, http://content.healthaffairs.org/cgi/reprint/hlthaff.w4.341v1.pdf; Turning Point, "About Turning Point," 2006, http://www.turningpointprogram.org/Pages/about.html. Turning Point was an initiative, started in 1997, of the Robert Wood Johnson Foundation and the W. K. Kellogg Foundation.

23. Centers for Disease Control and Prevention, "Legal Authorities for Quarantine and Isolation," January 29, 2010, http://www.cdc.gov/quarantine/AboutLawsRegulationsQuarantineIsolation.html.

24. Since the terror attacks of 9/11, many states have brought their public health laws into line with the Model State Emergency Health Powers Act, giving themselves the right to invoke mandatory powers such as quarantine and isolation. See K. Taylor-Clark, R. Blendon, A. Zaslavsky, and J. Benson, "Confidence in Crisis? Understanding Trust in Government and Public Attitudes toward Mandatory Health Powers," *Biosecurity and Bioterrorism: Biodefense Strategy, Practice and Science* 3, no. 2 (2005).

25. Schwartz and Schwartz, "Confronting Global Pandemics," 199.

26. Ibid., 198–201.

27. Official at Chinese National Center for Disease Control and Emergency Response Office, interview on February 8, 2010, by Shawn Shieh on behalf of the Global Infectious Disease Response System Project, Chris Ansell, Ann Keller and Art Reingold (principal investigators). NSF Project #0826995. Interviewee names were withheld at the request of the interviewees.

28. See Schwartz and Schwartz, "Confronting Global Pandemics," for a detailed description of the Chinese response to SARS.

29. Official of USCDC, interview, Beijing, July 13, 2010.

30. Official at China national CDC disease control and emergency response office, interview, Beijing, February 8, 2010.

31. C. K. Lee, epidemiologist and team leader of communicable disease surveillance and response for World Health Organization office in Beijing, interview on January 19,

2010, by Shawn Shieh on behalf of the Global Infectious Disease Response System Project, Chris Ansell, Ann Keller, and Art Reingold, principal investigators, NSF Project #0826995.

32. USCDC officer, Joint U.S.-China CDC Field Training Epidemiology project, interview by Shawn Shieh on January 29, 2010, on behalf of the Global Infectious Disease Response System Project, Chris Ansell, Ann Keller, and Art Reingold, principal investigators, NSF Project #0826995.

33. The role of residents committees (also known as neighborhood committees) is discussed extensively by Benjamin Read and C. M. Chen, "The State's Evolving Relationship with Urban Society: China's Neighborhood Organizations in Comparative Perspective," in *Urban China in Transition*, edited by J. R. Logan (Oxford: Blackwell, 2008).

34. Ben Read, "State-Linked Associational Life: Illuminating Blind Spots of Existing Paradigms," in *Local Organizations and Urban Governance in East and Southeast Asia: Straddling State and Society*, edited by Benjamin L. Read and Robert Pekkanen (London: Routledge, 2009), chap. 1.

35. William F. Chappell, Richard G. Forgette, David A. Swanson, and Mark V. Van Boening, "Determinants of Government Aid to Katrina Survivors: Evidence from Survey Data," *Southern Economic Journal* 72, no. 2 (2007): 344–62.

36. The argument here is that in China, the residents committees have a long-term relationship with the state and can be relatively easily mobilized. They are also ubiquitous. By contrast, the Red Cross is both more independent and less ubiquitous. This holds true for faith-based organizations, which are further constrained by being individual and thus unable to mount significant, well-strategized responses.

37. Chinese government's official Web portal, Mass Media, April 13, 2010, http://english.gov.cn/2006-02/08/content_182637.htm.

38. Preeti Bhattacharji, Carin Zissis, and Corinne Baldwin, "Media Censorship in China," *Council on Foreign Relations*, May 27, 2010.

39. Frank Ching, "China's Media Censorship," *Korea Times*, July 9, 2006.

40. Ann-Marie Brady, *Marketing Dictatorship: Propaganda and Thought Work in Contemporary China* (Lanham, Md.: Rowman & Littlefield, 2008), 13–15.

41. Ibid., 18.

42. Ibid., 19–21.

43. Sendhil Mullainathan and Andrei Shleifer, "The Market for News," *American Economic Review* 95, no. 4 (2005): 1031–53.

44. Peter Vasterman, C. Joris Yzermans, and Anja J. E. Dirkzwager, "The Role of the Media and Media Hypes in the Aftermath of Disasters," *Epidemiologic Review* 27, no. 1 (2005), 107–14.

45. Senior official, USCDC, interview, Beijing, July 13, 2010.

46. World Health Organization, *International Health Regulations*, 2nd ed. (Geneva: World Health Organization, 2005).

47. Ibid., 62.

48. Official, China National CDC disease control and emergency response office, interview, February 8, 2010.

49. USCDC official, interview by Shawn Shieh, Beijing, January 21, 2010. Global Infectious Disease Response System Project. The discussion here is of the civilian public health system, which is distinct from the military system. If an outbreak were to occur on a military base with high hospitalization rates in military hospitals, this

information would not be provided directly to the Ministry of Health. Rather, it would travel up the stovepipe to the State Council, which would likely inform the ministry. This might delay any information sharing between China and its international partners.

50. C. K. Lee, interview, Beijing, January 19, 2010; USCDC official, interview, Beijing, January 29, 2010.

51. The first proposal of this version was presented in January 1998; see David Fidler and Lawrence Gostin, "The New International Health Regulations: An Historic Development for International Law and Public Health," *Journal of Law, Medicine and Ethics* 34, no. 1 (2006): 85–94.

52. Ibid.

53. C. K. Lee, interview, Beijing, January 19, 2010. The National IHR Focal Point is charged with maintaining a continuous official communication channel between the WHO and state parties. In addition to this legal requirement, the national IHR focal point will need to ensure the analysis of national public health risks in terms of international impact, participate in collaborative risk assessment with the WHO, advise senior health and other government officials regarding notification to the WHO and implementation of WHO recommendations, and distribute information to and coordinate input from several national sectors and government departments." See World Health Organization, Regional Office for South-East Asia, "New International Health Regulations: An Historic Development for International Law and Public Health," http://www.searo.who.int/EN/Section10/Section2362_12864.htm.

54. Fidler and Gostin, "New International Health Regulations," 85–94.

55. U.S. Department of Health and Human Services, "International Health Regulations (2005)," Global Health.gov, http://www.globalhealth.gov/ihr/#how.

56. Robin M. Williams Jr., *American Society: A Sociological Interpretation*, 3rd ed. (New York: Alfred A. Knopf, 1970); Shalom H. Schwartz, "Cultural Value Differences: Some Implications for Work," *Applied Psychology: An International Review* 48, no. 1 (1999): 23–47.

57. Ibid.

58. Shalom H. Schwartz, "Causes of Culture: National Differences in Cultural Embeddedness," in *Quod Erat Demonstrandum: From Herodotus' Ethnographic Journeys to Cross-Cultural Research*, edited by A. Gari and K. Mylonas (Athens: Pedio Books, 2009), 3.

59. Ibid.

60. Shalom H. Schwartz, personal communication, March 15, 2009.

61. Compared with the standard deviations across countries on the two orientations, China is an extraordinary 2.6 standard deviations above the mean on hierarchy and almost two standard deviations below the mean on egalitarianism.

62. World Values Survey 2010, May 25, 2010, available at www.worldvaluessurvey.org.

63. Ibid.

64. The Reporters without Borders survey evaluates a country's record of press freedom; see http://en.rsf.org.

65. Two professors of public health, interview, Beijing, May 2005; four public health officials, interview, Shanghai, June 2005; physician, interview, Nanjing, June 2005. The view of the Chinese party-state losing its capacity to function effectively in a variety of spheres is argued by MinXin Pei, *China's Trapped Transition* (Cambridge, Mass.: Harvard University Press, 2006), chapter 5. For a contrasting view, see David Shambaugh,

*China's Communist Party: Atrophy and Adaptation* (Berkeley: University of California Press, 2005), chap. 8.

66. K. Taylor-Clark, R. Blendon, A. Zaslavsky, and J. Benson, "Confidence in Crisis? Understanding Trust in Government and Public Attitudes toward Mandatory State Health Powers," *Biosecurity and Bioterrorism: Biodefense Strategy, Practice, and Science* 3, no. 2 (2005): 138–46.

67. "Planning for Pandemic Influenza: Lessons from the Experiences of Thirteen Indiana Counties," Regenstrief Center for Healthcare Engineering, Purdue University, 2008, http://www.bepress.com/cgi/viewcontent.cgi?article=1430&context=jhsem.

68. L. Kahn, *Who's in Charge: Leadership during Epidemics, Bioterror Attacks, and Other Public Health Crises* (Santa Barbara, Calif.: ABC-CLIO, 2009), 162.

69. Ibid., 78.

70. S. Horwitz, "Walmart to the Rescue: Private Enterprise's Response to Hurricane Katrina," St. Lawrence University, Canton, N.Y., 2008, http://myslu.stlawu.edu/~shorwitz/Papers/Wal-Mart_to_the_Rescue.pdf.

71. J. Sutton, "A Complex Organizational Adaptation to the World Trade Center Disaster: An Analysis of Faith-Based Organizations," 2003, http://www.colorado.edu/hazards/publications/sp/sp39/sept11book_ch16_sutton.pdf.

72. I. Lupu and R. Tuttle, "The Faith-Based Initiative and the Constitution," *DePaul Law Review* 55, no. 1 (2005).

73. USCDC official, interview, Beijing, July 23, 2010.

74. Ibid.

75. CCDC national office official, interview, February 8, 2010.

76. Kevin B. O'Reilly, "Mandating Physician Immunization," June 28, 2010, http://www.ama-assn.org/amednews/2010/06/28/prsm0628.htm.

# Chapter 8

# Safe Harbor in a Risky World? China's Approach to Managing Food Safety Risk

*Elizabeth Wishnick*

With its booming, export-oriented economy, China typically is viewed as an engine of economic globalization. Transnational linkages also affect the Chinese state, however, by making it vulnerable to a wide range of new hazards, such as food safety risks, that arise as the unanticipated consequences of economic development. This chapter addresses Chinese risk management in the context of ongoing debates about China's contribution to global governance. After outlining the 2008 scandal over melamine contamination in milk in China, the paper examines the international response. It is argued that Chinese governmental practices pose unique challenges to food safety risk management. Three dimensions are examined: government-business relations, the role of information in risk management, and state-society relations.

Although food safety is a Chinese domestic policy concern, the globalization of the food and drug industries and China's emergence as a key player within these sectors have put the safety of Chinese food and pharmaceutical products on the foreign policy agenda of the United States and other countries. This was brought home in 2008 when at least eighty-one Americans died after taking Chinese-made counterfeit heparin, a blood-thinning drug made from pig intestines. In a July 2011 report, the U.S. Food and Drug Administration asserted that "the safety of America's imports of food and medical products remains under serious threat" as our reliance on imports from China, Mexico, and other countries far outpaces our capacity to monitor them.[1] Food safety issues have become a subject of United States–China diplomacy, providing new avenues for cooperation and creating new irritants in relations. Accordingly, this chapter also examines the role of international organizations, the United States, and other countries in managing food safety risks originating from China.

## China and Global Governance in a Changing World Order

China's role in the global order has been the subject of considerable debate in both the United States and China. More than five years ago, former deputy secretary of state Robert Zoellick challenged China to become "a responsible stakeholder." According to Zoellick, because China benefited from its involvement with the international community, now that it has emerged in a much strengthened position, the Chinese government has the responsibility to contribute to the resolution of global problems.[2] After initially focusing on economic integration (pursuing membership in the World Trade Organization and Asian regional economic groupings), over the past decade China has taken a series of important new steps such as expanding its role in United Nations peacekeeping operations and enhancing its soft power by establishing 400 Confucius Institutes in 108 countries that provide funding to promote study of the Chinese language and culture. In January 2010, China participated for the first time in a multinational naval effort to combat piracy off the coast of Somalia.

China's growing global engagement has led some American scholars to suggest that China could play a leading role, along with the United States, in solving the world's problems. Such a group of two (G-2) would give China a new role as "a legitimate architect" of the emerging economic order[3] and encourage China's more active involvement in conflict resolution in the Middle East and the Korean Peninsula.[4] Elizabeth Economy and Adam Segal argue, however, that the need for United States–China bilateral cooperation does not alter the fact that the international community must cooperate multilaterally to address some of the challenges posed by China itself on a range of global issues, including climate change and food safety.[5]

Some observers contend that, as China becomes more integrated regionally and globally, greater convergence between Chinese attitudes and Western norms about the use of force and other key security issues will develop. Others caution, however, that China's greater global engagement may have limited effects and may not be indicative of emerging agreement on standards of international behavior.[6] Finally, some analysts question whether integration in the liberal order will meet the needs of rising powers such as China, which may seek to fashion the international system in their own image.[7] Some scholars argue, for example, that the Chinese leadership is promoting its own values, a "Beijing Consensus" that would supplant the Washington Consensus, predicated on the belief of the superiority of a free market economy and a democratic political system.[8] In the wake of the 2008 financial crisis, critical statements made by some Chinese officials who questioned the wisdom of continued reliance on the U.S. economic model and the dollar lent credence to the viewpoint that China is advancing an alternative agenda.[9]

Although China is dissatisfied with what it perceives as U.S. hegemony in world affairs, what role China proposes to play remains unclear. Despite new signs of multilateral political and security engagement, China continues to place an emphasis on bilateral relationships to solve global and regional problems. This stems from the state-centric view of global politics that dominates Chinese policy analysis, despite the recognition of the increasing importance of transnational security threats and nonstate actors. Moreover, some Chinese observers are skeptical about the ulterior motives of global governance, which they see as seeking to institutionalize Western values and interests in the guise of developing frameworks and institutions to resolve global problems.[10]

The Chinese leadership's conception of a "harmonious world" has been promoted both to reassure the West of Beijing's peaceful intentions and to propose an alternative world order, one more in keeping with China's preferences for domestic and international governance. Chinese officials assert that their vision for a "harmonious world" presupposes a democratic international system, which they understand to mean the promotion of open and fair multilateral mechanisms for economic and collective security, respect for a diversity of political systems, and noninterference in the domestic affairs of other countries.[11] This concept of a "harmonious world" is fundamental to China's vision for the Shanghai Cooperation Organization (SCO), for example, the regional security organization that includes China, Russia, and the Central Asian states. The SCO rejects efforts to impose Western political frameworks—which the group calls "the export of development models"—and seeks instead to protect the diversity of civilizational approaches and promote "harmonious development."[12]

Although China shares many of the problems of developing states, as the world's second-largest economy it has emerged as a key player in the Group of Twenty (G-20). For Cui Liru, president of the China Institute of Contemporary International Relations, the eclipse of the "old dominating mechanism of the G-7 (-8)" and increasing prominence of the G-20 shows that a new, more balanced global governance mechanism is emerging.[13]

Chinese scholars have noted, however, that the more cooperative and multipolar world order poses additional challenges for their country, because China's leaders now must decide how and when to use their country's growing economic power globally.[14] This will require trade-offs, such as balancing Chinese global interests with those of the developing world. However, as the December 2009 Copenhagen summit highlighted, the growing divide on climate change between developing countries with larger and smaller economies makes it difficult for China to claim it speaks for the developing world as a whole.

Chinese leaders recognize that building a harmonious world will be no easy task, given the complicated mix of development, traditional security, and nontraditional security challenges their country faces. As the 2008 Chinese government white paper on defense explained, China faces unprecedented opportunities for peaceful development, economic globalization, and mutually beneficial economic cooperation, but also continues to confront traditional and nontraditional security threats. To cope with the latter, the white paper states that China would enhance its military capabilities as well as its national emergency management system, developed to respond to natural disasters and nontraditional security risks.[15]

In the face of unprecedented opportunities and challenges, China will hold high the banner of peace, development and cooperation, persist in taking the road of peaceful development, pursue the opening-up strategy of mutual benefit, and promote the building of a harmonious world with enduring peace and common prosperity; and it will persist in implementing the Scientific Outlook on Development in a bid to achieve integration of development with security, persist in giving due consideration to both traditional and non-traditional security issues, enhancing national strategic capabilities, and perfecting the national emergency management system.

In contrast to Western views, which emphasize the role of nonstate actors and transnational pressures, Chinese perspectives on nontraditional security emphasize the continued need for the state to provide protection for society against human security threats as well as the continued importance of maintaining sovereignty in the face of such challenges.[16] In light of a series of national emergencies in recent years, such as the 2003 severe acute respiratory syndrome (SARS) crisis, the 2008 Sichuan earthquake, and the 2008 melamine crisis, Chinese scholars and policymakers have begun to discuss the importance of public administration and risk management in disaster response.[17]

The concept of social risk first emerged in the 1980s in the work of European social theorists. The German sociologist Ulrich Beck pioneered the concept of a "world risk society" that he saw arising as a result of the unintended environmental consequences of rapid economic change.[18] In Beck's view, risk is both driven by increasing wealth (the ecological damage caused by the industrialization process and excess consumerism) and directly related to poverty (in terms of inadequate access to resources and their unsustainable use).[19] Because the dual nature of risk speaks to the development challenges that China now faces, scholars inside and outside China have turned to the concept of risk to capture the nontraditional security challenges that emerge from the modernization process itself.[20] For the Chinese government, managing risk requires hard choices, given that the very development process that creates risks for society is viewed as a priority for state security. Moreover, unlike Western societies that were the focus of the studies of social risk by European scholars, Chinese society has much less autonomy to respond to risk.

The Chinese government has focused on addressing the risks associated with poverty, and international agencies such as the World Bank credit its leaders with lifting half a billion people out of poverty from 1981 to 2004.[21] Given the challenge of poverty reduction in China and its large rural population, until recently the Chinese government has focused on achieving security of grain supplies to ensure food security, safeguard social stability, and avoid dependence on foreign imports, rather than on reducing food safety risk. However, the decentralization of the food industry in China and its inadequate regulation have exacerbated food safety risk for Chinese and foreign consumers alike.

Although China participates in many global efforts to improve food safety, as we will see in the 2008 case of milk contamination, Chinese government practices are at odds with global norms of transparency and accountability in food safety, with detrimental consequences for domestic consumers and a globalized food chain. In keeping with its understanding of a democratic world order as meaning opposition to interference in its domestic affairs, China's reluctance to release or publicize information about food safety incidents creates new challenges for global governance of food safety.

## Case Study: The 2008 Melamine Crisis Reexamined

On September 10, 2008, just after the close of the Beijing Olympics, China's official news agency reported that Sanlu Group, a state-owned enterprise and the largest seller of baby milk powder in China, was being investigated after infants in Gansu province developed kidney stones from drinking the product.[22] Intermediaries had laced the milk with melamine, a compound found in plastics and fertilizers. At the time, milk in China was tested for nitrogen to assess its protein content and the addition of melamine artificially boosted the amount of nitrogen found in the milk.[23]

Sanlu initially denied responsibility, then undertook a partial recall of 8,210 tons of milk powder produced prior to August 6. China's Ministry of Health initiated a total recall on September 13, prompting Sanlu to issue an apology.[24] China's top leaders then took an unusual series of steps to reassure the public. Free checkups for affected children and hotlines for parents were promised, President Hu Jintao visited a dairy farm to emphasize the need for vigilance about food safety, and Premier Wen Jiabao pledged a major government effort over the next two years to address food safety issues.[25] After apologizing on behalf of the government, Premier Wen promised: "We will never let the same situation repeat with any kind of food product,"[26] a promise that has proved impossible to keep.

More than three years after the Sanlu crisis first broke, melamine continues to be found in Chinese dairy products, despite the actions pledged by Chinese leaders and officials. In April 2011, Chinese police seized 26 tons of milk powder produced in Inner Mongolia and then resold to two other companies for use in ice cream because the product was contaminated with melamine.[27] In January 2010, Chinese authorities closed down one of the companies implicated in the 2008 scandal, Shanghai Panda Dairy

Company, when melamine was found again in its products.[28] This followed the arrest just two weeks before of three executives in a Shaanxi province dairy company that produced melamine-tainted milk powder.[29]

Ironically, as a "major brand," Sanlu had been exempt from quality control inspections and the quality of its products had just been showcased on *Weekly Quality Report*, a television program sponsored by China's quality control agency, the Administration of Quality Supervision, Inspection, and Quarantine (AQSIQ).[30] Ultimately twenty-two Chinese companies, including other leading brands such as Mengniu, Yili, and Bright Dairy, were implicated in the scandal, which sickened 294,000 Chinese children, killing six.[31] In the wake of the 2008 scandal, AQSIQ eliminated inspection exemptions for so-called "major brands" and its director resigned. A leading group on food safety was formed within the State Council, which launched a national investigation of Chinese milk products.[32] New safety and quality standards were also introduced for dairy products and animal feed.[33]

For her company's part in the scandal, Sanlu chairwoman and Shijiazhuang Party Secretary Tian Wenhua was fired, along with more than 36 other local party and state officials. Tian was ultimately sentenced to life in prison, and two intermediaries received death sentences for selling melamine-laced milk to the dairy companies. It became clear at Tian's trial that the company had been receiving complaints about the milk since 2007 and that she knew about the melamine contamination since at least May 2008.[34]

## The International Response to the Melamine Crisis

Dairy products constitute a small proportion of the food the United States imports from China, and mostly involve ingredients derived from milk, such as the casein substances used in coffee creamers, sports drinks, and power bars. Although in general the United States exports more food to China than it imports, China now is the third largest source of agricultural and seafood imports to the United States, after Canada and Mexico. The globalization of the food industry has proved to be a considerable challenge for the U.S. Food and Drug Administration (FDA), which is responsible for monitoring 80 percent of U.S. food imports. Typically the FDA inspects only 1 percent of these imports due to budget constraints.[35] From 2001 to 2007, only 33 Chinese food producers were inspected, out of a total of 1,034 inspections worldwide.[36] According to the FDA, it would cost more than $3 billion (approximately $16,700 per inspection) to inspect the

189,900 overseas facilities that produce and process foods destined for the U.S. market.[37] This is simply not feasible, considering that the FDA's entire fiscal year 2008 budget for food protection came to just $620 million.

In response to the concerns over melamine contamination in Chinese milk products, the FDA announced on November 13, 2008 that no Chinese milk products would be allowed into the United States until China could certify that they were free from melamine contamination.[38] The FDA has the right to refuse foreign shipments of foods that violate American safety standards. In fiscal year 2006, the United States refused 0.15 percent of Chinese food products, with seafood products constituting half of the 700 refused shipments. The Chinese government has interpreted the relatively low refusal rate as an indication that 99 percent of China's products are safe, although this does not take account of the extremely small proportion of inspected goods.[39]

Although the Chinese government assured Japan that no goods containing contaminated milk were exported to Japan, several companies found evidence of melamine in various types of pastries and other foods imported from China.[40] This led to product recalls and prompted two major Japanese food companies to suspend imports of Chinese milk products entirely. Coming just after a dispute over tainted dumplings imported from China in early 2008, the melamine contamination demonstrated that food safety was becoming an increasingly problematic issue in China-Japan relations.[41]

In the European Union, all imports of Chinese baby food containing milk products were banned. The EU also called for tests on all products containing more than 15 percent milk powder, even though European imports of such foods are relatively limited.[42] However, other polities found evidence of melamine in a much wider range of foods. In the last quarter of 2008 alone, Hong Kong reported contaminated fish feed and eggs; the United States complained of melamine in hog feed; and, after testing Chinese ingredients used in a wide range of processed foods, Malaysia found evidence of melamine in baking powder. Previously, in 2007 China had already admitted to problems with melamine in pet food.[43]

## Governmentality and Risk Management: State-Society Relations in China and Response to Global Risks

One of the more contradictory aspects of the Chinese government's response to food safety, environmental, and health risks has been its effort to involve society in resolving such risks,[44] while simultaneously increasing controls on the nongovernmental organizations (NGOs), public interest lawyers, journalists, and Netizens who are trying to call attention to these hazards. Scholars disagree about the degree to which the Chinese government is prepared to grant society a role in addressing the country's problems. Shaoguang Wang from the Chinese University of Hong Kong argues, for example, that the Chinese public is increasingly involved in agenda setting, to the point that the Chinese political system can no longer be called authoritarian.[45] Steve Tsang contends, however, that government responsiveness to public demands demonstrates the Chinese leadership's intent to retain control by preempting threats to political stability, a system he terms "consultative Leninism."[46] Within mainland China, scholars note the limited latitude that NGOs enjoy with respect to the state, although some argue that the NGOs and the government may have complementary interests.[47] A study by Kang Xiaoguang of Renmin University and Hang Heng of Zhengzhou University found that the Chinese government imposes "graduated controls" over NGOs depending on the degree to which individual groups are believed to benefit society or challenge the state.[48]

Michel Foucault coined the term "governmentality" to refer to the evolving process of redefining "what is within the competence of the state and what is not, the public versus the private."[49] In his view, the empowerment of civil society does not necessarily entail the weakening of state power. For Foucault, government involves more than assertions of sovereignty. Like the captain of a ship sailing in dangerous waters, the state's ultimate purpose is to find safe harbor and ensure the welfare of the population. To safeguard the population, the government relies on its own regulatory capacity and the support of institutions and groups outside the state, acquires information about emerging risks, and develops a security apparatus.[50]

As Nikolas Rose notes, part of the rationality of government is to evaluate what issues it should be responsible for and what should fall into the purview of firms, institutions, and localities. Accordingly, such groups are increasingly being asked to take responsibility for risk management.[51] Thus, a division of labor may develop where elements of society perform certain functions on behalf of the state and address particular risks. This does not mean that the Chinese state retreats as the role of nonstate actors increases. Instead, the state regroups and responds to the environment in new ways.[52] In the case of China, however, unlike in Western democracies,[53] it is much more difficult to argue that the empowerment of society reflects the rationality of government. In China, where society is state-led,[54] the Chinese Communist leadership typically interprets the independent exercise of power by groups within society as a challenge to its rule and seeks to coopt organizations such as NGOs, labor unions, entrepreneurs, and religious communities to prevent them from being separated from state control.

The following discussion explores the relationship between China's governmentality and its management of food safety risk during the 2008 melamine crisis. Four dimensions of Chinese governmentality are considered here: government-business relations, the role of information in risk management, and the roles of Chinese and international society in risk awareness. A concluding section examines the implications for United States–China relations.

## Government-Business Relations

In food safety, market factors constrain risk management. The Chinese food industry is increasingly a mix of state and private actors, all responding to market pressures. Moreover, the expansion of the role of the market has set limits on the government's ability to mobilize and implement new directives in response to a crisis.

The Chinese dairy sector has been booming in recent years, now that China's burgeoning middle class has discovered the health benefits of milk drinking. China is the world's third largest producer of milk, much of it generated by small companies struggling to remain competitive.[55] The Chinese dairy industry is remarkably fragmented and decentralized, involving a combination of public and private, large-scale and small-scale businesses engaged in fierce competition with one another.[56] Millions of small-scale farmers sell their product to intermediaries who collect the milk and then sell it to producers.[57] Chinese government regulations have been calling for consolidation of dairy firms, but the market share belonging to the ten largest processors declined from 50 percent in 2003 to 40 percent in 2008, with the rest divided among hundreds of smaller, less profitable firms.[58] The increased competition has benefited the larger producers, which earn the lion's share of profit and attract foreign investors.

Chinese analyses of the 2008 melamine crisis link food safety problems to the increasingly marketized economy and proliferation of small-scale producers. In the 2008 case, intermediaries competing for market share added melamine to hide the poor quality of their milk and boost sales, although it is unclear whether farmers actively connived with these brokers to receive a higher price for their milk.

To create a more stable market, increase overall profitability, and pool the costs involved in improving safety, a group of scholars at Renmin University advocated the formation of dairy cooperatives.[59] They note that currently 65 percent of milk producers are household farms and that 80 percent have between one and five cows.[60] According to a quality control official from Hebei Province, a key milk-producing region, small-scale producers face numerous disincentives that dissuade the majority from having their products inspected.[61] Western analysts note, however, that practices at China's large-scale factory livestock farms also present a wide range of threats to food safety due to the prevalence of poor environmental conditions, contaminated water and soil, and unsafe use of veterinary additives in sick animals.[62] In general, Chinese scholars urge their government to take a more comprehensive, "farm-to-table" approach to food safety, monitoring sites of food production in addition to inspecting final products.[63]

Foreign analysts focus, conversely, on the challenges to food safety caused by the state's involvement in the economy. Coverage of the melamine crisis noted that overlapping political and business responsibilities created disincentives for reporting food safety problems, especially during the Olympics, because the chairman and general manager of Sanlu, the state-owned company at the center of the crisis, also served as party secretary of Shijiazhuang, the city where the company was located and employed 10,000 people.[64] In terms of food safety regulation, foreign experts note that China has sought to improve government practices, but that producers and suppliers throughout the food industry also must be involved in food safety. Instead of being fully responsible for food safety, the Chinese government should work with food producers and suppliers, which need to be encouraged to play a bigger role.[65]

*Information and Risk Management*

The Chinese government has been inconsistent in its position on the role of information in risk management. After the 2003 SARS crisis, the Chinese government appeared chastened about the need to provide greater information on public health emergencies. New legislative reporting requirements were instituted, scholars urged improved flows of information to the public, and legislation granting the public the right to know—that is, to request and receive information from the government about issues of public concern—was passed on May 1, 2008.

On April 29, 2010, the Chinese legislature amended the state secrets law, a move that the official news agency characterized as promoting transparency by standardizing classification procedures. However, the law also strengthens requirements for Web-based companies to report leaks of state secrets, part of a series of recent legal measures the government aimed at preventing the Internet and cell phones from being used to spread information considered politically or socially harmful.[66] Indeed, political considerations continue to impede the public's right to know, as the scandal over melamine-tainted milk showed. As evidence of a problem with the milk supply mounted in the spring and summer of 2008, Chinese authorities quashed reporting of the issue due to their desire to avoid unfavorable publicity in the run-up to the Olympics, and only publicly acknowledged the problem after the games concluded.[67]

Chinese consumers often lack the knowledge to make informed decisions about the quality of products and, consequently, it may take considerable time before they realize that there is a safety problem.[68] In the 2008 melamine case, again, local media followed up on initial complaints about tainted milk products in June and July 2008, but then faced pressure by central party authorities to cease publishing such negative stories in the months leading up to the 2008 Olympics.[69] National news outlets such as Xinhua did not report the problem until after the Olympics, and then only after the New Zealand government had raised the issue on September 9.[70]

Chinese experts agree that consumers need to be informed more clearly about product safety, although they disagree on the mechanisms required. Some advocate a greater governmental role in establishing a database on food safety and developing an early warning system.[71] According to Zhao Naiji, a Guangzhou scholar, the government must protect consumers from opportunistic producers characteristic of a market economy, who may withhold safety information in order to get a better price for their products.[72] Nonetheless, he notes that overlapping responsibility for food safety by multiple agencies (the Ministry of Agriculture, the Ministry of Commerce, and the Ministry of Health, as well as AQSIQ) often leads to conflicts of interest, resulting in difficulties sharing information within the government, let alone with the public.[73] Others suggest that establishing a small group within the government to deal with food safety crises would improve its ability to collect and distribute information.[74] Such bodies have been set up since the melamine crisis, with inconclusive results. In 2009, a

National Food Safety Rectification Office, headed by Health Minister Chen Zhu, was established. A Food Safety Commission, chaired by Vice Premier Li Keqiang, also was created under the State Council in February 2010.[75]

The Chinese government response to recent food safety crises has emphasized improved official oversight, but some scholars contend that the media also can play a useful role in informing the public about food safety. An analysis of media coverage in Shanghai during three major food safety incidents—the 2001 mooncake-filling controversy, the 2004 powdered milk scandal, and the 2008 melamine crisis—found a lack of in-depth reporting, predominant reliance on government sources, and a focus on government remedies.[76] Noting the tendency of the Chinese media to accentuate the positive (*baoxi bu baoyou*), the study found fault with coverage of the food safety incidents for failing to involve expert analyses or adequately address the plight of victims.[77]

According to the authors, the media play a powerful role in the discussion of food safety—they can publicize information that is useful to the public but can also affect the fortunes of an entire industry or cause panic. Because coverage tends to emphasize government efforts to combat food safety problems and relies to a large extent on government sources, the study notes that, in practice, media coverage of such incidents typically serves two main purposes: crisis control and image control for the government.[78] As the authors point out, however, greater transparency in the media and multifaceted discussion involving input from experts and the public would help prevent future food safety crises from occurring.[79]

*The Role of Chinese Society in Risk Awareness*

Although risk theorists typically predict a societal upsurge against behavior that causes risk, in practice Chinese society faces many constraints in calling attention to food safety issues. As was noted above, the Chinese government limits press coverage of food safety incidents, leaving the public with inadequate information to make informed consumer choices and providing disincentives for companies to self-regulate.[80]

After the 2008 melamine crisis, some families of sick children filed suit, but the Chinese government pressured judges and lawyers not to take on product liability cases linked to the incident.[81] Some 3,000 of the plaintiffs accepted a $160 million (1.1 billion yuan) out-of-court settlement from the dairy companies ($29,200 for the death of a child, $4,000 for children who developed kidney stones or acute kidney failure, and $300 for children who suffered less severe symptoms).[82] A group of 550 parents petitioned the government to research the long-term health consequences of melamine exposure.[83] Others pressed on with civil suits against these firms as well as the retailers who sold their products, but only six of these cases had been accepted by late November 2009, and hearings were later postponed indefinitely.

Frustrated by the mainland system of justice, some claimants then filed suit in the United States and Hong Kong, but their suits and claims were rejected in both instances.[84] As one disappointed parent told the *South China Morning Post*, there would not be such food safety incidents if mainland residents "could seek justice from a fair and open legal system and the perpetrators were properly punished."[85] Although twenty-one people were convicted and two were executed for their role in the melamine scandal, Li Changjiang, the former head of AQSIQ, was appointed to a new, high-level position just fifteen months after being dismissed over his agency's handling of the melamine issue.[86] There are very few NGOs representing the rights of consumers or organizations encouraging industry to adopt best practices. One of the more established groups, the China Consumers Association (CCA), founded in 1984, is a national, state-organized NGO with 3,000 branch offices. The CCA promotes corporate social responsibility and assists the public with product liability cases. According to the group's annual report, in 2008 it received 638,477 complaints and obtained RMB 661.8 million ($98.5 million) in compensation for victims. Regarding food safety, the CCA claims to have conducted some investigations of problematic milk powder manufacturers, participated in testing of milk products, and commented on the food safety law.[87]

However, the Chinese authorities have sought to limit society-led efforts to address food safety incidents. On July 17, 2009, alleging violations of nonprofit law, Chinese authorities closed the Open Constitution Initiative (Gongmeng), which helped parents of sick children ultimately receive more compensation than initially proposed by the government. The group was assessed a huge bill of 1.42 million yuan ($207,900) for alleged late payment of taxes and its leaders were briefly detained.[88] A few months later, on November 13, Zhao Lianhai, a parent of a child sickened by melamine-laced milk, was detained by the Beijing police after setting up a Web site, "Home for Kidney Stone Babies," and organizing an online parental support group, "Milk Powder Group," on a popular social networking Web site. In March 2010, Zhao was tried for "creating a disturbance,"[89] and, on November 10, was finally sentenced to two and a half years for "inciting social disorder" through his Web site, his meetings with journalists, and his efforts to organize other affected parents.[90] As the above discussion shows, there were real limits to the accountability of the Chinese government to society in the aftermath of the 2008 melamine contamination scandal. Autonomous actions by individuals and groups were stymied, and only state-led efforts to provide a one-time settlement and information were tolerated and produced any redress for the victims.

### International Society and Food Safety in China

In the 2008 melamine crisis, international actors played a key role in informing Chinese and global publics. Fonterra, the New Zealand minority shareholder in Sanlu, first expressed concern to its local partners about milk contamination on August 2, 2008. When company officials failed to inform local authorities in Hebei Province, Fonterra raised the issue with the New Zealand embassy. Unfortunately for milk drinkers, Fonterra's warning came during the lead-up to the 2008 Olympic Games, when the Chinese Communist Party requested caution in reporting food safety issues.[91] Once New Zealand officials completed further investigations, they informed Prime Minister Helen Clark on September 5, who then directly informed the central government in Beijing on September 9.[92] The New Zealand government's role as a whistleblower was never reported in the Chinese media, however.[93] Fonterra, which had a good record for food safety in New Zealand, then found itself the target of criticism at home and (unsuccessful) lawsuits by Chinese victims.[94] The value of its shares plummeted and, once Sanlu went bankrupt, the New Zealand partner ended up having to write off the joint venture as a $200 million loss.[95] Although the company defended its behavior against accusations of being slow to respond, insisting it was following established procedures by going through channels and notifying the local partner first, Fonterra later contributed $8.4 million to a Chinese charity providing health care for mothers and infants in rural areas.[96]

Other major international brands—such as Cadbury, Lipton, Kraft, Mars, and Lotte—had to recall products made with Chinese milk. Some thirty countries, including the United States and the European Union, banned products containing milk or milk powder from China until exporters could demonstrate they were free of melamine. The Chinese government criticized the bans at a meeting of the World Trade Organization, arguing that they had no rational basis.[97] Indeed, developing countries often claim that food safety has become a nontariff barrier to trade because developed states falsely raise food safety issues to protect their domestic industries.[98]

Given the high cost and frequent incidence of recalls of Chinese products, some U.S. business analysts suggest that it is the international outsourcing manufacturers and importing companies that should act to ensure product safety. For example, in 2007 Mattel had to recall 21 million Chinese-made toys when they were found to contain lead-based paint, at a cost of $110 million. Other companies paid millions in settlements connected to the crisis that same year over melamine contamination in pet food.[99] Consequently, it would be more cost effective for outsourcing firms and importers to set up product safety units to develop standards, instruct subcontractors in quality control, restrict the common practice of further outsourcing by Chinese partners, and constantly monitor quality.[100]

International organizations such as the World Health Organization (WHO) and the Food and Agriculture Organization (FAO) also play an important role in promoting information-sharing and setting global standards for food safety, but their impact depends on timely response and compliance. For example, once Chinese and foreign media began covering the 2008 melamine crisis, the WHO asked Chinese authorities for information. The Chinese government promptly provided the requested information through the International Food Safety Authorities Network (INFOSAN).[101] Nonetheless, the information the Chinese government supplied the WHO showed that complaints had been registered about melamine in Chinese milk products at least since December 2007—nine months before the crisis broke.[102]

Moreover, the 2008 milk crisis revealed confusion in many countries about acceptable levels of melamine. Food safety agencies published conflicting guidelines about maximum levels requiring actions such as import bans or recalls. This demonstrated the need for further harmonization of scientific standards for food safety through the auspices of the Codex Alimentarius Commission, created in 1963 by the FAO and the WHO to establish codes of practice for food safety.[103] It took another two years—until July 2010—for the Codex Alimentarius Commission to agree on common standards for melamine in foods.[104] Chinese analysts note the importance of standardization and admit that their country is lagging in this area. According to research sponsored by the Chinese government published in 2010, currently only 40 percent of China's national food safety standards are in accord with international standards.[105]

It is also up to international organizations to hold China accountable for meeting those standards. Human Rights Watch sharply criticized the WHO and the International Olympics Committee for asserting in a 2010 report, *The Health Legacy of the 2008 Olympic Games*, that China should be praised because "no major outbreak of food-borne disease occurred during the Beijing Olympics." Despite the ongoing cover-up of the melamine crisis at the time of the Olympics and the subsequent repression of activists who sought compensation for the victims, the report calls China's handling of the Olympics "an instructive example of how mass events can be organized to promote health in a value-added way."[106]

## Implications for the United States

At a time when China has been trying to expand its soft power, regular food and product safety crises have had a negative impact on perceptions of Chinese brands. A Fortune/Interbrand survey taken in the United States after the melamine crisis found that two-thirds of respondents agreed with the statement that "the 'made in China' label hurt Chinese brands" due to perceptions of their low quality.[107] Even before the 2008 milk crisis, in the wake of recalls of products from China (poisoned toothpaste, pet food laced with melamine, contaminated seafood, and toys laden with lead paint), a Zogby poll of 4,508 Americans found that only 30 percent believed that Chinese food products were safe to eat, while 82 percent said they were concerned about purchasing Chinese goods due to the numerous media reports about poor product and food safety.[108]

An Associated Press/Ispos poll found that most respondents (79 percent) blamed the Chinese government for product safety problems and 64 percent said that China bore the greatest responsibility for these issues. Nonetheless, 75 percent said that the U.S. government was also to blame and 71 percent responded that consumers looking for the lowest price were at fault as well.[109] Thus Chinese food safety issues have become both a domestic and a foreign policy problem for the United States.

In December 2008, in response to criticism of its performance from Congress, the Government Accountability Office, and the public, the FDA issued a food protection plan to improve food safety and food defense, which enabled the agency to open three new offices in China staffed by 13 employees.[110] The Obama administration has sought to improve food safety in the United States and on January 11, 2011 signed the Food Safety Modernization Law, which imposes tougher standards on producers and calls for more extensive inspections (although the latter also would require increasing FDA funding levels at a time of overall budgetary constraint).

In addition to improving domestic food safety, U.S. policymakers have expanded cooperation with China in this area. After the May 2007 scandal about melamine in imports of Chinese-made pet food, food safety began to be discussed at the meetings of the United States-China Strategic Economic Dialogue. U.S. Treasury secretary Henry Paulson, who cochaired the meetings, called product and food safety the "No. 1 issue" on the agenda, which also included other highly contentious issues such as the exchange rate of the renminbi and the U.S. trade deficit with China.[111] Concerns over Chinese food safety only serve to exacerbate U.S. dissatisfaction with cheap Chinese imports and their successful challenges to better-quality (but higher-priced) U.S. products.

These initial discussions on food safety paved the way for the U.S. Department of Health and Human Services and China's AQSIQ to sign a bilateral agreement on food safety in December 2007. The agreement established mechanisms for information sharing on key Chinese food imports to the United States, including pet food, wheat gluten, corn gluten, low-acid canned foods, and farm-raised fish, as well as on U.S. food exports to China.[112] The agreement also set up a tracking system for containers of Chinese food products bound for the United States and a detention list of potentially risky products. Both sides are required to notify each other within 48 hours of a suspected food safety threat.[113] Moreover, U.S. food safety experts have been working with their Chinese counterparts to help China meet U.S. food safety standards, conducting training programs and helping China establish food additive standards and food safety analysis practices.[114]

In March 2008, six months before the melamine crisis became public, the U.S. Department of Health and Human Services, the FDA, and China's AQSIQ met in Beijing to map out an agenda for action. Because they decided that their initial priority was farm-raised fish (China is the second largest supplier of seafood for the U.S. market), the new agreement did not have an impact on the September 2008 melamine crisis. According to the original timetable established in March 2008, the United States planned to conduct a fact-finding mission prior to the opening of the 2008 Olympics in August, gaining a more thorough understanding of the regulatory environment in China. Based on this assessment, the U.S. side would then conduct training for Chinese officials in the fall of 2008. However, by that time, the melamine crisis was already in full swing.[115]

Nonetheless, the FDA took a series of unilateral steps to protect U.S. consumers from tainted milk products. Immediately after the Chinese government revealed the presence of melamine in locally produced infant formula, on September 12, 2008, the FDA issued a health information advisory. This was followed by a temporary ban on Chinese milk products on November 13 and the November 27 recall of items containing Chinese dairy products, including cookies, candy, cocoa, and pet snacks.[116] In issuing its advisories and recalls, the FDA was acting on information publicly provided by the Chinese government to its own media and the WHO, not in response to any early warning that should have been provided bilaterally according to the terms of the 2007 United States–China agreement.

## Conclusion

Beginning with the SARS crisis in 2003, the Chinese leadership has become increasingly aware of the need to manage nontraditional security risks, including food safety. Nonetheless, the Chinese government faces difficult trade-offs between state security and risk management due to the relationship between state and society in China. As the international community debates China's future role in global governance, it is important to bear in mind that Chinese governmental practices constrain its ability to respond effectively to emergencies at home and limit its participation in global efforts to manage transnational risks. Its unique patterns of government-business relations, as well as efforts to control information flows about food safety incidents and to restrict Chinese citizens from taking action about them, create particular challenges for food safety risk management.

The private sector within the Chinese food industry is made up of a large number of small producers and intermediaries, who typically are beyond the reach of the state's regulatory apparatus. Although larger state-owned firms should be better regulated, in the 2008 melamine scandal, Sanlu, a large state-owned company, also escaped scrutiny, on the strength of its brand and the political position of its chairwoman. Moreover, contrary to the predictions of the literature on risk, in China the media and society cannot be counted on to demand that the government address food safety hazards. Although the Chinese government recognizes the principle of the public's "right to know," in practice concerns over the negative consequences of revelations about food safety problems for social stability, the reputation of Chinese brands, and even the legitimacy of the Chinese government lead Chinese authorities to restrict investigative reporting of food safety incidents. News of the melamine crisis, falling right at the time of the 2008 Olympics, would have provided the exact opposite of the message the Chinese government was seeking to promote at the time about the safety of food for athletes and visitors. Subsequent attempts by melamine victims to call attention to their plight also demonstrated the unwillingness of the Chinese government to tolerate any independent activity to achieve compensation, other than those arrangements proposed by Chinese authorities or groups working with them.

International society has played a role in demanding greater transparency and regulation, but such efforts have largely been reactive rather than preventive, partly due to their inability to obtain needed advance warnings, but also due to the apparent reluctance of foreign partners such as Fonterra to press China for needed information and of international organizations to criticize China's handling of food safety incidents. Consequently, for countries like the United States, which depends on food imports from China, the issue of food safety risk management is likely to remain a prominent one on the bilateral agenda. Food safety has proved already to be an irritant in China's relations with the United States and other countries and has diminished the global appeal of Chinese brands. Nonetheless, bilateral measures alone may be insufficient to address food safety risk from China. Given the increasing globalization of the food chain, global food processors must do more to ensure the safety of their ingredients. This will require expanded inspection of food imports by industry and governments, improved domestic regulation of the food industry in the United States and other countries, as well as more effective efforts to engage China multilaterally on food safety issues.

## Notes

1. U.S. Food and Drug Administration, "Pathways to Global Product Safety and Quality," Washington, D.C., July 2011, 3. The FDA justified its fiscal year 2013 budget increase request to be able to "increase its capacity to detect and address risks of food and food ingredients manufactured in China and to ensure that these products do not harm Americans." See Mark Astley, "Proposed Budget Will Strengthen 'China Food Safety'—FDA," Food navigator-USA.com, February 14, 2012.

2. Robert B. Zoellick, "Whither China: From Membership to Responsibility?" speech to the National Committee on U.S.-China Relations, New York, September 21, 2005, http://www.ncuscr.org/recent-remarks-and-speeches.

3. C. Fred Bergsten, "A Partnership of Equals: How Washington Should Respond to China's Economic Challenge," *Foreign Affairs* 87, no. 4 (July–August 2008): 57–69.

4. Zbigniew Brzezinski, "The Group of Two that Could Change the World," *Financial Times*, January 13, 2009, http://www.ft.com/cms/s/0/d99369b8-e178-11dd-afa0-0000779fd2ac.html.

5. Elizabeth Economy and Adam Segal, "The G-2 Mirage," *Foreign Affairs* 88, no. 3 (May–June 2009): 14–23.

6. Joshua Kurlantzick and Devin Stewart, "Hu's on First?" *National Interest* 92 (November–December 2007): 63–67.

7. Naaznee Barma, Ely Ratner, and Steven Weber, "A World without the West," *National Interest* 90 (July–August 2007): 23–30.

8. Joshua Cooper Ramo, *The Beijing Consensus* (London: Foreign Policy Center, 2004).

9. Samuel S. Kim, "China and Globalization: Confronting Myriad Challenges and Opportunities," *Asian Perspective* 33, no. 3 (2009): 57.

10. Hongying Wang and James N. Rosenau, "China and Global Governance," *Asian Perspective* 33, no. 3 (2009): 5–41.

11. Hu Jintao, "Building towards a Harmonious World of Lasting Peace and Prosperity," speech at the United Nations Summit, New York, September 15, 2005, http://www.china-un.org/eng/xw/t212915.htm. See also Jean-Marc F. Blanchard and Sujian Guo, "'Harmonious World' and China's New Foreign Policy," in *"Harmonious World" and China's New Foreign Policy*, edited by Jean-Marc F. Blanchard and Suijan Guo (Plymouth, Mass.: Lexington Books, 2008), 1–19.

12. "Declaration on the Fifth Anniversary of the Shanghai Cooperation Organization," June 15, 2006, http://www.sectsco.org/EN/show.asp?id=94.

13. Cui Liru, "Globalization Era vs. International Order Transformation," translated by Ma Zongshi, *Contemporary International Relations* 19, no. 3 (May–June 2009): 4–5.

14. Jiao Shixin and Zhou Jinming, "Hou lengzhan shidai de jieshu? jiqi dui zhongguo de jianyi," *Shijie Zhenghi*, no. 12 (2009): 46.

15. "China's National Defense in 2008," Information Office of the State Council of the People's Republic of China, http://english.gov.cn/official/2009-01/20/content_1210227_3.htm.

16. Li Dongyan, "China's Approach to Non-Traditional Security (NTS)," http://ieas.berkeley.edu/events/pdf/2007.03.08_Li_Donyan.pdf.

17. See interview with Wang Yizhou, School of International Studies, Beijing University; and Yu Xiangfeng, College of Public Administration, Zhejiang University, "Social Change Needed to Meet New Security Threats," *Global Times*, February 1, 2010, http://opinion.globaltimes.cn/commentary/2010-02/502640.html.

18. Ulrich Beck, *World Risk Society* (Cambridge, Mass.: Polity Press, 1999), 3.

19. Ibid., 34–35.

20. Elizabeth Wishnick, "Competition and Cooperative Practices in Sino-Japanese Energy and Environmental Relations: Towards an Energy Security 'Risk Community,'" *Pacific Review* 22, no. 4 (2009): 401–28; Elizabeth Wishnick, "Of Milk and Spacemen:

The Paradox of Chinese Power in an Era of Risk," *Brown Journal of World Affairs* 15, no. 2 (Spring–Summer 2009): 211–23; Lei Zhong and Lijin Zhong, "Integrating and Prioritizing Environmental Risks in China's Risk Management Discourse," *Journal of Contemporary China* 19, no. 63 (2010): 119–36; Richard Suttmeier, "The 'Sixth Modernization'? China, Safety and the Management of Risks," *Asia Policy*, no. 6 (2008): 129–46.

21. "Speech by Christine Lagarde [managing director of the International Monetary Fund] to the Opening Ceremony, China Development Forum 2012," March 18, 2012, http://imf.org/external/np/speeches/2012/031812a.htm.

22. "China Starts Probe into Milk Powder after One Baby Dies," Xinhua, September 11, 2008, http://news.xinhuanet.com.

23. "Six Infants Possibly Died of Tainted Milk Powder," Xinhua, December 1, 2008, http://www.chinadaily.com.cn.

24. Vivian Wu, "78 Questioned over Melamine-Tainted Baby Milk," *South China Morning Post*, www.scmp.com.

25. Zhang Pinghui and Stephen Chen, "Wen Pledges to Restore Confidence in Food Safety within Two Years," *South China Morning Post*, November 1, 2008; Raymond Li, "Hu Urges Dairy Industry Vigilance on Symbolic Visit," *South China Morning Post*, October 1, 2008.

26. Stephen Chen, "Wen Apologizes to Victims of Tainted Milk; In State Broadcast, Leader Feels 'Extremely Guilty'," *South China Morning Post*, September 22, 2008.

27. "China Seizes 26 Tonnes of Melamine-Tainted Milk Powder," Reuters, April 27, 2011.

28. Guy Montague-Jones, "China Uncovers More Melamine Tainted Milk Powder," FoodQualityNews.com, January 4, 2010.

29. David Barboza, "Discovery of Melamine-Tainted Milk Shuts Down Shanghai Dairy," *New York Times*, January 2, 2010, available at www.nytimes.com.

30. He Huifeng, "Investigative TV Report Praised Sanlu," *South China Morning Post*, September 14, 2008, available at www.scmp.com.

31. "Six Infants Possibly Died of Tainted Milk Powder," Xinhua, December 1, 2008, available at www.chinadaily.com.cn.

32. Josephine Ma, "Watchdog Boss Takes the Blame: Milk Scandal Fells Product Safety Chief," *South China Morning Post*, September 23, 2008.

33. Andrew Jacobs, "China Issues Broad Rules to Improve Dairy Safety; Edicts Cover Industry from Breeding to Sales," *International Herald Tribune*, November 21, 2008, available at www.iht.com.

34. David Barboza, "Former Executive Pleads Guilty in China Milk Scandal," *New York Times*, January 1, 2009.

35. The Department of Agriculture is responsible for monitoring the remaining 20 percent of food imports, focusing on meats, poultry, and eggs.

36. U.S. Government Accountability Office, "Federal Oversight of Food Safety," Testimony before the Subcommittee on Oversight and Investigations, Committee on Energy and Commerce, House of Representatives, June 12, 2008, appendix 1, 1.

37. Ibid., 8.

38. Gardiner Harris and Andrew Martin, "U.S. Blocks Products with Milk from China," *New York Times*, November 14, 2008.

39. Geoffrey S. Becker, "Food and Agricultural Imports from China," *Congressional Research Service Report for Congress*, RL34080, September 26, 2008, 11.

40. "Food Safety under Fire," *Nikkei Weekly* (Japan), November 17, 2008.

41. James J. Przystup, "The Gyoza Caper: Part II," *Comparative Connections,* October 2008, 3–4; James J. Przystup, "Gyoza, Beans, and Aircraft Carriers," *Comparative Connections*, January 2009, 1–2, http://csis.org/program/comparative-connections.

42. "EU Bans Baby Food with Chinese Milk, Recalls Grow," *USA Today*, November 25, 2008, available at www.usatoday.com.

43. Andy Ho, "The Insidious Menace of Melamine," *Straits Times*, January 8, 2009; David Barboza, "Hong Kong Finds Tainted Chinese Fish Feed," *New York Times*, November 13, 2008.

44. E.g., see Information Office of the State Council of the People's Republic of China, "China's Policies and Actions to Address Climate Change," http://english.gov.cn/2008-10/29/content_1134544_8.htm, which praises the work of NGOs, whereas a 2009 white paper encourages voluntary community efforts; see "China's Actions on Disaster Prevention and Reduction," available at http://english.gov.cn/official/2009-05/11/content_1310629.htm,.

45. Shaoguang Wang, "Changing Models of China's Policy Agenda Setting," *Modern China* 34, no. 1 (2008): 81–82.

46. Steve Tsang, "Consultative Leninism: China's New Political Framework," *Journal of Contemporary China* 18, no. 62 (2009), 866.

47. Lai-Ha Chan, Pak K. Lee, and Gerald Chan, "Rethinking Global Governance: A China Model in the Making?" *Contemporary Politics* 14, no.1 (2008), 7. See also Wang Yizhou, "Domestic Progress and Foreign Policy in China," IRChina, 2005, http://irchina.org/en/xueren/china/view.asp?id=651.

48. Kang Xiaoguang and Han Heng, "Graduated Controls: The State-Society Relationship in Contemporary China," *Modern China* 34, no. 1 (2008): 36–55.

49. Michel Foucault, "La 'gouvernementalité'" (Governmentality), in *Dits et Écrits* (Speeches and Writings) *1954–1988*, vol. 3, *1976–1979* (Paris: Éditions Gallimard, 1994), 635–57; Graham Burchell, Colin Gordon, and Peter Miller, *The Foucault Effect: Studies in Governmentality with Two Lectures and an Interview with Michel Foucault* (Chicago: University of Chicago Press, 1991); Michel Foucault, "Le Sujet et le pouvoir" (The Subject and Power), in *Dits et Écrits 1954–1988*, vol. 4, *1980–1988* (Paris: Éditions Gallimard, 1994), 222–43.

50. Michel Foucault, *Security, Territory, Population: Lectures at the College of France, 1977–1978*, translated by Gregory Burchell (New York: Picador, 2007), 123.

51. Nikolas Rose, *Power of Freedom: Reframing Political Thought* (Cambridge: Cambridge University Press, 1999), 174, 236.

52. Gary Sigley, "Chinese Governmentalities: Government, Governance and the Socialist Market Economy," *Economy and Society* 35, no. 4 (2006): 497.

53. Ole Jacob Sending and Iver B. Neumann, "Governance to Governmentality: Analyzing NGOs, States, and Power," *International Studies Quarterly* 50, no. 3 (2006): 651–72.

54. Bernard Frolic, "State-Led Civil Society," in *Civil Society in China*, edited by Timothy Brook and Bernard M. Frolic (Armonk, N.Y.: M. E. Sharpe, 1997), 48, 56.

55. Economist Intelligence Unit, "Got Real Milk?" *Business China*, September 29, 2008, 1–3.

56. Hao Li and Xi Liu, "Regulatory Institutions and the Melamine Scandal: A Game Theory Perspective," *Organization Development Journal* 28, no. 2 (2010), http://www.questia.com/library/1P3-2042541641/regulatory-institutions-and-the-melamine-scandal.

57. In general, there are more than 400,000 food-producing companies in China (compared with 150,000 in the United States), only two-thirds of which are officially registered.

58. Economist Intelligence Unit, "Got Real Milk?"; Economist Intelligence Unit, "Got Safe Milk?" *Business China*, February 17, 2003, 6–7.

59. Kong Xiangzhi, Zhong Zhen, and Tan Zhixin, "Lun fazhan nongmin zhuanye hezuoshe yu nongchangpin zhiliang anquan wenti—yinaiyeweili" (On the development of farmers' professional cooperative and quality and safety of agricultural products—case study of dairy industry), *Tianjin shangye daxue xuebao* (Journal of Tianjin University of Commerce) 30, no. 4 (2010): 9.

60. Ibid., 10.

61. Inspection facilities are typically located in cities, far from these producers, and inspections are costly, especially for household farm operations. Moreover, small-scale producers lack training in food safety and fail to understand that sales of substandard products will lead to losses. To enhance their compliance with food safety standards, the official recommends requiring inspections, providing funding for small producers to implement standards, and instituting them at the village and district levels. Zhu Xiumin, "Zhiliang guandian: Cong jianyan zhushou tigao xiaozuofang de shipin anquan" (Quality viewpoint: Beginning with inspection, increase food safety of small producers), *Zhongguo zhiliang jishu jiandu* (China Quality Technology Control), no. 5 (2010): 60.

62. Linden J. Ellis and Jennifer L. Turner, " Surf and Turf: Environmental and Food Safety Concerns of China's Aquaculture and Animal Husbandry," *China Environment* no. 9 (2007), 20–28.

63. Li Yang, "Shipin anquan huanjingzhe shiji" (The Design of Food Safety Indicators), *Anyang gongxueyuan xuebao* (Journal of Anyang Institute of Technology) 9, no. 2 ( 2010), 19; Yu Liyan, Ren Yan, and Wang Dianhua, "Food Safety Regulatory System of Developed Countries and the Implications for China," *Management Science and Engineering* 4, no. 1 (2010), 37.

64. E.g., see Peter Enderwick, "Managing 'Quality Failure' in China: Lessons from the Dairy Industry Case," *International Journal of Emerging Markets* 4, no. 3 (2009): 224.

65. Rosita Dellios, Yang Xiaohua, and Yilmaz Nadir Kemal, "Food Safety and the Role of Government: Implications for CSR Policies in China," *iBusiness*, 1 (2009): 82.

66. Jonathan Ansfield, "China Passes Tighter Information Law," *New York Times*, April 29, 2010, http://www.nytimes.com/2010/04/30/world/asia/30leaks.html; Li Huizi and Cheng Zhuo, "China Narrows Definition of 'State Secrets' to Boost Gov't Transparency," Xinhua, April 29, 2010, http://news.xinhuanet.com/english2010/china/2010-04/29/c_13272939.htm.

67. See Wishnick, "Of Milk and Spacemen," 213.

68. Li and Xiu, "Regulatory Institutions," 3.

69. Josephine Ma, "Complaints Were Received in June but Nothing was Done," *South China Morning Post*, September 13, 2008, www.scmp.com; "Chinese Press Controls: Eating Their Words," *The Economist*, October 25, 2008, 52. Chinese Communist Party officials issued directives to journalists specifically placing food safety issues off limits during the Olympics. See Congressional-Executive Commission on the PRC, *2008 Report to Congress*, 59, www.cecc.gov.

70. "China Starts Probe into Milk Powder."

71. Zhang Xicai and Zhang Lixiang, "Shipin anquan weiji guanliji zhiguo jian yu duice yanjiu" (Food Security Crisis Management Mechanism and Proposals), *Luce jingji* (Grow economy) 7, no. 227 (2010): 60, 62; Zhao Naiji, "Wo guo shipin anquan zhengu jianguan zhidu tantao" (An investigation of my country's governmental food safety oversight system), *Jiandai shangmao gongye* (Modern Business Trade Industry) 9 (2010): 71.

72. Naiji, "Wo guo shipin anquan zhengu jianguan zhidu tantao," 70.

73. Ibid.

74. Xicai and Lixiang, "Shipin anquan weiji guanliji zhiguo jian yu duice yanjiu," 61.

75. "Food Safety Commission Established in China," February 12, 2010, www. chinacsr.com/en/2010/02/12/7162-food-safety-commission; "Chinese Vice-Premier Addresses State Council Food Safety Meeting," Xinhua, August 22, 2010.

76. Chen Dou and Zhou Shilin, "Shanghai zhuliu baozhi shipin anquan fenxi" (An analysis of food safety coverage in Shanghai's leading newspapers), *Jin Chuanmei* (Today's Mass Media) 10 (2010): 2–3. During the Autumn Festival in 2001, Chinese media revealed that the Nanjing manufacturer of the famous Guanshengyuan mooncakes was reusing year-old filling in the new season's product. The company was forced to halt production and recall its product. "Mooncake Filling Wanes Brand Name," *China Daily*, September 14, 2001, http://china.org.cn/english/19153.htm. In 2004, Xinhua reported that dozens of babies died of malnutrition in Fuyang and several other cities in eastern China after being fed counterfeit milk powder containing insufficient nutrients. "47 Detained for Selling Baby-Killer Milk," *China Daily*, May 5, 2004, http://www.chinadaily.com.cn/english/doc/2004-05/content_329449.htm.

77. Dou and Shilin, "Shanghai zhuliu baozhi shipin anquan fenxi," 2–3.

78. Ibid., 4–5.

79. Ibid., 1.

80. Linda J. Ellis and Jennifer L. Turner, *Sowing the Seeds: Opportunities for U.S.–China Cooperation on Food Safety* (Washington, D.C.: Woodrow Wilson International Center for Scholars, 2008), 27.

81. Yangsuk Karen Yoo, "Tainted Milk: What Kind of Justice for Victims' Families in China?" *Hastings International and Comparative Law Review* 33, no. 22 (2010): 555.

82. Edward Wong, "Milk Scandal in China Yields Cash for Payments," *New York Times*, January 17, 2009.

83. Peh Shing Huei, "Milk Scandal: Parents Seek Better Deals," *Straits Times*, January 24, 2009, available at www.straitstimes.com.

84. Associated Press, "Court Rejects Sanlu Victims," *Straits Times*, May 27, 2010, available at www.straitstimes.com; China Hearsay, China Law, Business, and Economics Commentary, "U.S. Melamine Litigation: Discussion of China Forum Non Conveniens," April 8, 2010, available at www.chinahearsay.com.

85. Verna Yu, "Parents Seek 'Justice' for Melamine Babies," *South China Morning Post*, July 10, 2010.

86. Ibid.

87. China Consumers' Association, "China Consumers' Association Annual Report 2008," April 9, 2010, http://www.cca.org.cn/english/EnNewsShow.jsp?id=161&cid=986.

88. "China vs. Civil Society," *Wall Street Journal*, July 21, 2009, available at www. onlinewsj.com. Two months before it was shut down, Gongmeng posted a report that criticized Chinese economic policies in Tibet. Edward Wong, "China Shuts Down Office of Volunteer Lawyers," *New York Times*, July 18, 2009, available at www.nytimes.com.

89. Human Rights in China, "Organizer of Families of Tainted Milk Powder Victims Detained," November 13, 2009, http://www.hrichina.org/public/contents/press?revision_id=172424&item_id=172422.

90. Andrew Jacobs, "China Sentences Activist in Milk Scandal to Prison," *New York Times*, November 10, 2010, available at www.nytimes.com.

91. Chinese Communist Party officials issued directives to journalists specifically placing food safety issues off limits during the Olympics. See Congressional-Executive Commission on the PRC, *2008 Report to Congress*, 59, available at www.cecc.gov.

92. Andrew Janes, "Delay Frustrates Fonterra Boss; Second Baby Dies from Contaminated Formula," *Dominion Post* (New Zealand), September 16, 2008, http://www.stuff.co.nz/dominionpost/.

93. Bill Schiller, "A Crisis Rooted in Two Chinas," The Star.com (Toronto), September 21, 2008.

94. Dan Eaton, "Fonterra Bungled Crisis, Says Clark; Countdown to a Crisis," *The Press* (New Zealand), September 23, 2008, available at www.thepress.co.nz.

95. Tim Cronshaw, "Fonterra Moves Cautiously to Develop China Project," *The Press* (New Zealand), February 12, 2010 (LexisNexis).

96. Andrew Janes, "Fonterra Pays $8 Million to Charity," *The Press* (New Zealand), October 11, 2008, available at www.thepress.co.nz.

97. "China Protests Milk Import Bans at WTO, Says Contamination Was Accidental," Associated Press, October 9, 2008 (Factiva).

98. Rosita Dellios, Xiaohua Yang, and Nadir Kemal Yilmaz, "Food Safety and the Role of Government: Implications for CSR Policies in China," *iBusiness* no. 1 (2009): 75.

99. Barry Berman and Kunal Swani, "Managing Product Safety of Imported Chinese Goods," *Business Horizons*, no. 53 (January–February 2010): 39–40.

100. Ibid., 43.

101. According to guidelines set by the FAO, the WHO has the responsibility for making emergency contacts during a food safety crisis. Information is then disseminated through the International Food Safety Authorities Network (INFOSAN), a network of 177 states established in 2004 to facilitate communication during food safety emergencies. "The International Food Safety Authorities Network (INFOSAN)," December 1, 2010, http://www.who.int/foodsafety/fs_management/infosan/en/.

102. Celine Marie-Elise Gossner et al., "The Melamine Incident: Implications for International Food and Feed Safety," *Environmental Health Perspectives* 117, no. 2 (2009): 6.

103. Ibid.

104. These are 1 milligram per kilogram of powdered infant formula and 2.5 milligrams per kilogram of other food products. Laura MacInnis, "Food Body Sets Rules for Bagged Salad, Melamine Use," Reuters, July 6, 2010, available at www.reuters.com.

105. Yu Liyan, Ren Yan, and Wang Dian-hua, "Food Safety Regulatory System of Developed Countries and the Implication for China," *Management Science and Engineering* 4, no. 1 (2010): 37–38.

106. Phelim Kine, "China's Public Health Whitewash," *The Guardian*, June 23, 2010, http://www.hrw.org/en/news/2010/06/23/chinas-public-health-whitewash-0.

107. Stephanie N. Mehta, "Study: Dairy Scandal Taints All Chinese Brands," *CNNMoney.com*, November 11, 2008.

108. Zogby, "Zogby Poll: 82 percent Concerned about Buying Goods from China," August 7, 2007, available at www.zogby.com.

109. Alan Fram, "Chinese Product Woes—Poll: Most Say United States Shares Blame," Associated Press, August 31, 2007, www.apfn.org/apfn/china-recalls/poll.htm.

110. U.S. Food and Drug Administration, "Food Protection Plan: One-Year Progress Summary," December 2008, www.fda.gov.

111. Cited in Steve Suppan, *U.S. China Agreement on Food Safety: Terms and Agreement* (Minneapolis: Institute for Agriculture and Food Safety, 2008), 3.

112. Ibid., 4.

113. Ellis and Turner, *Sowing the Seeds*, 38.

114. Caroline Scott-Thomas, "USP Signs MOU with Chinese Food Safety Agency," June 25, 2010, http://www.foodnavigator-usa.com/content/view/print/309541; Caroline Scott-Thomas, "U.S.-Based Food Safety Training for Foreign Food Manufacturers," May 24, 2010, http://www.foodnavigator-usa.com/content/view/print/304924.

115. Mary L. Nucci, Jocilyn E. Dellava, Cara L. Cuite, and William K. Hallman, "The U.S. Food Import System: Issues, Processes, and Proposals [Addendum: Imported Food Safety], Working Paper RR-0208-001 (Rutgers: New Jersey Experiment Station, 2008), 2.

116. U.S. Food and Drug Administration, "Melamine Contamination in China," January 5, 2009, http://www.fda.gov/NewsEvents/PublicHealthFocus/ucm179005.htm; Fred Gale and Jean C. Buzby, *Imports from China and Food Safety Issues*, U.S. Department of Agriculture, Economic Information Bulletin 52 (2009), 11.

# Chapter 9

# The Ambiguous Political Economy of Terrorism in Southeast Asia's Borderlands

*Justin V. Hastings*

By conventional standards, Southeast Asia is a fairly safe place. Governments have placed most territorial disputes on the back burner, there are no active interstate conflicts, armies do not face off against each other as in the endless cold (and occasional hot) wars of Northeast Asia, and countries generally talk to each other, in the Association of Southeast Asian Nations (ASEAN) and in other venues, when there are problems. Internal stability remains a concern for some countries, although even here there has been progress since the Asian financial crisis, with Indonesia consolidating its democracy and resolving internal conflicts in Aceh, Maluku, and Sulawesi (although Thailand seems to have degenerated as a stable polity). However, a major *nontraditional* security threat exists below the surface and along the peripheries of Southeast Asian states: the exploits of illicit nonstate groups such as terrorists, maritime pirates, smugglers, and insurgents.

Southeast Asia suffers from the strange problem of being both too developed and not developed enough, able to take advantage of modern communication, transportation, and markets but often still lacking in comprehensive state oversight. Consequently, it is an ideal operational environment for illicit actors such as pirates, terrorists, and smugglers. While the amount of danger such groups pose ebbs and flows over time, the conditions in the region that enable them to operate remain relatively constant. Illicit networks predate and transcend modern boundaries, provide livelihoods to people living on the periphery, and have now been made more efficient by modern communications and transportation technology. Illicit actors—smugglers, pirates, terrorists, and the like—are not simply suborning corrupt local officials. Sometimes they are actually part of the traditional social and political networks that undergird the economies of the border areas.

This chapter examines the institutions and relationships that characterize illicit and semi-illicit economies in two Southeast Asian border regions and looks, in turn, at how the cells of one terrorist group, Jemaah Islamiyah, have taken advantage of those economies to support their operations. The research presented here suggests that the degree to which terrorist cells are embedded in local political and economic networks in Southeast Asia varies inversely with the degree to which those illicit networks co-opt or are integrated into formal institutions of government and trade. Or to put it another way, terrorist cells do not become deeply involved in illicit economic networks that interact regularly with institutions of the state—for example, customs officials—even if those interactions typically involve corruption.

A better understanding of how these inherently transnational groups are embedded in local social, political, and economic networks will allow the United States and cooperating countries to target aid and development efforts more effectively, as well as avoid counterproductive security operations. If we do not have a proper understanding of the political economy of Southeast Asia's border regions, efforts encouraged by the United States to fight terrorists by cracking down on illicit flows of people, drugs, and weapons can raise the ire of local people along with causing economic hardships. Conversely, United States–supported and other economic development programs that do not take into account security concerns could backfire, and thus end up further empowering terrorists and criminals.

## The Scope of the Challenge

### Background

Most Southeast Asian countries, though not wealthy, are developed enough to take full advantage of modern communications and transportation technology. Singapore and Malaysia are attempting to become exporters of high technology, mobile phones have made inroads in the farthest reaches of Indonesia, and text messaging has become the primary means of long-distance communication across the region for all but the poorest of the poor. The region's cities and people are also connected in a dense web of transportation links. Low-cost air carriers have proliferated in the past ten years, and the islands of Indonesia, Singapore, Malaysia, and the Philippines have been connected by a network of ferries, cargo ships, and fishing boats for hundreds of years.[1] This technology supports fairly sophisticated transnational markets, not just in consumer goods like DVDs, but also in commodities such as tin and palm oil.

Southeast Asia's geography, broadly understood, has many characteristics that encourage legitimate cross-border movement and communication. Transportation links are fairly good, particularly for a region with only one or two fully developed countries. The archipelagic topography of the region, in premodern times, led to the development of sea-based trade routes and states rather than roads and land-based states,[2] and, in the past twenty years, has meant that the faster option of air travel has become increasingly popular and relatively cheap for well-funded organizations, including terrorist groups.[3] Mobile phones and, to a lesser extent, the Internet have a high degree of penetration, extending even to lightly populated islands in Indonesia.

Most relevant for nontraditional security threats, however, Southeast Asia's human and physical geography also encourages *illicit* cross-border movement and communication. Ethnic, social, and trade networks overlap with formal boundaries due to the colonial history of the region. Southeast Asian countries are faced with a fiction: the territory over which they claim sovereignty is often in no way the territory over which central governments have effective control. Large areas of the Philippines are under the control of insurgent groups, Indonesia struggles to patrol its waters, and insurgents have made southern Thailand a dangerous place for Buddhists.[4] This is due to accidents of both history and geography. Before the European colonial powers arrived in the region in the sixteenth century, indigenous states clung to the coasts of Southeast Asia's many islands, and derived most of their income and power from control of trade. To the extent that states controlled territory farther inland at all, state power was largely concentrated in a core area, with diminishing control toward the periphery. The Europeans introduced fixed territorial boundaries in the nineteenth century, but their efforts to enforce order along the borders led to adaptations by smugglers and others who continued their now-illicit movements.[5] Terrain that is difficult for states to police without significant resources—forbidding jungles and mountain ranges in Borneo and New Guinea, plus thousands of islands in Indonesia, Thailand, Malaysia, and the Philippines—dominates many of the border areas. The states that became independent in the twentieth century were thus left with swaths of territory on their peripheries that they were eager to keep out of the hands of other countries but could not control very well on their own. Indeed, noninterference was so important to Southeast Asian countries that it emerged as one of the pillars of the "ASEAN Way."[6]

Illicit Southeast Asian groups—terrorists, insurgents, pirates, and smugglers—have been able to achieve relatively high levels of sophistication because they take advantage of the full scope of technological and market tools that Southeast Asia has to offer in order to operate across these imperfectly controlled international boundaries. They inhabit a region that is developed enough to provide the tools that illicit networks need to operate over great distances and, should they so desire, make money—modern communications and transportation infrastructure, and commodities markets—but not so developed that governments have the financial resources, police and military personnel, and legal systems capable of consistently stopping sophisticated illicit groups from operating at all. Southeast Asian governments, even those of the Philippines and Indonesia, are too strong to be ignored entirely. Consequently, illicit groups establish support cells in the border areas where states' sovereignty claims and actual control are most at odds and draw on these cells for assistance in moving across borders. These areas are already crisscrossed by low-level trade networks based on routes and social ties that transcend the borders laid down by the colonial states. For illicit groups, operating efficiently requires becoming embedded in these local political and economic networks. But the extent to which they *are* embedded in these networks varies. In this chapter, I will focus specifically on terrorist cells' embeddedness in the region.

### Argument

We can think about terrorist cells as being embedded in the local environments of border regions in three senses. First, terrorist cells can use the same geographical routes and methods as smugglers and pirates to move people and illicit goods without any particular assistance from smugglers or pirates. Second, terrorists can "contract" with preexisting smuggling and pirate networks to move people and illicit goods by establishing personal ties with criminals or by simply hiring them. Third, terrorists can be integral parts of smuggling and piracy networks—that is, they can regularly engage in the illicit movement of people and goods unrelated to terrorist activities. Terrorists thus can have a complex relationship with crime and criminal networks, as has been established in other studies.[7]

The illicit and semi-illicit networks on which terrorist groups can depend can be institutionalized and even formalized locally in a number of ways.[8] Illicit networks can draw members from local ethnic groups or otherwise establish cultural, family, and social ties. They can maintain personal or business connections to local legitimate business networks and political officials by bribing or blackmailing them, or by carrying out business for them. The illicit networks can also use local trade routes, infrastructure, and methods to move people and goods, or to dispose of stolen or smuggled goods. These trade routes, infrastructure, and methods can be licit or illicit. However, it would be simplistic to consider networks either wholly licit or illicit. A network may have legitimate products it sells, for instance, along with its illegitimate products, or might import otherwise legal goods through illicit channels, bribing officials or simply finding ways to bypass import restrictions and tariffs. It might also use corrupt means to maintain its market for legitimate products. In short, illicit networks have an ambiguous relationship with state authorities, legitimate infrastructure, and markets. We can say that the more an illicit network (and by extension, the illicit economy of an area) co-opts the local state, expects the regular and frequent cooperation of local officials (including consistent results from that cooperation), and uses legitimate transportation and market infrastructure rather than providing its own, the more institutionalized it is.

In this chapter, I look at two border areas: (1) the area bounded by Johor in Malaysia (just north of Singapore on the Malayan Peninsula), Singapore, and Indonesia's Riau Islands (which include Batam); and (2) the border area consisting of Mindanao in the Philippines and the Indonesian province on the northern tip of Sulawesi, Sulawesi Utara (North Sulawesi) (figure 9.1). In the first region, illicit cross-border movement has been regularized and institutionalized to the point that both smuggling and labor migration operate in a gray market partially aided and abetted by the local government. In the second, illicit networks take advantage of transnational ethnic and social ties in order to carry out small-scale trade, and deal with the local authorities intermittently.

*Figure 9.1. Border Areas of Malaysia, Singapore, Indonesia, and the Philippines*

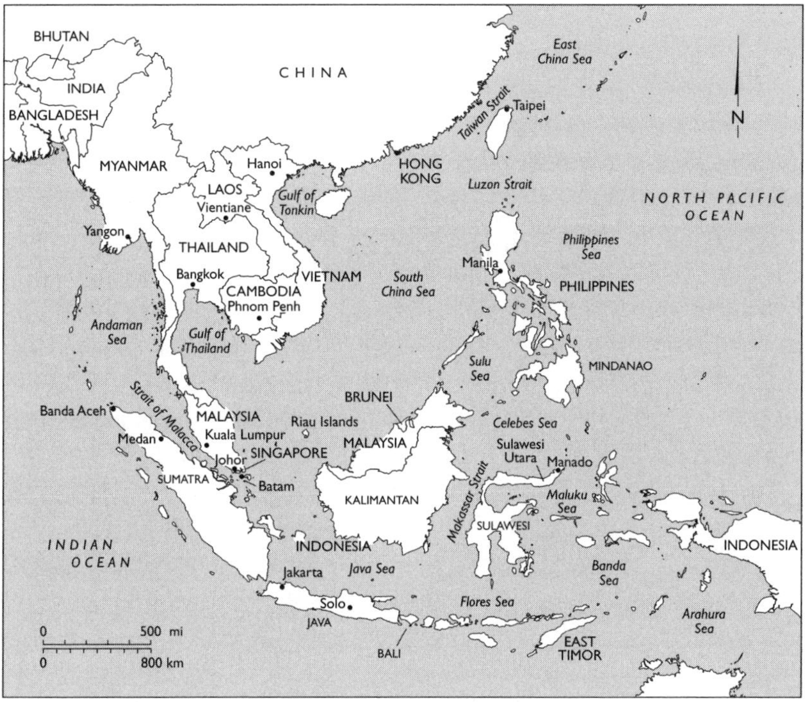

*Source:* National Bureau of Asian Research. Cartography by Bill Nelson.

The manner in which terrorist cells are embedded in the local political economic networks of Southeast Asia's border region can complicate both counterterrorism and economic development policies. Jemaah Islamiyah (JI) had operatives and activities in both of these border areas between the mid-1990s and the early 2000s. Because these terrorist cells were created by the same organization and operated at the same time, the underlying beliefs and goals of the group and the overarching structure and resources available to the cells from the organization were similar across different border areas. The task is thus to isolate the characteristics of the local illicit and semi-illicit political and economic networks in the border areas and examine how JI took advantage of them.

In Singapore, Johor, and Kepulauan Riau (the Riau Islands, also shortened to Kepri in Indonesian), JI was surprisingly uninvolved in the illicit economy. A few operatives used the routes and methods of illicit networks, but none used any services that would have required deep local ties. In Mindanao and Sulawesi Utara, however, JI integrated itself into the local illicit economy, building up local ethnic and social ties, constructing its own transportation infrastructure, and engaging in commerce.

## The Singapore–Johor Bahru–Kepulauan Riau Triangle

*Illicit networks.* Few smugglers on the Indonesian island of Batam are locals whose roots in the island stretch back generations; few inhabitants of Batam have lived there for more than a few decades. In the 1980s, before Batam was designated as a special economic zone in a bid to encourage foreign direct investment, the population of the island numbered in the low thousands. By 2009, it had passed 900,000.[9] There are "natives" of Batam, but they are few and far between. Batam's economic status means that migrants come from all over Indonesia to make their fortunes.[10]

The geography of Batam, which played a role in its rise as a special economic zone, also plays a role in how businessmen and others in the Riau Islands derive income. The potential profitability of both smuggling and piracy is boosted by the extreme proximity of Batam to Singapore and, to a lesser extent, the Malaysian state of Johor and the hundreds of islands in the Riau Archipelago. Additionally, the Riau Islands' position lies astride the Singapore Strait and, thus, the primary shipping lanes between the Middle East and East Asia. Smuggling networks in Batam move goods quickly and cheaply across the Singapore Strait from Singapore and Johor Bahru. The Singaporean government is known to ignore goods smuggled into the country as long as they are not explicitly illegal in Singapore (narcotics, guns, explosives) or among the few goods on which Singapore imposes tariffs (cigarettes, alcohol).[11] The smugglers bring back goods to Indonesia that would otherwise have high tariffs (consumer electronics) or are illegal in Indonesia (stolen cars).

Yet smuggling in Batam, while technically illegal, does not draw on networks that are wholly illicit. Businessmen in Batam engage in both legitimate and illicit activities, sometimes at the same time. One informant told of a time he was on a boat sailing between Singapore and Batam that had legitimate goods on top, visible to the customs officials (who came in the middle of the night and took a bribe), and smuggled goods hidden below.[12] Another informant produced and sold pirated video compact discs as well as engaged in dubious—but not illegal—activities such as running karaoke and video gambling parlors. His distribution network in the Riau Islands was sufficiently well formed that he could coordinate with other large pirated video compact disc producers to maintain the "quality" of their products.[13]

These semi-illicit networks also use a combination of illicit and legitimate infrastructure. During field research, several smugglers pointed out some of the "rat ports" (*pelabuhan tikus*), ports used to smuggle goods and hide pirate loot. Most were located in remote villages, but one was adjacent to a legitimate port, and another was down the road from a maritime police base. Others *were* in fact formal ports. Clearly the smugglers were not concerned with secrecy. The difference, according to informants, was between the relatively small volume of smuggled goods that could be brought in to legitimate ports (at least during the day) versus the expanded capacity of the totally illicit ports, which could handle entire ships' worth of smuggled goods at a given time.[14]

A local police official said that not only did he know who the biggest smugglers were, but he also knew the locations of their rat ports. There were, he said, sixty-four rat ports on Batam.[15] When asked why he did not arrest the smugglers, the police chief replied that if he cracked down on smuggling, he would earn the ire of the local population, who would be deprived not only of affordable foodstuffs like rice and cooking oil, but also of pirated DVDs and TVs stolen from Singapore. The local government was not in a position to provide for the welfare of the local population, given the high cost of living in Batam, and thus smuggled goods were necessary for sustaining the population.[16]

The labor migrant system in the Riau Islands similarly skirts the boundary between licit and illicit. Michele Ford and Lenora Lyons's research in Tanjung Pinang, the capital of Riau Islands province, has found that the process of obtaining a legal passport and local identity cards, exempting the holder from paying Indonesian exit taxes, has become formalized and institutionalized outside of the official labor migrant approval channel. Prospective migrants, often recruited by employment agencies, flood into Tanjung Pinang hoping to cross into Singapore and Malaysia to take low-skilled jobs. Although in theory the local government is supposed to send repatriated labor migrants and Indonesians deported by Singapore and Malaysia back to their provinces of origin, in reality intermediaries and illicit passport agencies have sprung up to provide the needed documents to migrants. The documents are legal, having been issued by local government officials who have contacts with the intermediaries and passport agents, and can be issued quickly—in some cases within one day.[17] This route to labor migration is known as *asli tapi palsu* (real but fake), or *aspal*; though technically illegal, it is sanctioned by a local government seeking an efficient way to deal with outside migrants and supported by a local population partially dependent on the jobs brought by the institutionalization of the process. Just as with smuggling networks, the networks that facilitate *aspal* operate on the line between licit and illicit because the local government and the population both view a pragmatic solution—to a problem in part created by central government regulations—as more important than the strict legal issues.[18]

*Terrorism networks.* Although JI was originally an Indonesia-based organization, Abu Bakar Ba'asyir and Abdullah Sungkar's exile from Indonesia in 1985 led them to build up cells of the group in Malaysia and Singapore, initially as a means of recruiting people to train in Afghanistan and then travel to Indonesia to fight for an Islamic state. Only later were these cells used as a means of establishing a pan–Southeast Asian organization.[19] These cells were involved in JI plots in Singapore and Indonesia in the late 1990s and early 2000s. Delving into how they drew on the illicit and semi-illicit networks discussed above to bring their goals to fruition will show how the nexus between terrorism and crime works in Southeast Asia's borderlands.

The JI maintained *wakalah*, brigade-level units, in Singapore and Johor. There was also a school affiliated with the group in Johor, which employed JI-affiliated teachers, and recruited new JI members until it was forced to close by the Malaysian government.[20] Although the group's cell was embedded in the local area, inasmuch as its members were actually from Singapore and Malaysia, with family ties to each other and other Islamists in the Malayan peninsula, there was surprisingly little interaction between the Johor *wakalah* and illicit networks.

The JI *wakalah* in Singapore mostly consisted of Singaporean citizens and some permanent residents of Malay or Muslim Indian origin. Singaporean members of JI seem to have been involved in a series of terrorist incidents: the successful Batam portion of the Christmas Eve bombings in 2000 (simultaneous attacks against Christian targets in eleven cities across western Indonesia), the failed Singapore bombing plots in 2001, the multiple escapes and plots of Mas Selamat Kastari and other Singapore fugitives, and the foiled Palembang bombing plot in 2008.[21] Because nearly all members of the Singapore *wakalah* were actually Singaporean, they were embedded in Singapore, inasmuch as they were part of the local ethnic groups (and the requisite social networks) and familiar with local legitimate transportation infrastructure.[22] The JI cell members were generally familiar with the most common routes and methods for smuggling goods into Singapore (one of their ideas for smuggling ammonium nitrate into Singapore was in trucks coming across the causeway between Johor Bahru and Singapore), but did *not* seem to have personal connections with local criminal networks.[23] During the period before the Batam plot, one of the JI Singapore members was tasked with taking the ferry between Batam and Singapore to survey potential routes for smuggling explosives into Singapore, but this potential route did not pan out before the Singapore plot was uncovered.[24]

Interestingly, JI did *not* maintain a *wakalah* in Batam. When JI carried out the Batam part of the Christmas Eve bombings in 2000, it had only one locally based contact who helped bomb plot members find housing and supplies on the island.[25] The rest of the people involved in the Batam attack were seconded from Singapore, other parts of Indonesia, and Malaysia. The Singaporean members of the Batam plot took ferries from and to Singapore, stayed in Batam for less than a month, and were largely tasked with support activities—leaving their apartment every morning as if going to work, reconnoitering potential targets, and acquiring legally available bomb components.[26] The Indonesian member of the bomb plot, Imam Samudra (later to become notorious for his part in the 2002 Bali bombings), seems to have had more connections, or at least familiarity with traveling and staying in Batam; he was able to obtain a passport on the island and stayed in cheap hostels on several visits.[27] The explosives needed for the bombs in Batam were brought by couriers from Jakarta without, it appears, using any illicit means of transportation or connections with the criminal underworld in Batam itself. JI was confident enough in its access to Batam and Johor that it planned to bring explosives through either or both areas on their way to Singapore,[28] but because those projects never came to fruition, we will never know if its couriers would have been able to smuggle explosives into Singapore.

Given the robust gray market in both smuggling and migration in the Riau Islands, it is surprising how light JI's footprint in the region was. While it had cells in Singapore and Johor, it never even tried to set up a cell in Batam. Imam Samudra may have used the *aspal* system to obtain his passport, and Mukhlas took an illicit ferry from Johor back to Indonesia, but that seems to have been the extent of JI's use of cross-border illicit networks. JI's operatives explored routes for smuggling explosives from Batam, but do not seem to have developed the contacts to have followed through on their plans. Within Indonesia, JI used its own couriers, but they had no need to cross from Batam to other countries. In short, JI sought to make use of illicit methods and routes, but otherwise was minimally embedded in the illicit economy of the region.

There are several possible explanations. Most JI members involved in JI activities in the Johor-Kepri-Singapore region were Malaysians and Singaporeans; they had no need for the networks designed to provide transport and documents to Indonesian migrants (and in fact, Mukhlas and Imam Samudra, both Indonesians, were the ones who did successfully contract out transport and documents to the gray economy). Given the costs of using illicit networks, it is possible that Batam's proximity to more developed economies in the form of Malaysia and Singapore meant that JI found it easier to send people in the reverse direction for its plots, obviating the need for illicit networks. The gray market itself may also have been a factor; the semiformal, institutionalized nature of the *aspal* system and, to a lesser extent, of smuggling allowed people from all over Indonesia (or other countries) to take advantage of them without being directly connected to local officials or local ethnic and social networks. In other words, if JI wanted to engage in certain illicit activities in the Riau Islands, it did not necessarily need to be deeply embedded.

## The Sulawesi Utara–Mindanao Region

*Illicit networks.* The smuggling networks of the Sulawesi Utara–Mindanao region are by and large designed to attend to the basic economic needs of the local inhabitants of Sulawesi Utara and the provinces of southern Mindanao, but more specifically of the inhabitants of the islands on either side of the border between Sulawesi and Mindanao. The northernmost island in Sangihe-Talaud, Marore, is only 40 nautical miles from Mindanao, allowing for relatively quick trips back and forth.[29] Smuggling in this area of Southeast Asia appears to be somewhat different from that of the Johor Bahru-Batam-Singapore Triangle.

Smuggling in the region is dominated by short-term operations: small businessmen move back and forth between Indonesia and the Philippines, staying in the other country for a few days at a time, and rely on connections with friends and relatives in both countries as a means of obtaining and then selling everyday goods.[30] The type of smuggling seen in the area is a reflection of the preexisting transborder social and economic networks. Filipinos live in the Sangihe-Talaud Islands, and a community of

Indonesians lives in Mindanao (12,000 were legally working and living in Mindanao in 2002), resulting in a transnational social network ready to support small-scale informal trade.[31]

Both sides of the border are relatively undeveloped, as are the Sangihe-Talaud Islands themselves. Neither side has much in the way of heavy industry, and economic production on the Indonesian side is geared toward primary commodities (unlike Kepulauan Riau, Singapore, and Johor), as is production in General Santos City on the Philippine side (known for its excellent tuna).[32] Much of what is smuggled, as a result, appears to be everyday goods such as agricultural, fishery, and small-scale manufactured products. One researcher reports that illegal trade is dominated by Indonesian traders—often ethnically Chinese—bringing small quantities of cigarettes to Mindanao, and returning to Indonesia with hard liquor.[33] The traders either use their own boats or hire one of the hundreds of fishing boats in the area to carry their wares.[34] In many cases, "bosses" in Indonesia have employees pilot small, two-person boats in the waters directly between Sangihe and Mindanao, delivering their goods to prearranged buyers, and buying from prearranged sellers. The vast majority of the people involved in transportation in these networks are young men who remain in the Philippines for less than five days. In most cases, they avoid any dealings with police and customs officers by maneuvering through the waters at night, along routes unlikely to be patrolled. Though officials can be bribed, the cost is apparently too high for many small-time smugglers to bear, and in any case, the trip to the nearest customs outpost in Marore makes the trip two to three times longer.[35]

The networks relied upon by smugglers are thus largely informal, with less involvement of the local governments than in Kepulauan Riau. Unlike Malaysia and Singapore, the Philippines are not a popular destination for Indonesian migrant workers or for high-value Indonesian commodities such as timber. Traditional trade appears to move informally and without contact with state authorities unless standard customs inspections reveal inconsistencies, at which point officials can be bribed. The relatively low level of reported crimes in Kepulauan Sangihe regency suggests that much smuggling occurs entirely off the books. From 2003 to 2007, there were only six reported weapons smuggling cases, three reported terrorism cases, and one case of criminal customs violations.[36] The issue for informal commerce, once operators have set up their networks, would appear to be less what smugglers have to do to penetrate Indonesia's border than who they have to cross to be caught.

*Terrorism networks.* The networks that both JI and other Islamist groups developed in eastern Indonesia and the southern Philippines were primarily designed to transport people to the southern Philippines, and to return both their transportees and locally acquired weapons back to Indonesia (and from there to other countries, if needed). JI devoted an entire *mantiqi* (Mantiqi III, the JI equivalent of a military division) in the late 1990s and early 2000s to eastern Indonesia and the Philippines to support the logistics of the organization and to provide training to the recruits once they actually arrived in Mindanao.[37] Although the *mantiqi* head was not based in Sulawesi Utara but in Sabah, Malaysia, one of the primary corridors by which JI moved weapons and people between Indonesia and the Philippines was the Sangihe-Talaud Islands, off the northern tip of Sulawesi. Within these islands, JI members had personal connections that allowed them to access both the networks and routes used to bypass state authority and move people and goods to and from the Philippines.

In 1997, for instance, JI's operative Mubarok made contact with a Filipino fisherman by the name of Sardjono. Sardjono was married to an Indonesian and lived in Peta in the Sangihe-Talaud Islands. Together, they bought a boat capable of transporting weapons and recruits, which is in fact just what it did for the next several years. Sardjono also functioned as a link on the route between Mindanao and Sulawesi Utara, even if he did not transport recruits himself. In December 1997, an operative by the name of Suryadi, loosely affiliated with JI, brought several other men and detonators from General Santos City on Mindanao to Nanusa in Talaud using a "traditional boat," apparently one of the many boats to ply international waters without formal consent from either the Philippine or Indonesian government. This time the Indonesian officials in Nanusa did search the boat, but were bribed into compliance. Sardjono received them in Peta and may have taken the operatives and the detonators on to the Sulawesi mainland.[38] On another occasion in 2000, Suryadi and other recruits he was accompanying took a regular ship (presumably a scheduled ferry) between General Santos City and Bitung, and bribed Philippine customs officials not to investigate a crate of "tuna fish" they were transporting.[39]

In Mindanao, JI seems to have had several operatives who, while Indonesian, lived in the Philippines for extended periods of time, and established contacts with indigenous insurgencies such as the Moro Islamic Liberation Front (MILF). Hambali, later a high-ranking JI officer, had been sent by Darul Islam to live with the MILF in the early 1990s and build up relationships that had begun when both Darul Islam and the MILF were training in Afghanistan in the 1980s.[40] Mustopa, the first head of JI's Mantiqi III, also had sufficient contacts in General Santos City to obtain weapons from local sellers and pass them on to operatives such as Suryadi.[41] As part of their cover and for income, JI and affiliated operatives would set up legitimate businesses—in Suryadi's case a jewelry import-export business.[42] This allowed them to make contacts with local economic networks and move weapons and explosives under the cover of legitimate trade, or at least informal trade that was not viewed as inherently dangerous by the authorities.

Consequently, JI's operatives were deeply embedded in the illicit networks of the Mindanao–Sulawesi Utara border area. They had longstanding contacts with the Moro Islamic Liberation Front and built up connections with arms dealers in General Santos City through relatively long stays in Mindanao. The recruitment of the local fisherman and forays into business show that JI operatives operated and gained cover by establishing ties and eventually integrating themselves into local ethnic, social, and business networks that stretched across national boundaries. The police could be bribed, just as in other parts of Indonesia and the Philippines, but there does not seem to have been a systematic effort to co-opt the local authorities.

JI chose to embed itself so meticulously in this region—compared with lesser embeddedness in other parts of Indonesia—possibly because it had no other choice. Local illicit networks, based on local ethnic and social ties and engaged in small-scale commerce, were not set up to be easily accessed by outsiders without considerable investment in building local connections. A deeper question is what caused illicit networks to take this particular form. Sparse state resources in the Mindanao-Sulut region of both Indonesia and the southern Philippines meant that enforcement on either side of the border was more haphazard than in the Riau islands. Co-opting the state might simply not have been the worth the cost in money and time, compared with simply evading it. The result was a noninstitutionalized environment for illicit networks. Moving between two developing countries—and relatively poor regions of those developing countries—would have marginal profits relative to trade to or from a more developed country and would not attract large-scale enterprises that would need to insinuate themselves into local power structures and demand regularized illicit services.

## Implications for Regional Governments

The differing experiences of JI cells in the illicit economies of Southeast Asian borderlands have a number of implications for how we think, not only about counterterrorism and economic development, but also about nontraditional security threats in general. As other analysts have suggested, nontraditional security threats in Asia are now emanating from malevolent nonstate actors such as terrorist groups and agency-less phenomena such as epidemics. Those threats are exacerbated by new technologies. However, those threats are also interconnected in ways that we do not necessarily expect. To take an example from this chapter, state weakness in Southeast Asia, particularly along international borders, does not create terrorism or transnational crime per se. Rather, imperfect state control in border areas creates different incentives for central governments versus local governments, providing a space in which illicit political and economic networks arise that may, given certain conditions, enable terrorist groups to operate more efficiently. Addressing a nontraditional security problem such as terrorism requires not only figuring out whether other problems are connected, but *how* they are connected, and whether a given policy designed to resolve one problem will have unintended side effects in others.

Getting the relationship between terrorism and illicit political and economic networks wrong can have deleterious effects on policies designed to deal with both. Blanket statements about terrorist infiltration of criminal organizations (or vice versa) are both unhelpful and untrue. Local governments have dealt with territorial control problems in different ways—in some cases, by not dealing with them at all, in others, as in the Riau islands, by semiformalizing gray markets in order to lower the time and financial resources needed for socially beneficial illicit movement and trade that were going to happen anyway. These gray markets may or may not actually help terrorist groups operate. This is an important but underappreciated insight: the temptation for states to deny terrorists sanctuary and ease of movement by cracking down on smuggling and tightening border controls may be ineffective or may backfire. Tightening border controls into and out of Batam and Bintan in a bid to stop the movement of terrorists, for instance, may complicate the local government's efforts to facilitate the movement of Indonesian migrant workers, and prevent those workers from earning income to support their families.

This insight is important as we turn to the question of Southeast Asian governments and what they can do about fighting transnational terrorism and the tools terrorists use to operate. At first glance, regional governments' fight against terrorism seems to have been more successful than not in the past decade: while the Philippines sees continuing problems with the Communist and Moro insurgencies, the MILF is willing to talk and make concessions of its own. For their part, Singapore and Malaysia rid their territory of JI operatives fairly quickly upon discovery in 2001 and 2002. In Indonesia, the relatively infrequent bombings since 2002 and the successful takedown of additional terrorists after each attack—bomb maker Azahari Husin in 2005 following the second Bali bombing, and ringleader Noordin Top in 2009 after the second Marriott bombing—suggest that thorough, efficient investigation and the work of Detachment 88, Indonesia's counterterrorism task force, have been successful in taking down active terrorist networks engaged in violent plots.

For all Indonesia's success in hunting down terrorists *inside* the country, there have been embarrassing lapses in stopping terrorists before they get *in* the country. A plot broken up in 2008 involved a Singaporean, and one of the perpetrators of the first Bali bombing was killed in a shootout in Jakarta in 2010 after apparently slipping back into Indonesia from the Philippines.[43] Border areas thus continue to be a problem. Even if the current generation of active JI-linked terrorists is successfully hunted down, the quietist faction of the organization, which currently favors a period of rebuilding and proselytizing rather than bombings, can continue to take advantage of the opportunities provided by the ambiguous political economy of the region's border areas, alongside other Islamist and separatist groups.[44]

The challenge of the borderlands is more complicated than simply "fixing" a potential terrorist haven. The mismatch between the claims that regional governments make over border areas and the actual control is not just a problem in Indonesia; Malaysia, Thailand, and the Philippines have similar gaps in reality and perception. The most obvious solution is simply to increase state capacity, or more specifically regional governments' ability to "broadcast power" in border areas with the same regularity and formality that they often do in core areas. This is easier said than done, in part because the lack of state capacity and resources is one reason why there is a mismatch in the first place.

But it is not simply a matter of state weakness. One of the primary problems for regional governments is that their own laws and regulations are creating arbitrage opportunities, and thus openings for gray and black markets. A common understanding of institutions in political economy is that their purpose is in large part to decrease transaction costs by decreasing the time and effort market actors need to find buyers and move goods, and by ensuring that contracts are enforced with regularity and consistency. Ideally the institutions in Southeast Asia that regulate commerce and movement across countries' borders—both the government organizations and the regulations—should decrease transaction costs or at least minimize them relative to the other purposes of those institutions, such as taxation and establishing sovereignty claims. In reality, many of these institutions actually seem to increase costs for the people involved. In the Sangihe-Talaud Islands in eastern Indonesia, for instance, processing through the sole official customs and immigration checkpoint near Mindanao involves a significant detour for local traders, leaving aside the costs to bribe corrupt officials. In Kepulauan Riau, the onerous and unrealistic regulations necessary for Indonesian workers to go overseas for contract labor legally mean that the vast majority of workers will never be able to go through official channels. Because the demand for emigration services far outweighs the legal supply, gray market agents step in. Just as important, local governments in Kepulauan Riau—and other border areas, such as Kalimantan Timur—cooperate with gray and even black market agents to move people through as efficiently as possible, and to avoid the workers' becoming a drain on their own resources.[45]

These "incentives" for illicit and semi-illicit commerce are not necessarily an accident. Regional governments both rich and poor have incentives for gray and black markets to exist in border areas. Aside from the rents extracted by customs and immigration officials and local governments from illicit trade on both sides of a border, gray and black markets allow poorer countries such as the Philippines and Indonesia to provide migrant workers and traders with a quick and relatively efficient pathway to wealthier countries and more job opportunities. These illicit markets also supply richer countries such as Singapore and Malaysia with access to cheap labor that can be periodically deported to their home countries.[46]

The labor, trade, and emigration regulations that help to create the illicit markets themselves serve an important purpose for central governments in Southeast Asia, in that the regulations accentuate and formalize the governments' sovereignty claims, even if they are enforced imperfectly or not at all. Formal regulations are especially important in sovereignty claims over territory that is disputed between two countries (i.e., in border areas) and areas where actual internal government control is limited. Regardless of the actual labor situation on the ground in Sabah, Malaysia, for instance, where thousands of Indonesians work semi-illegally in construction and on plantations, the Malaysian government will likely not relax formal regulations for Indonesians to enter the country as long as Indonesia and Malaysia have a territorial dispute over the waters off the coast of Sabah.

For governments that do want to decrease the allure of illicit economies, it may be feasible to reduce the transaction and opportunity costs associated with using fully legitimate routes. This could be accomplished through lower (or zero) tariffs and streamlined customs clearance procedures, perhaps targeted geographically at vulnerable land and sea border areas; looser import-export restrictions; and fewer regulations for expatriating migrant workers. It is not even clear why Indonesia, for instance, has *any* regulations governing when its citizens leave the country. The last area is one where regional government cooperation is needed—even if Indonesia were to loosen its expatriate worker regulations, without a clear and efficient process by which the workers could enter Singapore or Malaysia, illicit networks will still arise to provide services to would-be migrants leaving Indonesia.

In areas of weak or sparse state control but only small-scale smuggling, such as the Sulawesi Utara–Mindanao borderlands, one possibility involves establishing a targeted state presence along informal trade routes and regularizing the costs traders must bear. Another possibility is setting up customs checkpoints along informal trade routes so that traders do not have to waste time diverting from their routes. More generally, Indonesia and other developing countries in Southeast Asia should seek to move away from a model where customs officers' primary purpose is to raise revenue to one where their primary purpose is to secure the country's borders. The temptation for customs officers to accommodate bribe-paying importers is no doubt stronger when the importer is asking the officer to sign off on the nondeclaration or underinvoicing of what are otherwise legal goods rather than when the importer is asking that the officer ignore guns, ammunition, or explosives. While developing countries often rely on tariffs for revenue (with income tax being much more difficult to collect) and to protect fledgling domestic industries, the time may have come to dismantle that system in the interests of security. While rethinking customs enforcement is a tall order for the region's countries, it is not unthinkable: The ASEAN Free Trade Area has already eliminated (or drastically decreased) tariffs for its member countries on goods originating from within the ASEAN countries. Because all the ASEAN countries already theoretically are supportive of freer trade, rhetorically connecting freer trade with security imperatives may help convince the relevant players in the region.

Regional governments also have a potential ally in their efforts to alter environments that are supportive of terrorists: the illicit networks themselves. While current formal institutions in Southeast Asia's borderlands may not reduce transaction costs, the ethnic and social ties that straddle the borders *do* lubricate informal trade, and where informal institutions are particularly robust, the best approach may be to co-opt them. Of particular importance, while these networks are "illicit" from the central government's perspective, they are not necessarily illegitimate from the perspective of local residents, or even necessarily local governments (as the *aspal* system in Batam suggests), particularly because these informal trade networks are often older and more legitimate (and certainly more embedded in the local community) than the states themselves. In line with the changes in cross-border trade policy discussed above, Southeast Asian governments should seek ways to formalize informal trade networks. Central governments could derive greater local legitimacy from recognizing, in turn, the legitimacy of traditional local political and economic elites, and gaining their cooperation. This could lead to intelligence gains, because transnational networks grounded in ethnic and social ties will inevitably have better knowledge than outsiders of movements and transactions across the border. Co-opting cross-border trade networks would also allow for greater state presence in areas where state control was previously weak on the ground.

Finally, the divide between central and local governments is also critical, particularly in countries like Indonesia where local governments have been allocated more resources and assigned more responsibility over the past decade. Because, at least from the cases studied in this chapter, terrorist groups appear to be less embedded in highly institutionalized gray markets that have significant local state buy-in, it is possible that the central government may force its preferences for a crackdown on illicit economies with little effect on terrorist groups *and* a backlash from local governments. This could come about in several ways. If the terrorist group is really only using the same routes and methods as the illicit economic networks in a given area, but does not have ties with the illicit economic networks themselves, cracking down on the economic networks (in effect punishing them for the activities of the terrorist group) may not have much effect on the ability of the terrorist group to operate, and will also turn the population against the authorities, because crackdowns deny them the increased efficiencies and products that come from institutionalized gray markets. In Batam, for example, some local officials might view smuggling as a necessary evil,

even if corruption were eliminated and the state given more law enforcement resources. Batam officials have a strong interest in encouraging
cross-border commerce and movement into and out of Batam as a way of
promoting economic development.

Less institutionalized illicit economies, such as that of the Mindanao-
Sulut region, present different complications. In such areas, terrorist groups
face higher time and financial costs associated with taking advantage of
local conditions, but if they are genuinely embedded in local networks,
cracking down on illicit networks might have some genuine effect on the
ability of terrorists to operate. Aside from the economic impact, however,
there is the more fundamental problem that if the state had been able to
broadcast power over the territory in the first place, the informal commercial networks in which terrorist groups are embedded would look different,
and possibly less inviting.

## Implications for the United States

The United States has an interest in the political economy of terrorism in
Southeast Asia. The ability of terrorists to stage attacks in the region not
only risks destabilizing U.S. allies such as Thailand and the Philippines
and U.S. friends such as Singapore and Indonesia but also threatens U.S.
facilities. The U.S. embassies in Singapore and Indonesia and U.S. military
personnel working at Sembawang naval base in Singapore have all been
targeted by terrorists. Additionally, U.S. tourists in Bali and U.S. mission-
aries in the southern Philippines have been killed in terrorist actions. The
United States also has an interest in the indirect effects of terrorism: an
ongoing Islamist terrorist campaign, even if not ultimately successful in
attaining its stated goals, can embolden radical Islamist communities in the
region. Furthermore, if counterterrorism policies are not formulated and
implemented carefully, the general population in countries such as Malaysia and Indonesia may turn against the United States and its interests.

In the short term, the primary U.S. interest comes in seeing active terrorists hunted down and their networks dismantled. In the long term, the
United States has an interest in keeping new terrorist groups from spring-
ing up, and their partially dismantled networks from revitalizing. It is also
imperative to reshape the political, economic, and social environment in
Southeast Asia to make it difficult for terrorists to operate. This is not
merely an academic issue. JI is an offshoot of Darul Islam, an Islamic

nationalist movement that sprang up during the Indonesian War of Independence to fight first the Dutch, and later the secular Indonesian government. Darul Islam has existed since then in various forms—it sent recruits to Afghanistan and the Philippines in the 1980s and 1990s for training, and members of various Darul Islam groups helped JI carry out bombings in the 2000s.[47] Darul Islam continues to inspire new generations who want to see Indonesia become an Islamic state. While the temptation is for both the United States and allied governments to declare victory when a particular terrorist group such as JI is taken down, many of the movements from which terrorists and insurgents spring—notably Islamic fundamentalism and ethnic separatism—adopt the long view. They have waited decades. They can wait decades more.

In any case, the United States' levers for influencing what goes on in Southeast Asia are limited, and whatever policies it adopts must take this into account. Unlike in Northeast Asia, where the United States stations tens of thousands of military personnel on the soil of treaty allies, the U.S. footprint is very small in Southeast Asia—the only U.S. military deployments with more than one hundred personnel are in Singapore and the Philippines.[48] The region's strong attachment to both the legal particulars and symbolic aspects of national sovereignty and noninterference also makes direct U.S. military and even political interventions difficult. This was evidenced by the U.S. Navy's suggestion that it might patrol the Malacca Strait in 2004 to protect against pirates and generally keep the sea lanes of communication secure. The offer was rebuffed quickly and forcefully by Malaysia and Indonesia in particular.[49] The question thus becomes how the United States can protect its interests in fighting terrorists across the region in a way that will not offend regional government sensitivities but still be effective in achieving U.S. goals.

In the past decade, U.S. aid programs to Southeast Asian countries have been focused on political, economic, and military capacity building. In Indonesia, for example, the U.S. Agency for International Development provides funding for rural sector economic growth, election transparency and monitoring, health care, education, and environmental conservation.[50] The State Department has allocated millions of dollars to train and equip the Indonesian police counterterrorism unit, Detachment 88.[51] In 2005, after years of noncooperation due to the Indonesian military's behavior in East Timor, the Pentagon reinitiated training of Indonesian military personnel through the International Military Education Training program, with arms sales returning in 2006, and relations with Kopassus, the Indonesian special forces, restarting in 2010.[52] With U.S. support, the Indonesian police's Detachment 88 has had measurable success in hunting down active terrorists, while the U.S. Agency for International Development's programs have been focused on ameliorating health, economic, agricultural, and educational problems that affect developing countries. No current U.S. programs should necessarily be eliminated, but in the long term, the United States can create new programs to maximize their effectiveness both in developing certain areas of Southeast Asia and in diminishing the ability of terrorist groups to operate in the region.

Simply dumping more money into state capacity–building programs is not the answer. While many national and local governments in the region lack resources, as the case studies demonstrate, local governments in particular respond to realities on the ground in the ways that they do because their priorities are different than those of the national government—they are seeking to creatively solve problems that were in some cases created by national government policies. For programs that are designed to deal with both economic development and counterterrorism, the United States should target its aid at border areas with a history of terrorist operations, or areas with illicit commerce that could aid terrorists in the future. In Southeast Asia, this might include the two regions covered in this paper as well as the Malaysia-Thailand border and the Sabah–Philippines–Kalimantan Timur triangle.

Because of the inherently transnational nature of the networks that cross the border, the United States would do well to restructure program staff to avoid single-country stovepiping, and encourage engagement with multiple countries simultaneously, such as the Philippines and Indonesia in the Mindanao–Sulawesi Utara border area. Aid would be focused not only on border security, or even primarily on border security (more border guards, for instance, just means more opportunities for rent seeking), but on decreasing transaction costs associated with the use of formal political and economic institutions in border areas. This could include such measures as targeted anticorruption campaigns, streamlining and increasing transparency in bureaucratic procedures (which is especially important for the customs and immigration bureaucracies), and sponsoring programs that would encourage formal and informal ties among officials on both sides of borders.

The United States could also promote lower tariffs through free trade agreements with regional governments and perhaps even attempt to negotiate multilateral agreements targeted at specific commodities for which a tariff would otherwise create a gray or black market, such as rice and oil.

The U.S. government might also provide incentives for U.S. companies to invest in the border areas of Southeast Asia. The downside of such a policy is clear: Foreign companies have occasionally become targets for terrorists and insurgents, such as attacks on Exxon facilities by the Free Aceh Movement (Gerakin Aceh Merdeka) during its insurgency, and the security threats against Freeport-McMoRan's mining operations in Papua. At the same time, contact with Western business practices and their expectations of transparency and formal contracts may habituate local Southeast Asian transnational commercial networks to Western norms, just as the overseas Chinese (*huaqiao*) business conglomerates that arose in Hong Kong and Southeast Asia after World War II have gradually become more formalized as they compete in the global marketplace.

Finally, the United States can refocus and expand its funding and counterterrorism training to local police in border areas. The purpose would not be to re-create a national-level Detachment 88 in local areas—in fact, local police departments in Indonesia already have counterterrorism units.[53] Rather, where Detachment 88 functions essentially as a national-level SWAT team and investigative unit, local police in border areas could be trained to take advantage of their knowledge of local political and economic conditions to identify and fix (where appropriate) long-term weaknesses in border enforcement and transborder commercial networks that could be used by terrorists to move people and goods into and out of the country.

While the United States does have some leverage in the financial resources and military expertise associated with fighting active terrorists that it can provide to its friends and allies in the region, in all cases its influence is limited. The United States must tread carefully, with targeted programs and offers of help, if it is to be effective in pursuing its security objectives in Southeast Asia. The good news is that terrorist groups *are* dependent on illicit networks in many regions, and a more nuanced understanding of how terrorist organizations and illicit economies are intertwined can increase the efficiency of counterterrorism operations and mitigate the negative economic and political consequences of crackdowns, all while encouraging economic development.

## Notes

1. See, e.g., the astonishing growth of AirAsia and its various subsidiaries.
2. Anthony Reid, *Southeast in the Age of Commerce, 1450–1680, Volume 2: Expansion and Crisis* (New Haven, Conn.: Yale University Press, 1993).

3. See, e.g., the extensive use of air travel by Jemaah Islamiyah during the planning stages of several plots in 2000 and 2001, noted by Justin V. Hastings, "Geography, Globalization, and Terrorism: The Plots of Jemaah Islamiyah," *Security Studies* 17, no. 3 (July–September 2008): 505–30.

4. Angel Rabasa et al., *Ungoverned Territories: Understanding and Reducing Terrorism Risks* (Santa Monica, Calif.: RAND Corporation, 2007). In a chapter on the Philippines, authors discuss the lack of control the central government exercises over large parts of the southern islands.

5. Eric Tagliocozzo, *Secret Trades, Porous Borders* (New Haven, Conn.: Yale University Press, 2005).

6. Amitav Acharya, "Ideas, Identity, and Institution-Building: From the 'ASEAN Way' to the 'Asia-Pacific Way'?" *Pacific Review* 10, no. 3 (1997): 319–46.

7. Tamara Makarenko, *The Terror-Crime Nexus* (London: C. Hurst & Co., 2007); Paul J. Smith, ed., *Terrorism and Violence in Southeast Asia* (Armonk, N.Y.: M. E. Sharpe, 2005).

8. Phil Williams, "Transnational Organized Crime and the State," in *The Emergence of Private Authority in Global Governance*, edited by Rodney Bruce Hall and Thomas J. Biersteker (Cambridge: Cambridge University Press, 2002).

9. Badan Pusat Statistik Kabupaten Batam, "Batam Dalam Angka Tahun 2009" (Batam, Indonesia: Badan Perencanaan Pembangunan Daerah Kota Batam, 2009), 63

10. Matthew Sparke et al., "Triangulating the Borderless World: Geographies of Power in the Indonesia–Malaysia–Singapore Growth Triangle," *Transactions* (Institute of British Geographers) 29, no. 4 (2004): 485–98.

11. Author's interview, Singaporean police official, Singapore, July 2005.

12. Author's interview, Buddhist pandita, Jakarta, Indonesia, June 2004.

13. Author's interview, Chinese-Indonesian smuggler, Batam, Indonesia, August 2005.

14. Author's interview, Chinese-Indonesian "businessmen," Batam, Indonesia, August 2005.

15. Author's interview, Riau Islands provincial police official, Batam, Indonesia, November 2005.

16. Ibid.

17. Michele Ford and Lenore Lyons, "Travelling the Aspal Route: Grey Labour Migration through an Indonesian Border Town," in *The State and Illegality in Indonesia*, edited by Edward Aspinall and Gerry van Klinken (Leiden: KITLV Press, 2011).

18. Ibid. See also Michele Ford and Lenore Lyons, "Smuggling Cultures in the Indonesia-Singapore Borderlands," in *Illegal but Licit*, edited by B. Kalir and M. Sur (Amsterdam: Amsterdam University Press, in press).

19. International Crisis Group, *Jemaah Islamiyah in Southeast Asia: Damaged but Still Dangerous* (Jakarta: International Crisis Group, 2003); Justin V. Hastings, *No Man's Land: Globalization, Territory, and Clandestine Groups in Southeast Asia* (Ithaca, N.Y.: Cornell University Press, 2010), chaps. 4 and 8.

20. For a discussion of the Luqmanul Hakiem branch of Jemaah Islamiyah, see Justin Magouirk, Scott Atran, and Marc Sageman, "Connecting Terrorist Networks," *Studies in Conflict and Terrorism* 31 (2008): 1–16.

21. Hastings, "Geography, Globalization, and Terrorism."

22. Author's interview, Singaporean Internal Security Officials, Singapore, November 2005.

23. "The Jemaah Islamiyah Arrests and the Threat of Terrorism," Ministry of Home Affairs, Singapore, January 7, 2003; "Singapore Government Press Statement on Further Arrests under the Internal Security Act, 19 Sep 2002," Ministry of Home Affairs, Singapore, September 19, 2002.

24. *Surat Pernyataan Hashim Bin Abbas* (Singapore: Kepolisian Negara Republik Indonesia, 2002), 4–5.

25. "Berita Acara Pemeriksaan (Tersangka) Abdul Azis Bin Sihabudin Al. Abu Umar Al. Imam Samudra Al. Fais Yunshar Heri Al. Hendri Al. Kudama," Batam: Kepolisian Negara Republik Indonesia, Daerah Riau, Kota Besar Barelang, November 27, 2002, 5.

26. *Surat Pernyataan Ja'afar Bin Mistooki* (Singapore: Kepolisian Negara Republik Indonesia, 2002), 2–4.

27. "Berita Acara Pemeriksaan," 4.

28. See Hastings, "Geography, Globalization, and Terrorism," 526–27.

29. Suko Bandiyono, "Mobilitas Penduduk Sangihe," in *Dinamika Mobilitas Penduduk Di Wilayah Perbatasan*, edited by Mita Noveria et al. (Jakarta: Pusat Penelitian Kependudukan, LIPI, 2007), 81.

30. Haning Romdiati, "Perdagangan Ilegal Dan Mobilitas Penduduk Di Wilayah Perbatasan," in *Mobilitas Penduduk Di Wilayah Perbatasan Dan Kegiatan Ilegal*, edited by Mita Noveria et al. (Jakarta: Pusat Penelitian Kependudukan, LIPI, 2008), 124.

31. Ibid., 111.

32. General Santos City Government, "Tuna Industry," General Santos City Official Website, 2010, http://www.gensantos.gov.ph/tuna-industry/.

33. Romdiati, "Perdagangan Ilegal Dan Mobilitas Penduduk Di Wilayah Perbatasan," 112.

34. Ibid., 115.

35. Ibid., 126–27.

36. Badan Pusat Statistik Kabupaten Kepulauan Sangihe, *Sangihe Dalam Angka Tahun 2008* (Tahuna: Badan Pusat Statistik Kabupaten Kepulauan Sangihe, 2008), 118.

37. Nasir Abas, *Membongkar Jamaah Islamiyah: Pengakuan Mantan Anggota Ji* (Jakarta: Grafindo, 2005).

38. International Crisis Group, *Jemaah Islamiyah in Southeast Asia*, 19–21.

39. Ibid., 20–21.

40. Abas, *Membongkar Jamaah Islamiyah*, 143.

41. International Crisis Group, *Jemaah Islamiyah in Southeast Asia*, 20–21.

42. Author's interview, international nongovermental organization researcher on terrorism and insurgency, Singapore, April 2005; International Crisis Group, *Jemaah Islamiyah in Southeast Asia*, 21.

43. Jakarta Globe, "Dulmatin Posed as Livestock Trader While Running Guns to Aceh: Authorities," *Jakarta Globe*, March 11, 2010.

44. International Crisis Group, *Indonesia: Jemaah Islamiyah's Current Status* (Jakarta: International Crisis Group, 2007).

45. Awani Irewati, ed., *Kebijakan Luar Negeri Indonesia Terhadap Masalah Tki Ilegal Di Negara-Negara Asean* (Jakarta: Pusat Penelitian Politik, LIPI, 2003), 93, 104–5.

46. See, e.g., ibid.

47. International Crisis Group, "Recycling Militants in Indonesia: Darul Islam and the Australian Embassy Bombing," Jakarta, February 22, 2005; International Crisis Group, *Jemaah Islamiyah in Southeast Asia*.

48. International Institute for Strategic Studies, *The Military Balance* (London: International Institute for Strategic Studies, 2010), 43–44.

49. Mark Baker, "Malaysia Rebuffs U.S. Sea Force Plan," *The Age*, April 6, 2004.

50. U.S. Agency for International Development, "USAID Asia—Countries—Indonesia," USAID, 2010, http://www.usaid.gov/locations/asia/countries/indonesia/indonesia.html.

51. Ed Davies and Olivia Rondonuwu, "U.S.-Funded Detachment 88, Elite of Indonesia Security," Reuters, March 18, 2010.

52. Mustaqim Adamrah and Rendi R. Witular, "Kopassus Officially Off U.S. Military Embargo," *Jakarta Post*, July 23, 2010.

53. Author's interview, political-military analyst, Jakarta, December 2009.

# Chapter 10

# Managing New Security Challenges in Asia: Between Cybercrime and Cyberconflict

*Adam Segal*

In January 2010, Google announced that it, along with some thirty other companies, had been hacked and that the Gmail accounts of Chinese human rights activists had been accessed. A week later, in a wide-ranging speech about Internet freedom, Secretary of State Hillary Clinton declared U.S. interest in the free flow of information and called for countries or groups engaging in cyberattacks to "face consequences and international condemnation."[1] While Google traced the attack back to China, officials vocally denied that China was involved. Moreover, through an editorial in the *People's Daily*, Beijing criticized Clinton's speech as "naked political scheming," with the *Guangming Daily* protesting that the U.S. government "is relying on Internet technology as a tool to promote American values in other countries. An excuse for the use of this tool is the so-called 'free flow of information.'"[2]

The Google incident was the most public evidence that cyberconflict—the use of computer power for intelligence gathering or to attack the computer, communication, transportation, and energy networks of states or nongovernmental groups—had become a major arena of political and military contestation in Asia and beyond. Japanese and South Korean networks have been targeted after flare-ups over the Dokdo/Takeshima islets, Taiwanese computers are routinely probed, and 500,000 computers on the mainland were attacked in 2011, according to Chinese security officials. While much of the speculation about Stuxnet, a sophisticated computer worm that targets industrial control systems, has focused on Iran and its nuclear weapons program, the worm spread throughout Asia, infecting computers in India, Indonesia, and China. In the United States, hackers have accessed the networks of the Pentagon, White House, defense contractors, and utilities, as well as high technology, financial service, and oil companies.

The United States now has a declared national interest in a secure, open, and globally interconnected Web—one safe for not only economic exchange but also the flow of ideas. Stating the goal is much easier than achieving it, however, because attacks on and conducted over computer and communication networks exist in the overlap between "new" and "traditional" security challenges. As a result, policymakers are pushed outside of their comfort zones; not only do these threats present a technological challenge that many do not understand, but the policy solutions are an ever-changing mix that draws from several seemingly unrelated quivers—computer science, technical standards, trade policy, deterrence theory, and traditional diplomacy—all at once.

As many have already noted, the most obvious difference between the Internet and the other security domains is that cyberspace is manufactured. No one is creating more land, sea, air, or space, but technological, economic, and social change means that communication and computer networks are in constant flux. According to Michael Hayden, the former director of the U.S. Central Intelligence Agency, "Cyber was moving so fast that we were always in danger of building up precedent before we built up policy."[3] In addition, the diffusion of technologies has strengthened nonstate actors. Computer networks allow small groups to conduct offensive and surveillance operations that were once the sole purview of big states. As Alex Karp, the chief executive officer of Palantir Technologies, put it, "Software and technology have democratized espionage."[4]

Moreover, as Hathaway and Wills note in their introduction, cyberattacks are new in that they recognize neither international borders nor traditional definitions of sovereignty. Attacks are often traceable back to a national network system, and U.S. intelligence officials have suggested, for example, that they can identify particular Chinese groups behind the intrusions of government and private company networks, although in many cases it remains uncertain if these events are the work of independently operating "patriotic hackers," criminal groups, a national security agency, bored teenagers, or some combination of all four.[5] Attacks can be routed through multiple networks across several countries, all of which are usually owned and operated by private actors. No one agency, either national or multilateral, exerts authority over all parts of the Web; the Internet Corporation on Assigned Network Names, the organization responsible for the management of domain names and Internet Protocol addresses, for example, is a nongovernmental organization and plays a critical role in maintaining the stability and security of the domain name system.

The attribution problem—the difficulty of identifying who is behind an attack—also makes it difficult if not impossible to adopt many of the traditional tools of statecraft in the cyberrealm. Regional military stability, for example, has been maintained in part by deterrence and the capacity to hold valuable targets at risk in case of an attack, as well as the ability to distinguish between criminal act and warfare. But if states cannot identify who is behind an attack, then they cannot punish them and so cannot deter them from taking actions inimical to their interests. Besides, it is often difficult to decide whether an event is actually an attack or something else: A scan of a network can be espionage, crime, or preparation for a full-scale attack. The interconnectivity of the Web also makes collateral damage extremely difficult to predict and deterrence harder. Any counterstrike may also affect uninvolved third parties or lead to unexpected escalation, and so political leaders may be unwilling to risk a cyber-based response, further undermining deterrence. Moreover, the attribution problem makes verification difficult, weakening possible arms control agreements in cyberspace. Arms control agreements require participants to make mutual concessions, but participants are unlikely to forgo cyberexploitation or cyberattack capabilities in exchange for mutual restraint in the absence of better verification capabilities.

At the same time, the newness of cyber should not be overstated. States remain important actors; they are not powerless in the face of cyberspace, and in fact they are working to reassert their control and sovereignty over the Internet. The companies that develop and own the hardware and software of the Internet—as well as individuals who manipulate and send information—exist in the real world and so are subject to laws, regulations, and other instruments of state power. States can threaten, imprison, fine, and monitor individual users, and they can require that the physical infrastructure of the

Internet is configured to give them more control. Worried about the threat that the free flow of information poses to regime stability (in the case of China, Myanmar, and Vietnam) or that terrorists will abuse communication systems (India, the United States), states are insisting that service providers give security agencies the ability to monitor electronic traffic.[6]

Moreover, national rivalries and traditional geopolitical competition continue as cyberspace is quickly being militarized. With the establishment of the U.S. Cyber Command, the United States may be the furthest down this road. The Pentagon's 2011 Strategy for Operating in Cyberspace states that the U.S. military "will treat cyberspace as an operational domain to organize, train, and equip so that DoD can take full advantage of cyberspace's potential."[7] Still, other countries are not far behind. South Korea established an independent cyberwarfare command in 2010 to carry out planning, implementation, training, and research and development. Open-source Chinese writings speak of information warfare as a critical component of any military conflict. As a 2007 RAND Corporation study notes, People's Liberation Army (PLA) analysts speak of "soft-kill" and "hard-kill" methods in information warfare. Soft-kill methods include computer network attacks and electronic jamming, whereas hard-kill methods include directed energy weapons and explosives.[8] Chinese analysts believe that soft-kill methods are particularly useful against a stronger enemy; they give the PLA a longer strike range than it has with conventional weapons, and the attribution problem creates plausible deniability—the victim will not be "able to tell whether it's a child's prank or an attack from an enemy."[9]

The tension of viewing cybersecurity as a new security and a traditional security issue emerges in the competing analogies used to conceive of the problem and its policy solutions. Those who view it primarily through a national security perspective are more likely to refer to "cyberwar" and hark back to the 1950s and 1960s, to Project Solarium and to the work of nuclear deterrence theorists such as Herman Kahn and Bernard Brodie. As Mike McConnell, former director of the National Security Agency and National Intelligence, put it in a *Washington Post* article, "The cyber-war mirrors the nuclear challenge in terms of the potential economic and psychological effects. So, should our strategy be deterrence or preemption? The answer: both." With this framework in mind, McConnell identifies the attribution problem as critical, and suggests a radical reengineering of "the Internet to make attribution, geolocation, intelligence analysis and impact assessment—who did it, from where, why and what was the result—more manageable."[10]

In contrast, former cybersecurity czar Howard Schmidt said that cyberwar "is a terrible metaphor and . . . a terrible concept."[11] Greg Rattray and his coauthors argue that dealing with cyber is less like nuclear war and more like addressing global public health risks. While different models apply in wartime, the public health model "applies well in a range of peacetime scenarios in which cybersecurity involves defense against the spread of malware and botnet attacks—the cyberequivalent of 'preventive medicine.'"[12] The public health model does not discount the attribution problem, but it shifts focus from trying to quickly identify and punish attackers to the question of accountability, and the process of creating norms and cooperative agreements that change the incentives and operating environment of attacking states.

No matter what analogy is applied, it is clear that technology will change too quickly, and actors, be they individual hackers, criminal gangs, or states, will always find a way to exploit vulnerabilities. Cybersecurity will be a constant risk, and the United States will need to adopt a range of technological, security, commercial, and diplomatic strategies that manage the risks of attacks and increase resilience after the inevitable attack occurs. The rest of the chapter introduces the scope of the threat in Asia; the risk, so far, has primarily been economic and not oriented toward national security. As a result, there may be opportunities for the United States to build on national and regional responses to cybersecurity. The chapter concludes by suggesting a regional strategy for the United States that has a twofold focus: creating a more effective mechanism for combating crime, and developing norms of accepted state behavior in cyberspace.

## The Scope of the Challenge

Not surprisingly, the scope of the challenge depends on what is being discussed and the specific national context. While the term "cyberwar" is frequently used by the media, it makes more analytical sense to refer to "cyberconflict" and to divide that term into four categories of activities: crime, espionage, political hacking, and cyberwar.

Cybercrime already has a major detrimental impact on the global and regional economy; data theft and cybercrime cost global businesses more than $1 trillion in intellectual property annually, and computer attacks reportedly cost the U.S. economy $8 billion in 2009; these numbers include the value of customer and employee data, legal and financial records, and intellectual property as well as the time and expense of repairing and closing security vulnerabilities.[13] Eighty-three percent of Chinese Web users, 70 percent of Indians, and 70 percent of Singaporeans have been victims of some sort of cybercrime, including computer viruses, online credit card fraud, and identity theft, compared to 73 percent in the United States.[14] In another survey, 75 percent of companies in Asia reported cyberattacks over the course of a year.[15]

Espionage is conducted by both state and nonstate actors and is directed at political and military secrets as well as commercial intellectual property. Prominent attacks include the theft of details about the F-35 fighter, the attack on Google and thirty other technology companies, as well as what researchers at the University of Toronto have called GhostNet—computer espionage that affected more than 1,250 computers in 103 countries, although the majority of attacks appear to have been directed at the Dalai Lama and governments in South and Southeast Asia.[16] In 2010, South Korean intelligence reported attacks that appeared to be directed at officials and politicians involved in relations with the North, and Mitsubishi Heavy Industries and other Japanese defense contractors reported attacks in 2011.[17]

In political attacks, government Web sites, or sites closely associated with the state, political parties, social movements, or nongovernment organizations can be attacked by individuals and groups. The attacks that regularly occur when territorial disputes erupt between China and Japan, Japan and South Korea, or Indonesia and Malaysia are the most common forms of political hacking. Dissidents and government opponents can also be silenced. In Malaysia, the blog of government critic Datuk Seri Anwar Ibrahim's has been knocked offline by distributed denial of service (DDoS) attacks, an attack that makes a Web site unavailable or slows it down by flooding it with communication requests. DDoS attacks have also disabled the Web sites and blogs of critics of the Vietnamese Communist Party as well as BauxiteVietnam.info, an environmental Web site opposed to Vietnamese mining policy. Additionally, the Web sites of Survival and five other organizations—all of which hosted videos of Indonesian soldiers allegedly torturing native Papuans—were knocked offline in October 2010.[18]

Thus far, the region has not witnessed a real outbreak of cyberwar—the use of computer network operations to cause damage, destruction, or casualties for political effect by states or political groups. Cyberattacks are unlikely to be decisive, but they will provide advantage and, as demonstrated by the attacks on Georgian Web sites during the 2008 conflict with Russia, should be expected to be part of any future military conflicts.[19]

Instead of cyber as a weapon of mass destruction, the region has witnessed cyber as a weapon of mass disruption. Over the 2009 Fourth of July
weekend, for example, at least 11 major Web sites in South Korea including those of the Blue House, the Defense Ministry, the National Assembly,
the daily newspaper *Chosun Ilbo*, and the top Internet portal Naver.com as
well as the United States–based Web sites of the *Washington Post*, National
Security Agency, Department of Homeland Security, State Department,
and Nasdaq stock exchange all came under attack, with many crashing or
slowing to a crawl.[20] Yet these distributed denial of service attacks caused
no significant economic or political damage.

While most incidents have so far only had a relatively minor impact,
the potential threat to regional stability grows as power, finance, health,
and other critical systems grow more dependent on information and communication systems. As India's cybersecurity strategy states, "Many of
the critical services that are essential to the well-being of the economy are
increasingly becoming dependent on IT [information technology]."[21] In
the wake of the 2009 attacks on South Korea and the United States, Japan
announced "preparatory measures to be able to manage the state under
a large-scale cyberattack, in which the attack may threaten or actually
cause harm to life, physical injury, or the assets of the nation, or even the
country itself."[22]

In addition, the scope and sophistication of attacks are also increasing. As
Iain Lobban, director of the United Kingdom's Government Communications Headquarters (a defense intelligence agency), describes the problem,
80 percent of attacks can be solved by "observing basic network security
disciplines like keeping patches up to date." In contrast, the remaining 20
percent of "the threat is complex and not easily addressed by just building
the security walls higher and higher."[23] Stuxnet drew attention because it
appears to have compromised industrial control systems that were thought
to be relatively insulated from attack; many analysts also argued that the
code itself was more technologically sophisticated than anything previously seen out "in the wild."[24]

There are at least three additional dynamics of cyberattacks that threaten
regional stability: misperception, false flag attacks, and crisis aggravation.
South Korean officials, for example, quickly blamed the distributed denial
of service attacks that occurred in 2009 on North Korea. One theory was
that the attacks were retaliation for a new round of United Nations sanc-
tions, levied after North Korea's May 25 nuclear test. Computer experts,
however, cautioned that there was little evidence linking the attacks to

North Korea, and eventually a security company found the attacks involved 166,908 zombies, or compromised computers, from seventy-four countries, with the top three being South Korea, the United States, and China. North Korea was not on the list. The master server used in the attack was traced back to Miami. The fact that attacks can unfold in minutes if not seconds, while attribution is a slow and uncertain technical process, further desta-bilizes the situation. Pressured to "do something" quickly, leaders might launch what they see as a counterattack on their uninvolved and unwit-ting neighbor. Representative Peter Hoekstra, for example, claimed that the Fourth of July attack could not be the work of amateurs and urged a "show of force or strength" against North Korea.[25]

The desire to move quickly and to show force also creates the possibil-ity of "false flag" operations designed to get another state in trouble or to foment conflict between two other parties. Attacks that are the work of criminal gangs or patriotic hackers could be erroneously ascribed to another state, creating a regional crisis that quickly spins out of the control of policymakers in Beijing, Washington, Seoul, Taipei, or Tokyo.

The use of the Web as a weapon—or as an organizational or broad-cast tool for nonstate actors and political groups—also challenges foreign policymakers in the region. Web defacement and other attacks are now a regular part of interstate tension; in 2001 and 2005, for example, Chinese hackers defaced Japanese government Web sites after official visits to Yasukuni Shrine, and Japanese hackers targeted the Web site of the China Federation for Defending the Diaoyutai in 2004, 2005, and 2008. While in some instances states may exploit the actions of patriotic hackers to send a message, it is also possible that hacking can exacerbate crisis instability. Diplomats may try to signal their desire to de-escalate a conflict just as hackers take down an electrical grid.

How to control and channel attacks is now a particular focus for China. In the early stages of the crisis that erupted in September 2010, after Japan detained a fishing boat captain for colliding with a Japanese Coast Guard vessel, the Chinese authorities appear to have tried to prevent public pro-tests from spinning out of control. The Honker Union, a large group of Chinese hackers, announced that an attack on Japanese computers would not be useful; students were told not to protest; and the Web site of the China Federation for Defending the Diaoyutai was taken offline and anti-Japanese statements were erased from chat rooms. Still, by mid-September the Web sites of the Japanese Defense Ministry and the National Police Agency came under attack, and a week after Premier Wen Jiabao and Prime

Minister Kan met briefly in Brussels, the Chinese released some controls and there were protests in Zhengzhou, Xi'an, and Chengdu.

Finally, it is worth noting that dependence on and vulnerability to information technologies vary widely across the region. There is a significant digital divide in Asia, with Japan, South Korea, and Taiwan being some of the most wired societies in the world and boasting some of the most innovative IT companies. Malaysia has high Internet penetration and successful component and hardware manufacturers. China, India, Thailand, Indonesia, and Vietnam occupy a middle space, with relatively low penetration but a growing mass of Internet users and sophisticated commercial technologies. Meanwhile, Pakistan, Myanmar, Cambodia, North Korea, and Laos lag behind on both fronts. Internet penetration, for example, is extremely low in Myanmar, where there are 473,700 users, or 0.1 percent of the population, compared with South Korea, where there are 40.6 million users, or roughly 81 percent of the population.[26] North Korea has only three Internet service providers, and the country ranks 227th in terms of Internet access.[27]

## Differing Domestic Responses to Cybersecurity Challenges

As Nicholas Thomas notes, the countries in East Asia have different economic models, political systems, and rates of Internet connectivity and, thus, conceive of and respond to the cybersecurity challenge differently.[28] One-party, authoritarian states in particular are likely to think of security as having both an external component—threats from foreign hackers—and an internal component, viewing the free flow of information and unrestricted content as a threat to domestic stability and regime legitimacy. While the United States talks of cybersecurity, primarily meaning the defense of computers, networks, and infrastructure, China refers to information security, which includes content. A July 2010 report from the Chinese Academy of Social Sciences, *Development of China's New Media*, pointing to 2009 protests in Moldova and Iran, accuses the United States of using Twitter, Facebook, and other social media sites to foster instability.[29] The call of a State Department official to Twitter asking for the delay of scheduled maintenance during the protests in Tehran reinforced Beijing's sense that Twitter and other social media companies were tools of a U.S. policy of regime change. The Chinese have also protested the State Department's funding of circumvention software through the Global Internet Freedom Consortium, a group with ties to Falun Gong, which Beijing considers an evil cult.[30]

More liberal, open societies are also worried about internal threats, but this is usually framed as a concern about terrorists, criminal gangs, and others who might use connection technologies to plan and coordinate violent attacks, rather than concerns about political content transmitted over computer and cell phone networks. In the wake of the November 2008 attacks, Mumbai demanded that the firm until recently known as Research in Motion, the developer of the BlackBerry, set up servers locally and enable security agencies to monitor mail.

Different political systems pull in different directions, and domestic policies throughout the region encompass a range of responses that embrace varying political, economic, and cultural concerns. But the tension between two different conceptions of cybersecurity—as a traditional national security issue or as a nontraditional, transnational issue—is shared across the region. This is not a tension that has been resolved. States have so far tended to adopt solutions from both approaches or move back and forth between the two.

### Japan and South Korea

The South Korean and Japanese approaches to cybersecurity demonstrate similar threat perception, strategy, and institutional frameworks. In both countries, the primary threat is seen as crime, followed by espionage (both corporate and political), political hacking, and cyberwar. From 1995 until 2005, according to South Korean analysts and government officials, the threat was primarily "brunt force" attacks on government and business Web sites, especially through worms (self-replicating malware) and distributed denial of service attacks. The Korean Internet Security Center, housed in the Korean Communications Commission (KCC), was created after the slammer worm paralyzed the Internet for almost seven hours. Starting in 2005, attacks become more sophisticated and targeted, often involving a high degree of social engineering. All South Koreans must have registration numbers to use the Internet, and this is a very attractive target for hackers, especially in China, who use them to participate in South Korean online games and buy and sell products using virtual money. These identification numbers will become even more in demand as banking and other financial transactions in South Korea are moved to smart phones.[31]

The threat to Japan is also seen as growing in sophistication. For most of the decade, Japanese conceptions of cyber were closer to the public health model of quarantine and resilience. The 2006 First National Strategy on

Information Security listed three main objectives: the continued development of Japan as a major economic power, the realization of better lives
for the people through the use of IT, and ensuring national security from a
"new perspective."[32] The 2009 report *Secure Japan* embraces a resilience
model even tighter, describing an "'Accidents Assumed Society' with an
assumption that disasters may occur, rather than the previous activities
focused on preventative measures aiming at no accidents." Some outside
analysts complained at the time that the 2009 document gave short shrift to
national security concerns.[33]

By 2010, planning documents were tacking in the other direction, partly
because of personnel changes on the Information Security Policy Center
and several prominent large-scale data leaks, as well as concerns that Japan
could be subject to a large-scale attack. As the 2010 planning document
states, "Due to the large-scale cyberattack case in South Korea and U.S.
in July 2009, it is clear that the threat of information security has become
an issue of security assurance and crisis management while the risks faced
by information security are diverse, sophisticated and complex, and more
difficult to ensure information security through conventional efforts."[34]
Japanese government officials and analysts were focused on the threat of
targeted attacks—malicious emails or other exploits directed at specific
firms, many of which were seen to come from computers in China—as well
as broader attacks on infrastructure and national security.

In response to these threats, both South Korea and Japan have adopted
a similar institutional framework, a triad of defenses for government,
military, and private networks. In South Korea, the Ministry of Defense
is responsible for defending military networks and conducting offensive
operations. Critical infrastructure used by the government and the public sector is defended by the National Cyber Security Center, which is
under control of the National Intelligence Service. The responsibility for
protecting private networks is distributed to three agencies: the KCC, the
Korea Internet and Security Agency (KISA), and the Ministry of Knowledge Economy. Within KISA, the Korean Internet Security Center monitors domestic networks in real time and collects data from and coordinates
with the major Internet service providers and antivirus software firms.
At the top, the National Cybersecurity Strategy Council, chaired by the
head of the National Intelligence Service, is expected to coordinate policy
responses among all the ministries and agencies listed above as well as
the National Security Council Secretariat, Ministry of Administration and
Security, Ministry of Foreign Affairs and Trade, and Ministry of Justice.

The institutional framework in Japan mirrors that of South Korea. Established in 2005, the National Information Security Center (NISC)—chaired by the chief cabinet secretary and staffed by officials on loan from several ministries, including the Ministry of Economy, Trade, and Industry (METI); the Ministry of Defense; and the Ministry of Internal Affairs and Communications—coordinates policy at the top. It also sets the broad parameters for the protection of government networks, critical infrastructure, and the private sector. METI takes the lead on private sector and individual user security. The Ministry of Defense defends military networks. Apparently influenced by the establishment of the U.S. Cyber Command as well as the prominence of cyberwar in the 2010 Quadrennial Defense Review, the Ministry of Defense appointed a new coordinator for cyberplanning in the Joint Staff Office in 2010.

With these institutions in place, both countries face similar barriers to effective implementation and response. Outside analysts and government officials in both places speak of the difficulty of coordinating across different ministries and agencies. In Japan, this was in part the result of a lack of attention from the prime minister (and the constant turnover in the office from Koizumi to Noda), as well as the NISC's lack of authority over other ministries. In the wake of the announcement that Mitsubishi Heavy Industries had been breached, the NISC recommended the creation of computer-security-incident response teams in each government agency, as well as in companies with defense contracts, and the appointment of a chief information officer to coordinate their work. In South Korea, one analyst questioned the wisdom of distributing authority to KISA, the KCC, and the Ministry of Knowledge Economy: "It is better to have one control tower."[35]

There is also the difficulty of coordinating with private business, especially in the area of protecting infrastructure. The Japanese and South Korean governments set standards for security, and then it is up to businesses to meet them. Although by law South Korean companies are required to report attacks, companies—especially in the banking and financial sectors—often fail to comply and are reluctant to share information about specific malware.

Still, it is worth noting that both countries have adopted similar models of controlling botnets—a collection of computers that are used for illegal purposes without their owners' knowledge—which require a high degree of coordination among the government, vendor, and Internet service providers (ISPs). In Japan, the Cyber Clean Center runs decoy computers that collect and analyze malware. ISPs are notified that the attacks are coming from their customers' computers, which in turn inform the individual users, either through emails or regular mail, that they have been infected, directing them to a public site to download a disinfection tool. Response by the user is voluntary; of those who receive infection reports, about 40 percent access the Web site and about 30 percent download the removal tool.

## Malaysia and India

Compared to the Japanese and South Korean approaches, domestic terrorism and internal stability play a larger role in Malaysian and Indian thinking about cybersecurity. Also, because neither is a formal U.S. ally, they have more flexibility in promoting different forms of international cooperation.

Malaysia's definition of cyberthreats is less beholden to the state-centric, national security view than that found in Northeast Asia. "New cyberthreats," according to the National Cyber Security Policy document, "are in many ways significantly different from the more traditional risks that governments have been used to addressing."[36] Government officials break down the threat into hacks, fraud, denial of service, harassment, national security, sedition, and hate speech. Over 75 percent of incidents are referred to a law enforcement agency, which suggests the predominance of criminal, not military, threats.

That said, Malaysian officials refer to both the 2007 attacks on Estonia and the Stuxnet worm as the types of threats the National Cyber Security Policy was established to defend against.[37] The policy creates uniform security standards for protecting networked information systems in ten critical sectors: defense, banking and finance, communication, energy, transportation, water, health services, government, emergency services, and food and agriculture. More than three hundred government agencies that have responsibilities for these systems are required to meet uniform security standards (International Organization for Standards' Information Security Management System) by 2013. Coordinating the government's response is CyberSecurity Malaysia, which is administered by the Ministry of Science, Technology, and Innovation and is overseen by the National IT Council (chaired by the prime minister). In the case of a massive attack or a national crisis, the National Security Council directs the government response through the National Cyber Crisis Management Plan.

As with all the other cases, public-private partnership is extremely important. Malaysian officials boast that their response time for newly discovered malware is better than in most developed economies. The Cyber

Security Center, banks, the Malaysian Communications and Multimedia Commission (MCMC), Internet service providers, and the police all work closely together. "We can stop it within 24 hours," says Lieutenant Colonel Husin Jazri (retired), chief executive officer of CyberSecurity Malaysia. "If you talk about a 100-metre sprint, we are the fastest. Our cyberspace is well governed."[38] At the same time, Husin admitted that CyberSecurity Malaysia had no real sense of the scope of the problem. Bank Negara Malaysia, the Securities Commission, and MCMC collect their own data and information: "We have not been able to collate these statistics to see the bigger picture."[39]

Perhaps not surprisingly for a small country, Malaysia has also stressed the international dimension of cybersecurity. The International Multilateral Partnership Against Cyber Threats (IMPACT), which bills itself as the world's first global public-private partnership against cyberthreats, is a cooperative project with the International Telecommunication Union (ITU), the UN's agency for information and communication technologies. The initiative was announced by former prime minister Abdullah Ahmad Badawi in 2005, and the Malaysian government provided initial seed funding. Based in Cyberjaya, a science park located in the Multimedia Super Corridor about 50 kilometers south of Kuala Lumpur, IMPACT is now operationalizing the ITU's Global Cybersecurity Agenda, which involves developing legal framework, technical measures, and capacity building in member states, as well as building international cooperation. Currently, IMPACT provides security consulting for 48 of the ITU's 191 member states.

Although Indian policymakers refer to four types of attacks—crime, political hacking, sabotage, and espionage—cybersecurity is in large part shaped by concerns with two neighbors: Pakistan and China. After India's nuclear tests in 1998, Pakistani hackers attacked the Web sites of *Zee News* and *India Today*. After the terror attacks on Mumbai in 2008, the Pakistan Cyber Army hacked into the Web sites of the Indian Institute of Remote Sensing, the Center for Transportation Research and Management, and the Oil and Natural Gas Corporation of India. The attacks themselves have had a galvanizing effect on the Indian government; the terrorists used email and Google Earth to plan the attack, and since 2008 policymakers have struggled over how to prevent future attackers from exploiting communication technologies.

In addition, in 2010 it became publicly known that Indian diplomatic and military assets were the subject of a sustained espionage campaign apparently originating in Chengdu, China. Using Twitter, Facebook, Google Groups, and other social networking tools, hackers gained control over computers in the Indian military, the National Security Council Secretariat, and Indian embassies around the world.[40]

In response to these threats, the National Information Board (NIB) was set up in 2002. Chaired by the National Security Adviser, the NIB is the highest body to address cybersecurity issues in the country and consists of twenty-one members, mostly secretaries in the central government.[41] The National Technology Research Organization (NTRO) provides technical assistance and intelligence to the NIB, and the National Security Council Secretariat (NSCS) coordinates cybersecurity activities with the public and private sectors. The Computer Emergency Response Team–India (CERT-In)—within the Ministry of Communications and Information Technology's Department of Information Technology—is the lead agency for responding to and preventing attacks, especially on critical infrastructure defined as defense, finance, energy, transportation, and telecommunications networks.

After the Chinese espionage attacks became public in 2010, there were multiple calls for the creation of a cybercommand within the military as well as the use of Indian patriotic hackers. In August 2010, for example, the *Times of India* reported a high-level meeting, chaired by the national security adviser, Shiv Shankar Menon, and attended by the director of the Intelligence Bureau as well as senior officials of the telecommunications department and IT ministry, that considered recruiting and providing legal protection to "ethical hackers" who would be used to hack into the computers of hostile nations.[42] Interviewees in Delhi also reported that NTRO officials were soliciting hackers on Web sites and discussion groups, although others thought that, as a democracy with a free, vital press, India would be unable to exploit nonstate actors in the ways that China was reported to; eventually a reporter would find and reveal the link between the government and patriotic hackers, and the Indian government would be unable to deny it was involved in an attack.

Not surprisingly, given the geographical and bureaucratic size of India, cyberpolicy is seen to lack an overall strategy or policy coherence—or, as one think tank analyst put it, "No holistic view, no cyberstrategy."[43] The NIB rarely meets, and several interviewees reported a turf battle between CERT-In and the NTRO, whose activities are seen to be "shrouded in secrecy." As Subimal Bhattarcharjee put it, "The government is not able to demarcate a healthy work share between CERT-In and NTRO."[44] In February 2012, the *Times of India* reported that the Cabinet Committee on Security would clearly delineate responsibilities among CERT-In, NTRO, the Intelligence

Bureau, Military Intelligence, and other agencies fighting cyberintrusions, and in November of the same year the government announced the appointment of the first national cybersecurity coordinator.[45]

Contact and cooperation with the private sector are difficult because of the lack of a single coordinating point on the government side and the widely distributed nature of Indian infrastructure. One interviewee noted that it was almost impossible to believe that anyone, inside or outside of the government, had an adequate inventory of electrical power assets in the country, and he had no idea if the electrical industry had a critical infrastructure working group that interacted with the government. In October 2012, national security adviser Shiv Shankar Menon released the report of the joint working group on cybersecurity, which focused on improving public-private cooperation.[46]

There was, however, a very successful case of coordination during the Commonwealth Games in 2010. The Cyber Crisis Management Group, which operated from a command center set up on the seventh floor of the Games' organizing committee headquarters, defended six networks from a thousand attacks over twelve days. The group included cyberexperts from the intelligence agencies, the Delhi Police, and CERT-In, as well as vendors like Mahanagar Telephone Nigam Ltd., Electronics Corporation of India Ltd., and Telecommunications Consultants India Ltd.[47] Still, several outside analysts thought it would be very difficult to build out this model to any scale, given that it was successful largely because only a limited number of networks and organizations were involved.

## Regional Cooperation: Bilateral and Multilateral

Although the countries throughout the region are moving quite rapidly to develop national responses to cybersecurity, there is a widespread recognition that the challenge must be addressed through cooperation, either bilateral or multilateral. In 2005, for example, the United States and Japan agreed to annual meetings to strengthen cooperation against cyberattacks. In 2010, Japanese communications minister Kazuhiro Haraguchi and Julius Genachowski, chairman of the U.S. Federal Communications Commission, announced additional plans to combat attacks on government and business networks, with Japan's 2010 Information Strategy claiming that "international alliances must be reinforced as unprecedented borderless incidents are now more likely to occur."[48] Also in 2010, the Indian minister of state for communications and information technology, Sachin Pilot, suggested closer technological collaboration between Washington and Delhi, and during President Obama's visit to India in November the two sides announced their intention to "work together to promote a reliable information and communications infrastructure and the goal of free, fair and secure access to cyberspace."[49] Still, there is in much of the bilateral negotiations and pronouncements a sense that there is much to talk about, but very little concrete that gets accomplished, with the two sides failing to adopt any specific follow-up measures. With the United States–India announcement, for example, the most tangible example of cooperation was India's participation as an observer of U.S. Cyber Storm III, a biennial preparedness exercise.

The most developed cooperation mechanism is the Asia-Pacific Computer Emergency Response Team (APCERT). Each country in the region has its own computer emergency response team—Japan's is located in METI, South Korea's in KISA, Malaysia's in CyberSecurity Malaysia, and India's in the Department of Information Technology—which monitors traffic, responds to incidents, and coordinates with local Internet service providers. These teams then coordinate regionally and internationally. Full members of APCERT include China, Japan, South Korea, Taiwan, Brunei, India, Malaysia, Sri Lanka, Vietnam, the Philippines, Indonesia, Hong Kong, Singapore, Thailand, and Australia. The organization conducts annual drills in which the national computer emergency response teams test points of contacts and information-sharing procedures; in January 2010, for example, participants responded to a simulated attack on financial networks by detecting and analyzing the malware involved, and by shutting down and blocking systems hosting phishing sites or involved in DDoS attacks. Malaysia has also reached out to other Muslim-majority states, establishing the Organization of Islamic Conference Computer Emergency Response Team (known as OICCERT).

In 2004, Japan, South Korea, and China created a trilateral mechanism for cooperation in network and information security. Information and communication technology ministers met in Sapporo, Japan and agreed to develop a joint response to cyberattacks, as well as information exchanges on online privacy protection and national cyberpolicy. The three sides agreed to a stepped response mechanism—first, ISPs would coordinate; then, computer emergency response teams; and then, ministries—depending on the severity of attacks. Over the years, there have been several drills and real-life responses (e.g., hacking between South Korea and Japan over the Dokdo/Takeshima islets), but government officials in China, Japan, and South Korea all complained in interviews about specific instances in which their counterparts were not responsive enough or local authorities did little to pursue or stop hackers attacking foreign networks, though the agreements seemed more robust in the wake of tensions in the East China Sea in 2012.

The Association of Southeast Asian Nations (ASEAN) Regional Forum organizes an annual seminar on cyberterrorism, with members promising "to share intelligence, expertise and skills on fighting cyber-crime, and look at laws to prevent terrorist attacks being planned or encouraged through computer networks."[50] According to the "2009–15 Roadmap for an ASEAN Community," ASEAN will also foster cooperation among member nations' law enforcement agencies and promote the adoption of cybercrime legislation. Though ASEAN has primarily focused on terrorism, the Asia-Pacific Economic Cooperation forum (APEC) has concentrated more on crime; APEC's Cyber Security Strategy, developed by the Telecommunication and Information Working Group, encourages members to build up "comprehensive substantive, procedural, and mutual assistance laws and policies."[51] Programs include identifying best practices, helping developing economies in the region build their own national computer emergency response teams, and capacity building in cybercrime prosecution and judgment.

Although regional mechanisms are important, they primarily focus on information sharing, training, consultation, and coordination; they lack sanction and enforcement. These agreements are unlikely, in the near term, to move beyond greater coordination without shared definitions of legitimate action on the Internet. To rephrase a cliché for the Information Age, one state's patriotic hacker is another's cyberterrorist. Moreover, too many states now benefit strategically from a relatively uncontrolled cyberspace. This may change as states begin to recognize their own vulnerability to cyberattacks, but this is likely to be a long, drawn-out process.

## Principles of Action

In May 2011, the White House released its "International Strategy for Cyberspace."[52] The document clearly stated U.S. interests in cyberspace as working "to promote an open, interoperable, secure, and reliable information and communications infrastructure." These goals are to be pursued through diplomacy, defense, and development, and U.S. officials are to concentrate their efforts in seven areas: international standards and open markets; network defense; law enforcement; military alliances and cooperative security; Internet governance; international development and capacity building; and the support of Internet freedom and privacy. The document is stronger on process than actual strategy. The strategy is very focused on how the United States should do things: "distributed systems require distributed action"; the United States will engage as many actors in as many forums as possible; sometimes Washington will work with close allies, while in other instances it will engage potential adversaries; the ITU may be a suitable venue for discussing technical issues, while regional groupings may be more appropriate for security concerns; the United States will need to work with the private sector as well as nongovernmental groups such as the Internet Engineering Task Force, an open, international community of network designers, operators, vendors, and researchers that addresses the technical issues of the Internet. There is little discussion, however, on guidelines for what the priorities should be—is it more important to work with countries such as India and Brazil on technology standards or to come to some agreement with Russia and China on cyberconflict? The United States should and can do both, but eventually decisions are going to have to be made about time, resources, and the inevitable trade-offs between competing goals.[53]

The United States must also realize that its own actions will have a massive effect on shaping international behavior. Washington cannot expect others to rein in criminal behavior when American computers are the source of many cybercrimes. According to the security firm Kaspersky Labs, the United States surpassed China in the first quarter of 2010 as the largest source of malicious programs; 28 percent of the 1.9 million servers it found distributing malware were located in the United States.[54] In one survey of 600 IT and security executives around the world, it was the United States they feared the most, with 36 percent of all respondents saying that it represented their "greatest concern" to networks in their country; China followed, at 33 percent.

Similarly, the United States probably has the most sophisticated cyberweapons capabilities in the world, and thus its actions will directly affect the strategic analysis of other states. During his confirmation hearing as head of the U.S. Cyber Command, Lieutenant General Keith Alexander declared it was "not about the militarization of cyberspace," but rather safeguarding vital systems. Though this statement was clearly meant to reassure Beijing, Moscow, and others and to dampen an arms race, it is likely to have little impact. In his written answers submitted to the committee before the hearing, Alexander stated that foreign nations' military command-and-control networks, power grids, banks and other financial institutions, and transportation and national telecommunication networks are "all potential targets of military attack, both kinetic and cyber, under the right circumstances."[55] As Jack Goldsmith has argued, "U.S. cybersecurity policymakers are in the habit of thinking too much about those who attack us and too little about our attacks on others."[56]

With a distributed process and a sense of its own global impact, the United States should work to shrink the space for cybercrime and develop norms for state action. These two areas are, as others have pointed out, connected. Criminal activity provides a cover for some state activity like espionage and political attacks against dissidents, like the DDoS attacks on Twitter that were directed at the Georgian blogger known as CYXYMU.[57] Espionage networks in particular exploit criminal techniques both to "distance themselves from attribution and strategically cultivate a climate of uncertainty." In addition, in the "absence of norms, principles, and rules of mutual restraint at a global level, a vacuum exists for subterranean exploits to fill."[58] With no state willing to define clearly what types of behavior should or should not be allowed, almost anything becomes permissible.

## Cybercrime

International efforts to control cybercrime center around the Council of Europe's Convention on Cybercrime. The convention establishes a baseline set of laws that parties to the treaty agree to pass, criminalizing computer crimes such as illegal access and interception, data and system interference, misuse of devices, forgery, fraud, child pornography, and intellectual property offenses. It also requires signatories to cooperate in the investigation and prosecution of such crimes. This convergence of laws was expected to ensure that there is no safe harbor for criminals.

In effect, however, the convention has not worked. States can opt out of the duty to cooperate if the request infringes on sovereignty, security, or other critical interests. As a recent National Research Council study concluded, "A signatory nation may decline to cooperate with its obligations under the convention on fairly broad grounds, and the convention lacks an enforcement mechanism to assure that signatories will indeed cooperate in accordance with their obligations."[59] Every country in the world was invited to sign, but even with relatively lax enforcement requirements, only twenty-nine countries have ratified, including the United States, with seventeen signatories in the process of consideration, including Japan. China and Russia have refused to sign, with Moscow protesting against a provision that would let foreign investigators work directly with network operators, avoiding government officials.[60] India has complained that it was not part of the convention's creation, and Japan's hesitancy in ratifying seems to stem from the convention's European provenance.

A more effective model for cyber might be built on the experience of the Financial Action Task Force (FATF), which was developed in an effort to combat money laundering.[61] Established in 1989 by the Group of Seven and some other countries, the FATF now includes thirty-four countries, which conduct a majority of the world's financial transactions. The FATF exports best practices—forty recommended regulations—but members are also subject to self-evaluation and peer review in a multilateral process. When states fail to conform to accepted standards, members of the FATF can threaten the loss of access to international financial networks. There are also regional organizations that provide similar services.

In the case of cyber, the United States and other states could work to develop accepted standards of behavior, based on the Council of Europe's Convention on Cybercrime as well as other recognized Asian best practices. States might choose to stop exchanging traffic with the networks of states that do not make significant progress in eliminating criminal havens (i.e., depeering). These provisions would not be fail-safe; as with traditional sanction regimes, states will find ways out of their isolation, perhaps through finding other suppliers. Offending states could also reroute traffic, but there would be reputational costs, as states would be clearly defined as violators of cybercrime norms. More broadly, the U.S. government would root the anticrime efforts within specific regional institutions and understandings.

## Norms of Behavior

It will not be enough, however, just to address the issue of criminals and cybercrime. Rather, state action helps structure the space for cybercrime and other illegal behavior. Most of the rules of cyberconflict—what legitimate targets are, how states control escalation and signal intentions, and what types of cyberattacks would constitute an act of war—are unknown.

The United States must work with its allies as well as potential adversaries in Asia to develop accepted norms of behavior.

After several previous refusals, in December 2009 the United States agreed to enter into discussion with Russia about a cyber arms control agreement.[62] It is likely, however, that U.S. negotiators believe there is little chance that the discussions will lead to anything like an arms controls agreement for cyberspace, because the barriers to any agreement are very high. As Jack Goldsmith has noted, there is the problem of mutual concessions. The United States talks primarily about preventing attacks on critical infrastructure like the power grid or financial systems; the Russians and the Chinese worry about these vulnerabilities but are also interested in censoring content. Washington provides support for "hacktivists" to circumvent content filters and views this behavior as benign, whereas "the Chinese view them on a par with the Google hack." [63] As a result, in any negotiations, Russia and Beijing are likely to demand that the United States limit its support for digital activists in return for controlling its patriotic hackers, a requirement Washington is unlikely to meet.

Even if states decided to work toward an arms control agreement, they would have little confidence in its effectiveness. Verification of attribution is extremely difficult. Signers of an agreement could mask an attack, rendering compliance very difficult to verify in any reasonable amount of time.[64] The lines between an attack, a probe (scouting for vulnerabilities), and espionage are very thin. The technologies used in most attacks are commercial and widely available; laptop computers, Internet connection, and programming tools are cheap and easy to conceal. Many tools for exploitation and espionage are available on the black market.

Finally, the growing importance of information in warfare makes attacks on digital infrastructure too valuable for a state to renounce. China in particular sees cyber as a useful tool against a stronger adversary. Since the 1991 Persian Gulf War, "PLA military strategists have emphasized using asymmetric approaches to level the playing field against technologically superior opponents."[65] Chinese defense analysts believe attacks on information systems can have widespread effects and thus are a strong deterrent, especially because they believe that the United States is much more dependent on these systems than is China.

Despite the difficulties of shaping an arms control accord, it still makes sense for the United States to engage both its allies and potential adversaries in discussions of norms of behavior that might create mutual understandings, reduce unintended outcomes, control escalation, and prevent miscalculation. The first move would be greater transparency in military doctrine regarding the use of cyberattacks. As previously noted, the United States is already widely seen to be both the most powerful force in cyberspace and intent on limiting room for others to maneuver. Moreover, given current technological capabilities, defense is at a major disadvantage, and so there is a push for the research and deployment of "active defenses"—offensive cyberweapons that can be used against an attacker before an attack is ever launched.[66] Because it is difficult to differentiate between offensive and defense capabilities, countries are likely to respond to new research-and-development projects by developing their own weapons for even more effective attacks, creating a classic security dilemma.

Few militaries, as James Lewis has noted, will be willing to discuss potential offensive operations. But at a general level, discussions about what targets are considered legitimate, which targets should be off limits, and how the authority for attacks is distributed will help reduce misperception. As suggested by Robert Knake, the United States, along with all other users, has a stake in maintaining the security of the root servers.[67] Thirteen root servers help resolve the request for a Web site name into an Internet address for all top-level domains (.com, .net, .us, .jp, .cn); they are currently vulnerable to penetration attempts and DDoS attacks.

Similarly, states need to begin to more clearly define what the threshold of an attack is—what types of attacks constitute an act of war and what types are seen as being escalatory. This is a particularly important discussion for the United States to have with its allies Japan and South Korea; one of the issues raised by the large-scale DDoS attacks on Estonia was whether the country should, or could, have invoked Article 5 of the NATO Charter, in which members agree that an "armed attack against one or more of them . . . shall be considered an attack against them all." At the time, NATO and international law lacked an accepted definition of cyberattack (as is the case today). In the end, Estonia appealed for technical assistance in dealing with the attacks, not for NATO to mount some type of counteroperation.

Moreover, as Eneken Tikk has argued, it would have been irresponsible, and counterproductive, for Estonia to invoke Article 5 with "no clear vision about the expected outcome."[68] Estonia did not perceive itself as being at war, but rather informed NATO of a new type of risk and asked the organization to come up with a position on future attacks. It seems unlikely that the United States and its allies have—as of yet—agreed on what constitutes a cyberattack, and what the responsibilities of each party are. In early 2010, a senior Japanese official reported that the Ministry of Defense was still waiting for the United States to take the lead in crafting a shared definition of an attack that crossed the threshold.[69]

There are some signs that China in particular may be receptive to an opening from the United States on cyber. China was one of fifteen countries along with India and South Korea that agreed in July 2010 to a set of recommendations on how to move forward in international discussions on cybersecurity. The proposal included discussions about how different nations view the Internet; cyberwar; computer security; improving the infrastructure and security of less developed countries; and developing a common terminology.[70] At the same time, China appears to be signaling that it is willing to enter into discussions with the United States about the rules of the road. After returning from a visit to Beijing in the summer of 2010, Senators Dianne Feinstein, Mark Udall, and Kay Hagan reported that Wu Bangguo, National People's Congress Standing Committee chairman, suggested that cybersecurity be added to the topics discussed at the annual Strategic and Economic Dialogue between the United States and China.[71]

It took several decades of engagement and pressure to get Beijing to move on proliferation, but there may be some lessons from the past.[72] In both cases, Beijing turned a blind eye to, and possibly encouraged, illegal markets for strategic, ideological, and economic reasons. As with cyberattacks, sales to Iran, North Korea, and other rogue states were an attractive asymmetrical weapon. In addition, there was a degree of plausible deniability; the Chinese domestic market was so large, Beijing could claim it had no knowledge and little control over some of the companies doing the selling.

Washington has at least three reasons to think that it might come to some type of agreement with Beijing on cyberissues.[73] First, there are signs that Beijing is increasingly worried about its own growing vulnerability to cyberattacks. According to Liu Zhengrong, deputy director general of the Internet Affairs Bureau of the State Council Information Office, "Internet-related crimes are showing a steady upward trend," and China "suffers big economic losses from hacking networks and viruses."[74]

Second, there are competing interests within the Chinese government. The strongest incentive for some form of cooperation is probably economic. Chinese firms are themselves threatened by hacking, and because they want to expand globally, they also have a stake in international security norms. So for every discussion about the governance of the Internet, there are a series of minidebates between those who have a more mercantilist view of the world and those willing to pursue Chinese goals through collaboration and open trade. The United States wants this second group to prevail as much as possible.

The third reason is that, for image and status concerns, Beijing has traditionally not liked being on the outside of international agreements and can often be brought in by highlighting the disparity between China's position and international norms. In climate change negotiations, for example, China presents itself as a developing country and as a representative of the Group of Seventy-Seven, and so the group exerts some influence over Chinese behavior. For example, following protests from leaders of the group, China relinquished its claim to any payment from a global climate fund after years of insisting on some share of the money. Pushing China toward accepted norms is, of course, easier to do when there are in fact widely accepted international norms. These are currently lacking in cyberspace, but Washington's participation in international discussions about state behavior and responsibility could begin to help shape an international consensus that Beijing feels uncomfortable standing outside of.

## Conclusion

States in Asia have been proactive in addressing the cybersecurity issue both domestically and multilaterally, and there is much that United States should embrace and expand. An approach more oriented toward national security clearly has a role, with the traditional allies of the United States along with potential adversaries. Together, these actors must begin to define the types of attacks that cross the threshold of armed conflict and suggest how states might actually respond. The United States, widely perceived by the rest of the world as possessing the most technologically sophisticated attack capabilities, will, however, need to take the lead in defining the state norms of cyberconflict. Interviewees in Seoul and Tokyo, for example, pointed to establishment of the U.S. Cyber Command as having an influence on national decisionmaking and institution building. Public statements from Department of Defense officials about U.S. doctrine and strategy will have a pervasive, if hard-to-measure, impact on how states in the region think about and plan for cyberwar.

In the short term, however, the United States will gain more traction if it frames cybersecurity as a new, cooperative security issue, downplaying and diminishing talk of "cyberwar." At this point, the region appears open to a new security approach, whether it is based in public health, low insurgency conflict, or some other model. Of course, there is likely to be some swinging of the pendulum, as has happened in Japan. There, after the 2009 attacks on South Korea and the United States, the language of cyber shifted from resilience and recovery to national security. But it is early enough in the process that the United States can embrace and promote a regional approach that is open, transparent, and cooperative.

It will, however, be difficult for the United States to pursue both approaches at the same time; in fact, the first is likely to undermine any efforts to build the second. Policymakers in Tokyo and Seoul, much less Beijing, are going to be suspicious of collaborative approaches if they believe Washington is prioritizing offensive capabilities over all other possible responses to cybersecurity. The most lasting impact of the Stuxnet virus may not be on the Iranian centrifuges at Natanz but in the growing assumption that the United States was involved in designing the malware, either alone or with Israel.[75] Given the high degree of dependence of the American economy and military strength on information and communication networks, the United States is likely to be the biggest loser in a world where states feel there are no boundaries on permissible behavior. It makes sense to try to develop constraining norms sooner rather than later.

## Notes

1. Hillary Rodham Clinton, "Remarks on Internet Freedom," Newseum, Washington, D.C., January 21, 2010, http://www.state.gov/secretary/rm/2010/01/135519.htm.

2. *China Daily* quoted in "China Paper Slams U.S. for Cyber Role in Iran Unrest," Reuters, January 24, 2010, http://www.reuters.com/article/idUSTRE60N0V320100124.

3. Ellen Nakashima, "Dismantling of Saudi-CIA Web Site Illustrates Need for Clearer Cyberwar Policies," *Washington Post*, March 19, 2010.

4. "A Conversation with Alex Karp, CEO Palantir Technologies," *Charlie Rose Show*, August 11, 2009, http://www.charlierose.com/view/interview/10549.

5. Office of the National Counterintelligence Executive, "Foreign Spies Stealing U.S. Economic Secrets in Cyberspace," October 11, 2011 http://www.dni.gov/reports/20111103_report_fecie.pdf; Siobhan Gorman, "U.S. Homes in on China Spying," *Wall Street Journal*, December 13, 2011.

6. "India Asks RIM, Google, Skype to Set Up Local Servers," Bloomberg News, September 2, 2010, http://www.bloomberg.com/news/2010-09-01/india-asks-rim-google-skype-to-set-up-local-servers-update1.html; Charlie Savage, "U.S. Wants to Make It Easier to Wiretap the Internet," *New York Times*, September 27, 2010.

7. U.S. Department of Defense, "Department of Defense Strategy for Operating in Cyberspace," July 2011, http://www.defense.gov/home/features/2011/0411_cyberstrategy/docs/DoD_Strategy_for_Operating_in_Cyberspace_July_2011.pdf.

8. RAND Corporation, "Entering the Dragon's Lair," 2007, xvi, http://www.rand.org/pubs/monographs/2007/RAND_MG524.pdf.

9. Quoted by James Mulvenon, "PLA Computer Network Operations: Scenarios, Doctrines, Organizations, and Capability, in *Beyond the Strait: PLA Missions Other Than Taiwan*," 258.

10. Mike McConnell, "How to Win the Cyber-War We're Losing," *Washington Post*, February 28, 2010.

11. Ryan Singel, "White House Cyber Czar: 'There is No Cyberwar,'" *Wired*, March 2010, http://www.wired.com/threatlevel/2010/03/schmidt-cyberwar/.

12. Greg Rattray, Chris Evans, and Jason Healey, "American Security in the Cyber Commons," in *Contested Commons: The Future of American Power in a Multipolar World*, edited by Abraham M. Denmark et al. (Washington, D.C.: Center for a New American Security, 2010), 151, http://www.cnas.org/files/documents/publications/CNAS%20Contested%20Commons_1.pdf.

13. Anastasia Ustinova, "Russian Cybercrime Thrives as Soviet-Era Schools Spawn Hackers," Bloomberg, October 6, 2010, http://www.bloomberg.com/news/2010-10-05/russian-cybercrime-thrives-as-soviet-era-schools-spawn-world-s-top-hackers.html.

14. Norton Cybercrime Report, *The Human Impact*, 2010, http://us.norton.com/content/en/us/home_homeoffice/media/pdf/cybercrime_report/Norton_USA-Human%20Impact-A4_Aug4-2.pdf; Sharath Kumar, "Cyber Crime: China, India Most Affected Nations," http://www.ciol.com/Security/Vulnerabilities/News-Reports/Cybercrime-China-India-most-affected-nations/141165/0/; Tyler Thia, "70 Percent of S'pore Net Users Hit by Cybercrime," *ZDNet Asia*, September 9, 2010.

15. Symantec, "Symantec State of Enterprise Security Study," February 24, 2010, http://security.networksasia.net/content/where-enterprise-security-heading-2010.

16. "Tracking GhostNet: Investigating a Cyber Espionage Network," *Information Warfare Monitor*, 2009, http://www.scribd.com/doc/13731776/Tracking-GhostNet-Investigating-a-Cyber-Espionage-Network.

17. Neil Ungerleider, "South Korea's Power Structure Hacked, Digital Trail Leads to China," *Fast Company*, October 2010, http://www.fastcompany.com/1696014/chinese-hackers-target-south-korean-diplomats; "Japan's Defense Industry Hit by Its First Cyber Attack," Reuters, September 19, 2011, http://www.reuters.com/article/2011/09/19/mitsubishiheavy-computer-idUSL3E7KJ0BD20110919.

18. "Malaysian Government Critics Silenced with DDoS Attacks," *InfoSecurity*, September 15, 2010, http://www.infosecurity-magazine.com/view/12466/malaysian-government-critics-silenced-with-ddos-attacks/?goback=.gmp_2677290.gde_2677290_member_29715679; "Google: Critics of Vietnam Mine Face Online Attack," Associated Press, March 31, 2010; John Leyden, "Tribal Rights Charity Weathers DDoS Assault," *The Register*, October 28, 2010.

19. James Lewis, "Multilateral Agreements to Constrain Cyberconflict," *Arms Control Today*, June 2010, http://www.armscontrol.org/act/2010_06/Lewis.

20. Matthew Shaer, "North Korean Hackers Blamed for Sweeping Cyber Attack on U.S. Networks," *Christian Science Monitor*, July 8, 2009, http://www.csmonitor.com/Innovation/Horizons/2009/0708/north-korean-hackers-blamed-for-sweeping-cyber-attack-on-us-networks; Choe Sang-Hun, "Cyberattacks Jam Government and Commercial Websites in U.S. and South Korea," *New York Times*, July 8, 2009, http://www.nytimes.com/2009/07/09/technology/09cyber.html.

21. Indian Department of Information Technology, "Cybersecurity: Strategic Approach," n.d., http://www.mit.gov.in/content/strategic-approach.

22. "Information Security 2010," Information Security Policy Center, July 22, 2010, http://www.nisc.go.jp/eng/index.html.

23. U.K. Government Communications Headquarters, "Iain Lobban, Director of United Kingdom's Government Communications Headquarters, Makes a Cyber Speech at the IISS, October 12, 2010, http://www.gchq.gov.uk/Press/Pages/IISS-CyberSpeech.aspx.

24. William J. Broad, John Markoff, and David E. Sanger, "Israeli Test on Worm Called Crucial in Iran Nuclear Delay," *New York Times*, January 15, 2011.

25. John Leyden, "Congressman Calls for 'Cyber-Reprisals' against North Korea," *Register*, July 13, 2009, http://www.theregister.co.uk/2009/07/13/korean_ddos/.

26. "Internet World Stats," June 2010, http://www.internetworldstats.com/asia/kr.htm and http://www.internetworldstats.com/asia/mm.htm.

27. James Lewis, "Speak Loudly and Carry a Small Stick: The North Korean Cyber Menace," *38 North*, September 7, 2010, http://38north.org/2010/09/speak-loudly-and-carry-a-small-stick-the-north-korean-cyber-menace/.

28. Nicholas Thomas, "Cyber Security in East Asia: Governing Anarchy," *Asian Security* 5, no. 1 (2009): 3–23.

29. Anita Chang, "China Group Says U.S. Uses Facebook to Sow Unrest," Associated Press, July 9, 2010, http://www.salon.com/news/2010/07/09/as_china_social_media.

30. John Pomfret, "U.S. Risks China's Ire with Decision to Fund Software Maker Tied to Falun Gong," *Washington Post*, May 12, 2010, http://www.washingtonpost.com/wpdyn/content/article/2010/05/11/AR2010051105154.html.

31. Interview with a senior official, Korean Communications Commission, Seoul, March 2010.

32. National Information Security Policy Center, "First National Information Security Strategy," Tokyo, February 2, 2006, www.nisc.go.jp/eng/pdf/national_strategy_001_eng.pdf.

33. Interview with a professor, Keio University, Tokyo, March 2010.

34. "Information Security 2010," Information Security Policy Center, July 22, 2010, http://www.nisc.go.jp/eng/index.html.

35. Interview with a professor, Korea University, Seoul, March 2010.

36. Ministry of Science, Technology, and Innovation, National Cyber Security Policy, n.d., http://nitc.mosti.gov.my/portalnitc/index.php?option=com_content&view=article&id=22&Itemid=93.

37. Rob O'Brien, "Prime Minister's Office Targets Infosecurity Threats," November 11, 2010, http://www.futuregov.asia/articles/2010/nov/11/malaysia-positions-itself-cyber-security-hub/.

38. "World Wide Threat," *Malaysian Business*, July 1, 2009.

39. Ibid.

40. Steven Adair et al., "Shadows in the Cloud: Investigating Cyber Espionage 2.0," Joint Report: Information Warfare Monitor and Shadowserver Foundation, April 6, 2010.

41. Subimal Bhattacharjee, "The Strategic Dimensions of Cyber Security in the Indian Context," *Strategic Analysis*, 33, no. 2 (2009), 196–201.

42. "Desi Hackers Join Indian Cyber Army," *Times of India*, August 5, 2010.

43. Interview with a senior fellow, Institute for Defence Studies and Analyses, Delhi, October 18, 2010.

44. Bhattacharjee, "Strategic Dimensions."

45. "Government Draws Up Multi-Layered Plan to Strengthen Cyber Security," *Times of India*, February 12, 2012, http://articles.timesofindia.indiatimes.com/2012-02-07/india/31033732_1_cyber-attacks-cyber-security-cert; Josy Joseph, "Gulshan Rai Tipped to Be First Coordinator of National Cybersecurity Agency," *Times of India*, November 4, 2012, http://articles.timesofindia.indiatimes.com/2012-11-04/india/34908267_1_cyber-security-cyber-threat-national-technical-research-organisation.

46. Subimal Bhattacharjee, "Managing India's Cybersecurity Problems," LiveMint, October 16, 2012, http://www.livemint.com/Opinion/XIvim27KMgpKffESs11HFL/Managing-Indias-cyber-security-problems.html.

47. Ritu Sarin, "1,000 Cyber Attacks on Games, Most from China," *India Express*, October 16, 2010.

48. National Information Security Center, "Information Strategy 2010," Washington, D.C., 2010, http://www.nisc.go.jp/eng/pdf/is2010_eng.pdf.

49. White House, "Fact Sheet on U.S.-India Strengthening Cooperation on Cybersecurity," November 8, 2010, http://www.whitehouse.gov/sites/default/files/Fact_Sheet_on_U.S-India_Strengthening_Cooperation_On_Cybersecurity.docx.

50. "ASEAN Regional Forum, Co-Chairs' Summary Report of the Fourth ASEAN Regional Forum Seminar on Cyber Terrorism," Busan, South Korea, October 16–19, 2007.

51. APEC Telecommunications and Information Working Group, "APEC Cybersecurity Strategy," August 19–23, 2002, Moscow, http://unpan1.un.org/intradoc/groups/public/documents/APCITY/UNPAN012298.pdf.

52. See Barack H. Obama, "International Strategy for Cyberspace: Prosperity, Security, and Openness in a Networked World," White House, Washington, D.C., May 2011, http://www.whitehouse.gov/sites/default/files/rss_viewer/international_strategy_for_cyberspace.pdf.

53. Adam Segal, "Open, Interoperable, Secure, and Reliable," *Asia Unbound*, May 17, 2011, http://blogs.cfr.org/asia/2011/05/17/open-interoperable-secure-and-reliable/#more-4270.

54. Bryan Acohido, "U.S. Replaces China as Top Source of Malicious Servers," *USA Today*, June 3, 2010.

55. U.S. Senate, "Advanced Questions for Lieutenant General Keith Alexander, USA Nominee for Commander, United States Cyber Command," http://www.senate.gov/~armed_services/statemnt/2010/04%20April/Alexander%2004-15-10.pdf.

56. Jack Goldsmith, "Can We Stop the Global Cyber Arms Race?" *Washington Post*, February 1, 2010, http://www.washingtonpost.com/wp-dyn/content/article/2010/01/31/AR2010013101834.html.

57. Jenna Wortham and Andrew E. Kramer, "Professor Main Target of Assault on Twitter," *New York Times*, August 8, 2009, http://www.nytimes.com/2009/08/08/technology/internet/08twitter.html.

58. "Shadows in the Cloud: Investigating Cyber Espionage 2.0," *Information Warfare Monitor* and *Shadowserver Foundation*, April 6, 2010, http://shadows-in-the-cloud.net.

59. William A. Owens et al., *Technology, Policy, Law, and Ethics Regarding U.S. Acquisition and Use of Cyberattack Capabilities* (Washington, D.C.: National Research Council, 2009), 24.

60. David Talbot, "Global Gridlock on Cyber Crime," *Technology Review*, July–August 2010, http://www.technologyreview.com/computing/25584/?a=f.

61. Roderic Broadhurst and Peter Grabosky, eds., *Cyber-Crime: The Challenge in Asia* (Hong Kong: Hong Kong University Press, 2005), 291; James Andrew Lewis, *Cyber Security: Turning National Solutions into International Cooperation* (Washington, D.C.: Center for Strategic and International Studies, 2003); Robert Knake, *Internet Governance in an Age of Cyber Insecurity,* Council Special Report 56 (New York: Council on Foreign Relations, 2010).

62. John Markoff and Andrew E. Kramer, "In Shift, U.S. Talks to Russia on Internet Security," *New York Times*, December 13, 2009, http://www.nytimes.com/2009/12/13/science/13cyber.html.

63. Jack Goldsmith, "The New Vulnerability," *New Republic*, June 7, 2010, http://www.tnr.com/article/books-and-arts/75262/the-new-vulnerability.

64. David Elliott, "Weighing the Case for a Convention to Limit Cyberwarfare," *Arms Control Today*, November 2009, http://www.armscontrol.org/act/2009_11/Elliott.

65. Office of the Secretary of Defense, "Military Power of the People's Republic of China 2008," Annual Report to Congress, http://www.defense.gov/pubs/pdfs/China_Military_Report_08.pdf.

66. William Lynn III, "Defending a New Domain: The Pentagon's Cyberstrategy," *Foreign Affairs*, September–October 2010, http://www.foreignaffairs.com/articles/66552/william-j-lynn-iii/defending-a-new-domain.

67. James Lewis, "Multilateral Agreements to Constrain Cyberconflict," *Arms Control Today*, June 2010, http://www.armscontrol.org/act/2010_06/Lewis; Knake, *Internet Governance.*

68. "Why Estonia Did Not Invoke Article 5," March 25, 2009, http://www.eneken tikk.net/2009/03/why-estonia-did-not-invoke-article-5.html.

69. Interview with a senior official, Ministry of Defense, Tokyo, March 2010.

70. John Markoff, "Step Taken to End Impasse over Cybersecurity Talks," *New York Times*, July 16, 2010, http://www.nytimes.com/2010/07/17/world/17cyber.html.

71. Dianne Feinstein, Mark Udall, and Kay Hagan, "U.S. and China Must Lead on Cybersecurity," *San Francisco Chronicle*, July 9, 2010, http://articles.sfgate.com/2010-07-09/opinion/21943516_1_wu-bangguo-united-states-and-china-cybersecurity.

72. Adam Segal, "Apples Are to Oranges as Cyber Is to?" *Asia Unbound*, May 3, 2010, http://blogs.cfr.org/asia/2010/05/03/apples-are-to-oranges-as-cyber-is-to/.

73. Adam Segal, "China and the Shared Domains," paper presented at the "Intelligence Community and Cyberspace: Traditions, Boundaries, and Governance Conference," Office of the Director of National Intelligence, Washington, D.C., August 9, 2010.

74. "China Addresses 'Severe Cyber Security Threats,'" *China Daily*, May 6, 2010, http://www.chinadaily.com.cn/china/2010-05/06/content_9814131.htm.

75. Broad, Markoff, and Sanger, "Israeli Test."

# Contributors

**Justin V. Hastings** is assistant professor at the Georgia Institute of Technology's Sam Nunn School of International Affairs. He received his Ph.D. in political science from the University of California, Berkeley.

**Robert M. Hathaway** is director of the Asia Program at the Woodrow Wilson International Center for Scholars. He received his Ph.D. in history from the University of North Carolina.

**Yanzhong Huang** is associate professor at the John C. Whitehead School of Diplomacy and International Relations at Seton Hall University and senior fellow for global health at the Council on Foreign Relations. He received his Ph.D. in political science from the University of Chicago.

**David Pietz** is associate professor of history at Washington State University and director of its Asia Program. He received his Ph.D. in history from Washington University in Saint Louis.

**Kenneth Pomeranz** is University Professor in History and the College at the University of Chicago. He received his Ph.D. in history from Yale University.

**Robert S. Pomeroy** is professor of agricultural and resource economics at the University of Connecticut, sea grant fisheries extension specialist at the Connecticut Sea Grant Program, and principal scientist at the WorldFish Center in Penang, Malaysia. He received his Ph.D. in natural resource economics from Cornell University.

**Jonathan Schwartz** is associate professor of political science at the State University of New York at New Paltz. He received his Ph.D. in political science from the University of Toronto.

**Rachel D. Schwartz** is assistant professor of biosecurity and disaster preparedness at the Institute for Biosecurity of the School of Public Health at Saint Louis University. She received her Ph.D. in English literature from Washington University in Saint Louis.

**Adam Segal** is Maurice R. Greenberg Senior Fellow for China at the Council on Foreign Relations. He received his Ph.D. in government from Cornell University.

**Eric A. Strahorn** is associate professor of South Asian and world history at Florida Gulf Coast University. He received his Ph.D. in history from the University of Iowa.

**Michael Wills** is vice president of research and operations at the National Bureau of Asian Research. He received his B.A. in Chinese studies from the University of Oxford.

**Elizabeth Wishnick** is associate professor of political science and law at Montclair State University and senior research scholar at the Weatherhead East Asian Institute at Columbia University. She received her Ph.D. in political science from Columbia University.

# Index

Administration on Quality Supervision, Inspections, and Quarantine (AQSIQ, China), 127, 177, 188

Afghanistan: and Indus River Basin, 77, 81, 91–93; U.S. military presence in, 6, 79

Africa: China's resource diplomacy in, 60, 63–64; and piracy, 172. *See also specific countries*

"Agreement on Cooperation on Addressing Climate Change" (China-India), 82

agriculture: and biofuels production, 62; Chinese exports to United States, 177; and floods, 50$n$40; and food security, 37–38; genetic engineering of crops, 38; and Himalayan dams, 32–33; in North China Plain, 55; overseas land acquisitions for, 18, 63–64; self-sufficiency goals of, 60, 61; and water supply, 16, 59–60, 61–62. *See also* irrigation

Ahmed, M., 110

air travel restrictions, 123–24

Alexander, Keith, 242, 243

al-Qaeda, 2, 6, 90

alternative energy, 62

American Legion, 163

American National Red Cross, 154, 168$n$36

anthrax attacks in U.S. (2001), 135

antibiotics, 70

APCERT (Asia-Pacific Computer Emergency Response Team), 240

APEC (Asia-Pacific Economic Cooperation), 112, 241

AQSIQ. *See* Administration on Quality Supervision, Inspections, and Quarantine

aquaculture, 70–71, 188

aquifers, 26. *See also* groundwater

Argentina: grain production in, 63; H1N1 flu epidemic response in, 131

ASEAN. *See* Association of Southeast Asian Nations

Asian Development Bank, 42, 58

Asian influenza (1957–58), 146

Asia-Pacific Computer Emergency Response Team (APCERT), 240

Asia-Pacific Economic Cooperation (APEC), 112, 241

Asia-Pacific Fishery Commission, 112

*aspal* system, 206, 207

Associated Press/Ispos poll on Chinese product safety, 187

Association of Southeast Asian Nations (ASEAN): and cybersecurity, 241; and fisheries management, 99; free trade area, 215; and security challenges cooperation, 2, 12; and terrorism, 198; Treaty of Amity and Cooperation, 69